STEPS ON THE PATH TO ENLIGHTENMENT

Steps on the Path to Enlightenment
A Commentary on Tsongkhapa's Lamrim Chenmo

Volume 1: The Foundation Practices
Volume 2: Karma
Volume 3: The Way of the Bodhisattva
Volume 4: Śamatha
Volume 5: Insight

STEPS
ON THE PATH TO
ENLIGHTENMENT

A Commentary on Tsongkhapa's
Lamrim Chenmo

Volume 4: Śamatha

GESHE LHUNDUB SOPA
with James Blumenthal

Wisdom Publications
199 Elm Street
Somerville, MA 02144 USA
wisdompubs.org

Library of Congress Cataloging-in-Publication Data for Volume 1
Lhundub Sopa, Geshe, 1925–
  Steps on the path to enlightenment : a commentary on Tsongkhapa's
Lamrim chenmo / Geshe Lhundub Sopa ; David Patt, senior editor ; Beth Newman,
editor.
    p. cm.
Includes bibliographical references and index.
  ISBN 0-86171-303-6 (alk. paper)
  1. Tsoṅ-kha-pa Blo-bzaṅ-grags-pa, 1357–1419. Lam rim chen mo. 2.
Lam-rim. I. Patt, David. II. Newman, Beth. III. Tsoṅ-kha-pa
Blo-bzaṅ-grags-pa, 1357–1419. Lamrim chenmo. IV. Title.
  BQ7950.T754L359 2003
  294.3′444—dc22

2003017363

ISBNs for Volume 4: Śamatha
ISBN 978-1-61429-287-6   ebook ISBN 978-1-61429-311-8
20 19 18 17 16
5 4 3 2 1

Cover and interior design by Gopa & Ted2, Inc.
Set in Diacritical Garamond Premier Pro 10.5/13.
Photos of Geshe Sopa are courtesy of Kalleen Mortensen.

Wisdom Publications' books are printed on acid-free paper and meet
the guidelines for permanence and durability of the Production Guidelines
for Book Longevity of the Council on Library Resources.

This book was produced with environmental mindfulness. We have elected to print this
title on 30% PCW recycled paper. As a result, we have saved the following resources: 9
trees, 1 million BTUs of energy, 744 lbs. of greenhouse gases, 4,039 gallons of water, and
270 lbs. of solid waste. For more information, please visit our website, wisdompubs.org.

Printed in the United States of America.

Contents

Foreword

THE *Great Treatise on the Stages of the Path to Enlightenment* (*Lamrim Chenmo*), composed by Tsongkhapa and explained here by Geshe Lhundub Sopa, is a commentary on the *Lamp for the Path to Enlightenment* by Atiśa. The primary goal of these teachings is to discipline and transform the mind. These texts have their source in the sutras and the other teachings of the Buddha himself, but their special virtue is that they convey the thought of the Buddha in a format that is easy to apply in actual practice.

The authors of these wonderful texts composed them in order to help all living beings. Since they developed the altruistic attitude to benefit mother sentient beings, we too should follow their example, irrespective of our own weak situation.

The Buddha and the great teachers who followed him gave clear instructions on how to proceed from a state of suffering to a state of peace and happiness. Following such teachings of the great masters of the past, Atiśa summarized them in his famous text, the *Lamp for the Path to Enlightenment*. It is a wonderful text, and Atiśa's disciples such as Dromtonpa and Potowa put what it teaches into practice. It was then transmitted through the Kadam lineages, finally coming down to Tsongkhapa.

Tsongkhapa was an unparalleled scholar who composed the *Great Treatise on the Stages of the Path to Enlightenment*, the marvelous text explained here in the manner of the great masters of Nālandā monastic university. We are indeed fortunate after so much time to have access to such a great work and to be able to read and think about what it contains. With this publication of Geshe Sopa's commentary, Tsongkhapa's words are brought to life and illuminated for a modern audience, continuing the lineages of scripture and realization that the Buddha set in motion more than 2,500 years ago.

The two principal aspects of practice described here are a proper understanding of emptiness and the awakening mind of *bodhicitta*. A correct understanding of the view of emptiness is very important, for whether you are taking refuge, or cultivating the awakening mind of bodhicitta, all other practices are enhanced by such an understanding. At the same time, it is extremely important that our insight into the ultimate nature of reality is supported by compassion and the awakening mind of *bodhicitta.*

In my own case, regardless of my limited capacity, I try my best to develop these two minds: the wisdom understanding emptiness, and *bodhicitta*—the wish to achieve enlightenment for the sake of all sentient beings. Merely trying to approach and cultivate these two minds brings greater peace and happiness. The development of these two minds is really the heart of Buddhist practice. It is the essential meaning of this *Stages of the Path to Enlightenment.* If we were to examine all the sutras and words of the Buddha, along with the subsequent treatises that are commentaries on them, we would find that they can be summed up in these two practices. Therefore, we should study these teachings motivated by an aspiration to achieve enlightenment for the sake of all sentient beings.

Today, Buddhism is spreading throughout the Western world, encountering new cultures and new languages. During such a period of transition it is very important that the Dharma be transmitted by scholars and practitioners who possess a deep and vast understanding of the teachings, because that is the only way to protect the authenticity and purity of the teachings.

Atiśa exemplified this role by bringing the pure teachings from the great monastic centers of North India and establishing them in Tibet in an authentic and complete form that was, at the same time, suitably adapted to the Tibetan personality. He reestablished monasticism in Tibet and emphasized ethical conduct as the heart of Buddhist training. He dispelled the many misconceptions and erroneous customs that had entered the practice of the Dharma in Tibet. In this way he reestablished the pure Buddhadharma in many places where it had been lost, and enhanced it where it survived.

Requested by Jangchub Ö to give a teaching that would be beneficial to the Tibetan people in general, Atiśa composed the *Lamp for the Path to Enlightenment,* which condensed the essential points of both sutras and tantras into a step-by-step method that would be easy to follow. This text inaugurated the grand tradition of the study and practice of the stages of the path method in Tibet. Atiśa also worked with his Tibetan students on the translation of many texts from Sanskrit into Tibetan and so made a rich contribution to the flourishing of Buddhism in the Land of Snows.

Geshe Sopa, the author of this commentary on the *Lamrim Chenmo,* was one of the several good students of Geshe Lhundrub Tabke and was therefore chosen to debate with me during my final examination. Geshe Lhundrub Tabke, who became the abbot of Sera Je, was in turn one of the several good students of Geshe Tsangpa Lhundrub Tsondru, who was a renowned scholar at the time of the Thirteenth Dalai Lama and later ascended the throne of

Ganden Tripa. Geshe Sopa is therefore the third generation of high-quality scholarship commencing from Geshe Tsangpa Lhundrub Tsondru, and he continues the excellent tradition today.

Geshe Sopa is an exemplary heir of Atiśa's tradition conveying the pure Dharma to a new world in an authentic and useful way. He has been a pioneer among those bringing Buddhism to the West. He left for America in 1962. In due course, Geshe Sopa was invited to the University of Wisconsin, where he became one of the first Tibetan language instructors at an American university. He later rose to become a tenured faculty member, and his career as a Professor of Buddhist Studies eventually spanned more than thirty years.

All Tibetans should feel honored and proud that Geshe Sopa, a man from far-away Tibet, could rise to the highest levels of Western academic attainment largely on the basis of his Tibetan monastic education combined with his own brilliance and personal qualities. Publication of this excellent series of books is a fitting tribute to an illustrious career.

Tenzin Gyatso, the Fourteenth Dalai Lama

Editor's Acknowledgments

I AM GRATEFUL first and last to my teacher Geshe Lhundub Sopa Rinpoche for inviting me to assist with this volume of commentary on the *Lamrim Chenmo*. Geshe-la is a teacher in all the best and most meaningful senses of the word. He is not only learned beyond compare, he perfectly embodies the teachings in his every deed as he skillfully passes them on to students with kindness, patience, wisdom, and compassion. I will never be able to fully repay his kindness to me, but I hope my contribution to seeing this book to fruition will be a small start.

The achievement of śamatha marks a critical point on any Buddhist's path to liberation. It is on the basis of achieving śamatha that a direct realization of selflessness can be achieved, and thus liberation from the afflictions that keep us bound in samsara is possible. I hope that those who read this volume find the teachings of Tsongkhapa, Geshe-la, and the many great masters whose words they cite as insightful and inspiring as I have in the preparation of this book.

It is a rare blessing to receive teachings such as these from an individual who is both incredibly learned in the scholastics of the subject and equally able to teach from deep personal experience. During my dozens of hours of discussing the contents of this book with Geshe-la, it was abundantly clear that he was teaching from both perspectives simultaneously.

A number of Geshe-la's students at Deer Park in Madison, Wisconsin, contributed to this volume in a variety of ways, from assistance with transcription, to editorial suggestions, to locating citations for the many textual quotations Geshe-la made from memory in oral teachings. Specifically I would like to thank Beth Newman, Frank Barone, Anne Chavez, Namdrol (Miranda) Adams, Ven. Jampa (Alicia Vogel), Rodney Stevenson, and Ven. George Churinoff. Despite the excellence of the teachings and outstanding help I have received from so many in the preparation of this volume, there are surely some mistakes remaining in a book this size. Any errors that remain are undoubtedly my own.

I would also like to thank the inspirational teacher and great spiritual friend Lama Thubten Zopa Rinpoche for his unending moral and financial support of this project. Completion of this book would not have been possible were it not for his kindness and generosity. Many individuals at Wisdom Publications also contributed in a variety of ways to this volume, including David Kittelstrom, Tim McNeill, and Keri Cole.

As taught by the Buddha, Tsongkhapa, and many others, the results can be tremendously beneficial when sincere practice is accompanied by great learning and understanding. Practice without understanding or learning can be useful but has its limitations. In this spirit and in the spirit of the Mahayana tradition, it is my most sincere hope that this volume will be useful to many as they use these tools in progress toward the achievement of buddhahood for the benefit of all sentient beings. As the Buddha said in the *Individual Liberation Sutra*, "There is bliss in the forest for those of great learning."

Sarva Maṅgalaṃ
James Blumenthal

Publisher's Note

Both Geshe Lhundub Sopa and Professor James Blumenthal passed away in 2014 before this volume reached the final stages of publication. They each left behind a legacy of learning, teaching, and institution building, sowing the seeds of Dharma insight for generations to come, and they are sorely missed by those whose lives they touched. Wisdom is honored to be able to publish this volume as part of their generous legacy, and we are grateful for the assistance of Beth Newman in helping us bring the work to completion.

Technical Notes

REFERENCES

All works mentioned are referenced by their titles in English. Although there are many ways to render a particular title, we have employed the versions used in Cutler's translation of the *Lamrim Chenmo—The Great Treatise on the Stages of the Path to Enlightenment*—to make it simple for the reader to use the two works together.

At the first mention of a particular work we provide the title in its language of composition. Again, although scholars may find some irregularities, for the ease of the general reader we have followed the Sanskrit titles as they appear in *The Great Treatise on the Stages of the Path to Enlightenment*. The bibliography allows the reader to find an English title and see the same title in Sanskrit (if applicable) and/or Tibetan.

Quotations not drawn from *The Great Treatise on the Stages of the Path to Enlightenment* are cited by the English title, chapter, and stanza or page number. Quotations drawn from *The Great Treatise on the Stages of the Path to Enlightenment* are not cited in notes. Since we utilize the subject headings from Cutler's translation for the ease of the reader, such quotations can be easily found in those volumes.

PRONUNCIATION

Terms from Sanskrit and Tibetan that have become part of the English language appear without diacritic marks or Tibetan spelling.

Tibetan technical terms and names are spelled phonetically for ease of use of non-Tibetan speakers. Sanskrit technical terms that are not commonly used in English appear in this work with diacritic marks. These terms appear in the glossary in English alphabetical order.

The following rough guide to Sanskrit pronunciation is from *The Wonder That Was India* by A. L. Basham.

The vowels *ā, ī, ū, e, ai, o,* and *au* are long and have approximately the same pronunciation as in Italian, or as the vowels in the English words, *calm, machine, rule, prey, time, go,* and *cow,* respectively. The vowels *a, i,* and *u* are short and equivalent to the vowels in the English words *cut*, *bit*, and *bull*. Ṛ is classed as a short vowel and pronounced as *ri* as *rich*.

The aspirated consonants *th* and *ph* are pronounced as they are in the words *pothole* and *shepherd*; they are never pronounced as the English *thin* or *photo*. *C* is pronounced *ch* as in *church*. *Ś* and *ṣ* are both generally pronounced as *sh* as in *shape*. The distinction between the other subdotted retroflex consonants (*ṭ*, *ṭh*, *ḍ*, *ḍh*, *ṇ*) and the dentals (without subdots) is not important to the general reader.

STYLISTIC NOTE

Steps on the Path to Enlightenment is based on an oral commentary on Tsongkhapa's *Lamrim Chenmo* that Geshe Sopa gave to his students over the course of more than a decade. In turning Geshe-la's presentation into a series of books, the editors have chosen to use an informal second-person voice. In contrast, the Tibetan language generally leaves person understood and is often rendered with an abstract third person: "one can do this" or "one should do that." We chose the second-person style in order to preserve something of the oral nature of the original and to create a more intimate bond between the author and the reader. The intent of Tsongkhapa and of Geshe Sopa was to give those who wish to embark on the path to enlightenment advice on how to proceed. This advice is offered here in the direct address of a teacher to his students.

STRUCTURE OF THE BOOK

The outline of headings in this book is drawn from Tsongkhapa's own outline of the *Lamrim Chenmo*. The chapter breaks and the format of the outline correspond to *The Great Treatise on the Stages of the Path to Enlightenment*, the English translation of the root text. The chapter numbers of this book correspond to volume 3 of that root text translation. The full outline for this volume is reproduced in the appendix.

Introduction

THE BUDDHA'S ADVICE is the best medicine. Ordinary medicine can cure temporary illnesses and minor pains, but the Buddha's spiritual teachings have all the methods contained within them to completely eradicate our spiritual malaise from the root. When people recognize their spiritual dilemma and want to be completely free from misery and suffering, not temporarily but forever, then they will find no better medicine than the holy teachings of the Buddha.

The Buddha's teachings are not a single medication or just one remedy. Sentient beings have so many types and sources of suffering. This is because our minds are filled with many kinds of confusion and misunderstanding. From this ignorance arise desire, hatred, jealousy, pride, and all types of mental afflictions. This mental disease in turn causes us to engage in all sorts of actions, or *karma*, that shape our future experiences and create all the pain, misery, and trouble in the world. The cure is the complete removal of this karma and the mental afflictions that drive it. In other words, karma is rooted in the mental afflictions, and these in turn are rooted in ignorance. By eradicating ignorance and the actions it drives, the Buddha's teachings are antidotes to misery, suffering, and dissatisfaction.

If we take the teachings seriously and follow the directions as the Buddha prescribed and did himself, then complete and real freedom can be achieved. If we do not follow the Buddha's instructions, the antidotes to our spiritual dilemma, then we are like sick people carrying around the medicine we need but never taking it. This analogy is made in the *King of Samādhi Sutra* (*Samādhi-rāja-sūtra*):

> Though I have taught the most excellent Dharma,
> If having heard it, you do not practice it properly,
> You are like a patient holding a bag full of medicine
> Who still cannot cure his disease.[1]

Nāgārjuna (ca. second century C.E.) used the same medical analogy. Different medicines cure different illnesses, but whatever your degree and type of sickness, you must take the right medicine in order to be cured. Likewise, the

Buddha taught specific antidotes for each of the mental delusions and harmful emotions that afflict sentient beings. If you listen to, study, and understand the teachings and then seriously practice them, you can eradicate suffering and its causes from the root. If you do not take the teachings seriously and put them into practice—even though the teachings have the capacity to cure the illness—they will not help. The medicine can only help if you take it.

Generally it is said that the Buddhist teachings describe 84,000 types of mental afflictions and 84,000 antidotes. The way to use these teachings properly can be difficult to understand for beginners, so commentaries and the guidance of a qualified teacher are useful. The *lamrim*, or "stages of the path," teachings arrange the Buddhist path in a particular order to show people where to start and how to proceed. They show the remedies to common problems encountered at each stage. The lamrim is a special Buddhist manual that draws the essence of all the teachings from a wide variety of sources and arranges them into practical, graduated stages. It is like a big treasure of teachings on every subject necessary for attaining liberation.

The *Lamrim Chenmo* (*The Great Treatise on the Stages of the Path to Enlightenment*) by Tsongkhapa (1357–1419) is a complete Mahayana guide that outlines each step of the path from the very beginning until the achievement of enlightenment. Generally speaking the text describes three levels of spiritual beings: small-scope beings, intermediate-scope beings, and great-scope beings. This way of presenting types of beings was first described by Atiśa (980–1054) in his text *Lamp for the Path to Enlightenment* (*Bodhi-patha-pradīpa*). Tsongkhapa describes the *Lamrim Chenmo* as a commentary on Atiśa's text. These three types of beings are differentiated according to their goals.

Small-scope beings are of two types: those concerned only with the samsaric pleasures of this life and those concerned with the next life. The first type of person focuses on worldly pleasures, such as the accumulation of wealth, fame, and praise. They think these will bring them real happiness and are completely absorbed in pursuing these worldly pleasures. They have no interest in any spiritual path that looks beyond satisfaction in the present life. They think they have nothing else to worry about. But that is not the case. The lamrim teachings demonstrate that when this life ends, it is not the end of our existence. Our lives continue.

The second type of small-scope being considers what will happen after death and generates a healthy fear of what might happen in the next life. In particular these practitioners fear lower rebirth. Understanding karma and the nature of samsara, they want to take advantage of the opportunities this life affords to protect against a miserable existence in the next life. They engage in various practices, such as taking refuge in the Buddha, in order to protect themselves from future suffering. This is the range of practice for the second type of small-scope beings; they have a religious inclination but of a lesser sort than the higher scopes.

Middle-scope beings clearly see the problems of falling to a lower rebirth, but they also see that higher rebirths, too, are under the control of karma and part of the cycle of samsara. Since a higher rebirth is temporary, it is not enough for beings of the middle scope. Recognizing that the impure circle of life in samsara is controlled by karma and the afflicted mind, they seek complete emancipation from it. Therefore, they listen, study, and meditate on the teachings in order to break free by cutting out samsara's roots: ignorance and its byproducts—karma and the afflictions. They dedicate every effort along the spiritual path toward their own personal liberation.

The last type is the great-scope being. Great-scope beings understand that from beginningless time, all sentient beings have suffered in samsara under the control of karma and the afflictions, and they wish to free all beings from this suffering. Beings of great spiritual scope generate great love and compassion for others; their love for others is even greater than for themselves. When this great love and compassion arises, they desire to help everybody achieve the everlasting happiness and peace of buddhahood or enlightenment. Since their goal is to be of maximum benefit to others, and they realize they cannot do much for others until they themselves achieve buddhahood, they practice to reach this goal as quickly as possible.

Everybody has the potential to remove the causes of their misery and suffering. Therefore, everybody has the potential to achieve buddhahood. The causes of suffering are not permanent or absolute. Karma and the mental afflictions—attachment, hatred, and so forth—are not permanent parts of the mind. They arise in the mind on the basis of ignorance. Ignorance also is not immutable. It can be destroyed and replaced with wisdom. Once the ignorance is destroyed, then the mental afflictions will not arise again. Once ignorance is removed, its results will cease to be generated.

In this vein, the Indian saint Śāntideva says that all the mental afflictions come from the wrong, egoistic view—grasping at notions of "I" and "mine." This is ignorance. This selfish and self-centered perspective is the cause of every negative emotion. The mind of this egoistic view is obscured or muddied, but that deception can be removed. The Buddha used many analogies to explain this. For example, just as we can distinguish between the sky that is temporarily obscured by clouds and the pure sky, we can distinguish the mind temporarily obscured by ignorance from the pure nature of the mind. Clouds are not the nature of sky, and ignorance is not the nature of the mind. Likewise we can use the analogy of muddy water: remove the mud and pure water remains. Yet another analogy is that of gold and dirt. The nature of the mind—like gold—is shining and pure. Sentient beings' minds are pure by nature, and yet the dirt of ignorance can obscure their luminosity.

The possibility of emancipation and enlightenment is the very heart of this teaching. Temporarily our minds have varying degrees of muddiness—some more, some less—and buddhas' minds have no mud at all. But even buddhas, before attaining buddhahood, had minds muddied with ignorance. Like the buddhas, we all have this same original purity of mind, and since impurities can be removed, we all have the potential to become buddhas. This potential is called *buddha nature*.

Those seeking enlightenment need to ask what the method is for achieving this state. Though the number 84,000 for the delusions and the methods to eliminate them may be more evocative than literal, we must study and learn and finally understand the antidotes the Buddha taught. Knowing the methods for alleviating suffering begins with understanding its causes. When we understand these causes and generate the wish to be free from them, we begin to develop compassion for ourselves and others.

Those who seek enlightenment should start with the practices of the small scope and ascend through the lamrim practices and methods step by step. The *Lamrim Chenmo* presents Mahayana Buddhist teachings. The practice and final goal of the Mahayana is based on love and compassion and, more specifically, the wish to free all beings. Called *bodhicitta*, or the "spirit of enlightenment," the altruistic aspiration for buddhahood is the essence of the Mahayana.

Without some kind of experience and understanding, how can you lead others? Thus, Mahayana practitioners say, "For the purpose of ultimately helping others, I will train myself in wisdom and compassion and free myself from the various obstacles that keep me in bondage. I will achieve the highest knowledge by removing these obstacles. Once they are removed, then without error I can help other sentient beings who still suffer. Thus I will strive to attain buddhahood so that I can benefit other sentient beings." This is the path of the authentic Mahayana practitioner.

In the beginning of the second chapter of his *Commentary on the "Compendium of Valid Cognition"* (*Pramāṇa-vārttika*), Dharmakīrti discusses how achieving the goal will be extremely difficult if you don't know the methods of practice. Before you can succeed in leading sentient beings to freedom, you must go there yourself. Not only must you be skilled at the steps on the path, you need to have perfected them. Otherwise you will not be able to help others perfectly. You may have loving compassion and the wish to free all beings, but if you have not trained in the methods that activate that goal and have no personal experience of it, then it remains a mere wish. Therefore Dharmakīrti encourages us to train in these methods and practice with a sense of urgency.

Tsongkhapa explains the benefits of both study and meditation because some people are confused about what is necessary in practice. Some say you do not need to study. They seem to think that if you just sit in meditation and try to clear your mind, that is enough. That is misguided. Others who are quite scholarly think that intellectual knowledge alone will bring about these great qualities. But this is not the case either. Tsongkhapa gives an extensive explanation detailing the importance of cultivating strength in both meditation and knowledge.

When bodhicitta—the mind that aspires to attain enlightenment as quickly as possible in order to benefit others—spontaneously arises in you virtually all the time, then your actions will naturally go toward that purpose. Since the compassion of that bodhicitta mind is for numberless sentient beings, the benefits of the practice of generating bodhicitta are enormous. The attitude is great; its goal is limitless. With such a goal, every moment becomes very powerful.

So what are the trainings of bodhisattvas, those who have bodhicitta as their motivation? Perhaps foremost is the taking of the bodhisattva vow and then training in that. The bodhisattva vow contains within it all of the bodhisattva's practices. This includes avoiding negative actions and training in the six perfections: generosity, ethical discipline, patience, perseverance, meditative stability, and wisdom. We have discussed these perfections quite extensively in the previous volume and gone into many details on how bodhisattvas train, particularly in the first four of these.

Tsongkhapa dedicates the final two chapters of the *Lamrim Chenmo* to the last two perfections, meditative stability (*dhyāna*) and wisdom (*prajñā*). Almost half of the text involves how to train in the concentrated mind and in the wisdom knowing the ultimate truth of emptiness. Meditative stabilization is addressed specifically through the cultivation of calm abiding, or *śamatha*, the mind resting in single-pointed focus. The perfection of wisdom is addressed through the cultivation of special insight (*vipaśyanā*) into emptiness. The present volume presents Tsongkhapa's chapter on cultivating the serenity of śamatha, while volume 5 of this series presents the chapter on developing the insight called vipaśyanā. Tsongkhapa bases his explanation on the teachings of the great paṇḍitas and yogis of ancient India. He makes extensive use of quotations from a variety of Indian texts to illuminate his explanation and illustrate the authoritative nature of his sources. We will also follow this method.

The cultivation of śamatha is critical to the path to enlightenment. It is the foundation of all effective meditation, including the meditation on emptiness, and it is thus a cornerstone of liberation. Since Tsongkhapa is starting a significant subject and a new chapter at this point in his treatise, he begins with a brief homage to his most venerable gurus, who possess great compassion. This homage is made in light of the next two chapters, the final section of the *Lamrim Chenmo*.

There are a great many terms for meditation in Buddhism. Even the specific practice of concentration meditation goes by a variety of names. The word *samādhi*, for instance, refers in a general way to a stable, single-pointed mind. The word *dhyāna*, and its Pali parallel *jhāna*, refer to the four meditative absorptions of the form realm, but the term is also the name of the fifth bodhisattva perfection, that of meditative stability. The Sanskrit term *śamatha* is rendered as *zhi gnas* in Tibetan (pronounced *sheenay*) and has a somewhat more specific definition. The Tibetan term is composed of *zhi*, which means "calm" or "peace," and *gnas*, which means "to abide" or "stay." Normally the mind is distracted and running all over the place; it is anything but calm or still. "Calm" here refers to freedom from the distractions that dominate our normal state of mind. Together the two parts of the term refers to the ability of a mind to stay focused on an object of observation with complete freedom from distraction and mental laxity. In other words, it refers to the state where the mind is able to remain concentrated without any excitement or dullness at all.

The actual state of śamatha is achieved only after extensive training over a long time. A mind that has achieved śamatha is able to remain spontaneously on its object of focus for as long as it likes. This single-pointed concentration is accompanied by a very subtle and deep feeling of physical and mental bliss. In addition, along with this single-pointed awareness and subtle bliss is a physical and mental pliancy that perfectly facilitates effective meditation. These qualities of śamatha and the methods for achieving them will be discussed at length in this volume.

The final chapter of the *Lamrim Chenmo* on the special insight called *vipaśyanā* is in Tibetan *lhag mthong* (pronounced *lock-tohng*). *Lhag mthong* literally means "superior seeing." It is a type of wisdom that knows reality directly and nonconceptually, but it is cultivated through discerning analysis stabilized within meditation. Vipaśyanā is the key to liberation, but it depends upon śamatha for its successful cultivation. We need both to achieve enlightenment.

Everybody who has ever achieved liberation has done so on the basis of śamatha and vipaśyanā. Without śamatha, if you use analytical meditation to analyze whether an object is permanent or impermanent, real or unreal, and so on, you are easily distracted. Vipaśyanā cannot be fully realized without a foundation of śamatha. Conversely, if we train only in śamatha, then the afflictions cannot be removed and liberation is not possible. However, when we combine śamatha with the special insight of vipaśyanā, we progress quickly, and freedom from samsara will be achieved.

❖ 1 ❖

Śamatha and Vipaśyanā

2″ In particular, how to train in the last two perfections
   (a) The benefits of cultivating śamatha and vipaśyanā
   (b) How śamatha and vipaśyanā include all states of meditative
      concentration
   (c) The nature of śamatha and vipaśyanā
   (d) Why it is necessary to cultivate both
   (e) How to be certain about their order
   (f) How to train in each (chapters 2–6 and volume 5)

2″ IN PARTICULAR, HOW TO TRAIN IN THE LAST TWO PERFECTIONS

ŚAMATHA AND VIPAŚYANĀ are the cornerstones of the Buddhist path in virtually all Buddhist traditions. As was noted above, a key way that the Mahayana traditions outline the path to buddhahood is by way of the six perfections: generosity, ethical discipline, patience, perseverance, meditative stability, and wisdom. These last two perfections are pursued with the practices of śamatha and vipaśyanā.

It is highly rewarding to understand the deep meaning of these wonderful teachings that Tsongkhapa has offered to us. Śāntideva illustrates this point with an apt analogy. He says that just as the skin of sugar cane does not have the sweet essence of the sugar, so too a spiritual practice that consists of a mere surface knowledge of teachings, prayers, and so forth misses the sweet essence of the deep meaning. If you acquire only intellectual knowledge of Buddhist practice, you will not achieve its goals.

The primary purpose of Buddhist practice is to rid yourself of the mental afflictions that are the main source of your suffering and misery. Unlike animals, who are concerned only with their own temporary pleasure, human beings can see a deeper spiritual meaning in life. Humans can choose to pursue the superior goal of perfect everlasting happiness for all sentient beings. They can recognize that temporary happiness is not ultimately satisfying. Suffering may be reduced temporarily in one area, only to arise again someplace else. Humans must go deeper to find the root causes of misery and pull them out completely.

According to Buddhism, the root cause of suffering is not outside of us; it is within. The internal causes of our suffering are mental afflictions such as greed, hatred, and jealousy, all of which are grounded in ignorance. As long as these mental afflictions dominate our minds and our lives, we will experience misery. We will see problems everywhere, inside and outside. Only with spiritual practice can we free ourselves from these afflictions and finally become perfect buddhas.

Once the mind is freed from all afflictions and obstacles to knowledge, it is perfect. The mind is then omniscient, compassionate, and loving. It then embodies all the positive enlightened qualities of a buddha, while all the negative qualities along with their sources are removed. This is the main spiritual goal of all the teachings of Buddhism; this goal can be accomplished with a human mind. After all, the Buddha appeared in the world as a human being.

(a) THE BENEFITS OF CULTIVATING ŚAMATHA AND VIPAŚYANĀ

When Tsongkhapa explains the practice of any one of the six perfections, he begins by explaining the benefits of engaging in that practice and taking it to heart. It is important to know the benefits of doing an activity in any serious aspect of life, but especially for spiritual practice. In fact, it is important to see both sides: the benefits of doing the practice and the disadvantages of not doing the practice. For by seeing the great advantages of a practice and the disadvantages of neglecting it, we are inclined to put greater effort into it and persevere through hardships and difficulties. Therefore it is important to see the benefits of cultivating both śamatha and vipaśyanā.

Śamatha is achieved when you are able to remain focused single-pointedly on your object of meditation for as long as you wish with complete clarity and without any excitement or mental laxity. Wisdom realizing the true nature of reality is cultivated in reliance upon śamatha; it cannot be developed without it. Only when the achievement of śamatha is combined with the wisdom that knows reality can you begin to remove the mental afflictions keeping you bound to samsara. You then have a great opportunity to make significant spiritual progress, to achieve emancipation, and even to achieve the enlightened state of complete buddhahood.

At the beginning of his chapter on meditative stability in *Engaging in the Bodhisattva Deeds* (*Bodhisattva-caryā-avatāra*), Śāntideva said:

> Knowing that mental afflictions are completely destroyed
> By the wisdom that rests firmly on śamatha,
> Begin by seeking śamatha.
> Śamatha is established with joyous nonattachment to the world.

An uncontrollable mind that is scattered, going here and there, cannot serve as a foundation for the wisdom that uproots the afflictions. When you properly employ the techniques for developing śamatha taught in the *Lamrim Chenmo*, your mind can achieve great stability. By analogy, just as a wild untamed elephant can cause a lot of damage, if your mind is out of control, it can cause you a great many problems in this life and the next. In contrast, a tamed elephant can help you do many things, and the same is true for your mind. Once it is trained to concentrate, it can serve as the basis for developing vipaśyanā. All of the mental afflictions are rooted in ignorance, which is the opposite of insight. By removing ignorance from the root with wisdom, you can completely and permanently remove the mental afflictions. When all of the mental afflictions are removed, you will have achieved liberation.

There are also temporary antidotes to the afflictions. Concentrating on love, compassion, and patience can reduce hatred and anger. Meditation on the impurity of objects and impermanence is an antidote to attachment. These antidotes can subdue these afflictions for a time. However, in order remove these afflictions entirely from the root, the ignorance upon which they are grounded must be removed by the power of wisdom. Therefore, you should try to cultivate śamatha as the basis for the wisdom that uproots mental afflictions. This is what Śāntideva is saying in the quotation above.

Tsongkhapa's way of explaining śamatha is very detailed. As he explains, these teachings on śamatha were originally taught by Śākyamuni Buddha, recorded in the sutras, and then explained in more detail in the great Indian commentaries. Tsongkhapa investigates and analyzes these scriptural explanations in order to support their various statements with sound logic. Then he explains how to practice śamatha and describes the immediate and long-term results of such practice. This is all part of the extensive explanation of the *Lamrim Chenmo*. Tsongkhapa says:

All of the mundane and supramundane good qualities of the Mahayana and Hinayana are the result of śamatha and vipaśyanā.

When Tsongkhapa mentions the Hinayana, he is referring to practitioners whose spiritual focus is on freedom and emancipation for themselves. The Hinayana is called the *small vehicle* because the scope of that practice is relatively small; it is only for oneself. In contrast, the main goal of the Mahayana, the *great vehicle*, is to help all sentient beings achieve freedom. Mahayana practitioners known as *bodhisattvas* recognize that all sentient beings have been their dear mothers in previous lives. Thus they have great compassion and practice with the goal of liberating all sentient beings. For that purpose, they try to achieve the highest goal of buddhahood.

Mundane good qualities are spiritual attainments developed on the path by non-āryas, those whose insight into selflessness is not yet direct. There are other qualities that are attained by āryas, the "noble ones," who have realized selflessness directly. These are the supramundane qualities that lead to nirvana and buddhahood. The mundane qualities are a result of strengthening your concentration; the supramundane qualities are the result of cultivating insight into the nature of reality on the basis of that concentration. All good, wholesome, and virtuous qualities and merits are the result of śamatha and vipaśyanā. This includes all of our mental development and spiritual realizations from the mundane to supramundane levels, including even buddhahood itself.

This point is also made in the *Sutra Unraveling the Intended Meaning* (*Saṃdhi-nirmocana-sūtra*):

> Maitreya, you should know that all mundane and supramundane virtuous qualities, whether of śrāvakas, bodhisattvas, or tathāgatas, are the result of śamatha and vipaśyanā.

Having made such claims about the incredible value of śamatha and vipaśyanā, Tsongkhapa rhetorically asks how all good qualities can be the result of śamatha and vipaśyanā if śamatha and vipaśyanā themselves are good qualities that are achieved through meditation. In response to this question, Tsongkhapa replies that we must first understand the terms. The nature of *śamatha* is a stabilized mind that is able to remain on an object for as long as the meditator likes. There are nine stages of training, which serve as milestones of your progress in the cultivation of śamatha. The actual state of śamatha is the culmination of training through these nine stages, which we discuss below. As you progress through the nine stages, many excellent qualities arise: an increasing ability of the mind to control negativities, an increasing ability to stay vividly and clearly on the object of meditation without distraction or sleepiness for as long as you wish, and once śamatha is achieved there is the ability to meditate comfortably for as long as you like since the body is in complete harmony with the mind. This last quality is called the *bliss of śamatha*, a sort of sensual pleasure. The harmony of body and mind that results from śamatha is an example of a mundane, or worldly, virtuous quality in that it can be achieved by non-āryas.

All successful meditation requires some degree of mental stabilization. There must be some stability for benefit to arise from any meditation, even if actual śamatha is not yet achieved. So when any sort of meditation practice is used as a means to cultivate virtuous qualities, we can say those qualities depend on the cultivation of śamatha. Vipaśyanā is insight that realizes the nature of reality. Any insight that distinguishes the relative and ultimate nature of things—and the virtuous qualities that follow from such insight—is said to arise from vipaśyanā. In this sense, we can talk about three types of wisdom:

1. *Wisdom that arises from hearing* is the wisdom that you gain from listening to teachings from a teacher and from studying Dharma books and so forth. This phrase arose in a time when it was not easy to get copies of books. To study the teachings you had to hear them from a teacher or guru. Today books are much more accessible and the study of texts is included here as well. From this sort of activity a certain a degree of wisdom arises, and from that understanding good qualities arise.

2. *Wisdom that arises from contemplation* is the wisdom that results from contemplating the wisdom that is generated from what you heard from teachers and read in books. When you seriously think about the meaning of these teachings, examine them, and analyze them through logical reasoning and personal experience, the wisdom that arises from contemplation arises. For example, you can use logical analysis in meditation on the four noble truths or impermanence and achieve some insight that is an aspect of vipaśyanā. And from this, good qualities arise.

3. *Wisdom that arises from meditation* refers to the wisdom that arises from meditating after hearing the teachings and analyzing them. The mind that engages in meditation is already trained in the subject under consideration from developing the wisdoms that arise from hearing and contemplating. The purpose of meditating is to become so deeply familiar with a topic that you eventually understand it internally and spontaneously. A direct realization of an aspect of the truth produces

certain special effects. The qualities that arise from meditating on a direct realization of selflessness with the support of śamatha—the actual state of the union of śamatha and vipaśyanā—is supramundane in that it can cut the roots of samsaric existence.

This is what was meant in the sutras when the Buddha claimed that all virtuous qualities are a result of śamatha and vipaśyanā.

Another sutra, the *Sutra of Cultivating Faith in the Mahayana* (*Mahāyāna-prasāda-prabhāvanā-sūtra*), makes this same point:

> Child of good lineage, this list should inform you that faith in the Mahayana of the bodhisattvas—and indeed, everything resulting from the Mahayana—comes from accurately reflecting on facts and meaning with an undistracted mind.

An undistracted mind is single-pointed and concentrated. As the result of concentration, it is focused and stabilized and has aspects of the actual state of śamatha. "Accurately reflecting" refers to insight. The mind that properly examines, discerns, and utilizes analytical meditation is an aspect of vipaśyanā.

So this sutra makes the same point that Tsongkhapa does above. All the virtuous qualities of both the Hinayana and the Mahayana arise in dependence upon aspects of śamatha and vipaśyanā. That is to say, the virtuous qualities of both Hinayana and Mahayana practitioners arise from continuous effort to cultivate meditative stabilization and wisdom. In the struggle against internal faults such as ignorance, wisdom is the main weapon we must use. But in order for wisdom to be powerful, it must have śamatha as its basis. If a person has some wisdom but does not have mental stability, then wisdom will not function up to its full potential. To cut down a tree, you need a sharp axe. A sharp axe blade is like vipaśyanā. But a sharp axe blade is not enough; you must also have a good handle and strong arms—the mental stability of śamatha. When you have both śamatha and vipaśyanā, you can achieve the goals of both the Hinayana and Mahayana. This is what is meant by the claim that all the mundane and supramundane goals of the spiritual path arise from the basis of śamatha and vipaśyanā.

In order to clear away any potential confusion regarding this topic, Tsongkhapa quotes a variety of sutras. This detailed explanation elaborates how both śamatha and vipaśyanā can be classified in two ways: actual and partial. In order to reach the actual, or real, śamatha, there are nine stages of training and corresponding accomplishment. Each of these levels is a form of partial śamatha. Then, on the side of vipaśyanā, there are analytic meditations that are geared toward analyzing and seeing the nature and depth of reality. These analytic practices are all parts of vipaśyanā. So every yogic practice is included in one or both of these. In this vein, the *Sutra Unraveling the Intended Meaning* states:

> Once people have cultivated vipaśyanā
> And śamatha, they are free
> From the bondage of dysfunctional tendencies
> And from the bondage of signs.

"Dysfunctional tendencies" are the seeds of mental afflictions such as anger, hatred, pride, and jealousy. These dysfunctional tendencies are not always present in your consciousness, but the potential for them to arise in your mind is always there until you achieve nirvana, the state of an *arhat*, one who has eliminated suffering and its causes. For example, you may not always feel hate for an enemy, but the potential for hatred is present. These dysfunctional tendencies are like seeds: a seed will not become a sprout until certain conditions of soil, sunlight, moisture, and so on are present. These potentials are variously referred to as "stains in our minds," "dysfunctional tendencies," "predispositions," or "the bondage of bad habits." The "bondage of signs" is the actual mental affliction that occurs when the potential meets the conditions that enable it to manifest.

These two types of bondage are present when your mind is not yet perfected. All sorts of suffering come from them. By practicing śamatha and vipaśyanā, your mind begins to separate from these forms of bondage. The way to temporarily free your mind from these types of bondage is through the practice of śamatha. When you cultivate vipaśyanā in addition to the practice of śamatha, you become truly and completely free. Through the various levels of meditation, you remove the delusions and attain the state of buddhahood, which is completely free from bondage. There is no other way to remove these delusions. No one—not a person, god, or Buddha—can do it for you. Only mental training can remove these fetters. When you accustom yourself to the practice of the stages of śamatha and vipaśyanā, you learn to free your mind from the bondage of the two types of obstacles described in the sutra.

The Indian commentator Ratnākaraśānti said that vipaśyanā eliminates the bondage of dysfunctional tendencies and śamatha eliminates the bondage of signs. In other words, the state of śamatha subdues the afflictions temporarily, but only when it is combined with vipaśyanā are mental afflictions removed from the root. It is easier to get rid of your manifest mental afflictions than it is to get rid of their seeds. A present mental affliction can be temporarily subdued through an assortment of practices—like concentrating on its opposite, trying to avoid certain conditions, meditating on love and compassion, or applying various other antidotes. However, removing the gross manifestations of the mental afflictions—the bondage of signs—does not necessarily mean that the delusions are completely uprooted. In order to get rid of them from the root, you need to cultivate the penetrating wisdom that sees reality. Only when śamatha is firm and you cultivate vipaśyanā do you begin to remove the bondage of dysfunctional tendencies from the root. Therefore, if you want to remove the mental afflictions both in their present manifestations and their potential for arising again, you must cultivate śamatha and vipaśyanā together.

In summary, the benefit of cultivating both śamatha and vipaśyanā is that, working in union, they are the antidotes to the source of samsara.

(b) How śamatha and vipaśyanā include all states of meditative concentration

Among the six perfections in general, and the practice of śamatha and vipaśyanā in particular, there are many types of meditative achievement. If we look at this from the perspective of the three vehicles—Hinayana, Mahayana, and Tantrayana—we can also discern many meditation techniques and achievements. The bases of all of these attainments are aspects of śamatha and vipaśyanā. Tsongkhapa says there are myriad leaves, flowers, and branches on a tree, yet they all are features of the tree. In the same way, the Buddha taught many forms of meditative concentration in Hinayana and Mahayana sutras and in the tantras, each with a specific function, purpose, result, approach, name, and so forth, yet all are aspects of the general categories of śamatha and vipaśyanā. The Buddha says in the *Sutra Unraveling the Intended Meaning:*

> Know that śamatha and vipaśyanā include all of the many aspects of the states of meditative concentration that I have taught for śrāvakas, bodhisattvas, and tathāgatas.

Likewise, Kamalaśīla wrote in his second *Stages of Meditation (Bhāvanā-krama)*:

> Since those two include all states of meditative concentration, all yogis should at all times definitely rely upon śamatha and vipaśyanā.

When you practice the Dharma, you rely on śamatha and vipaśyanā. They are the foundation, like the trunk and roots of a tree. Eventually other branches will grow as you emphasize specific aspects of these two practices. One branch may seem separate from another, but they are all connected to the same trunk. Different meditators may appear to focus upon completely different practices, but all Buddhist meditation practices are branches of śamatha and vipaśyanā.

(c) The nature of śamatha and vipaśyanā

This third topic explains what śamatha and vipaśyanā are in general. Tsongkhapa begins his explanation of śamatha with a quotation from the *Sutra Unraveling the Intended Meaning*:

> While you dwell in solitude and properly direct your attention inward, you attend to just those topics upon which you have carefully reflected. Your attention is mentally engaged by continuously attending inwardly. The state of mind wherein you do this and stay this way often, and in which both physical and mental pliancy arise, is called *śamatha*. Therefore bodhisattvas strive to achieve śamatha.

This is a very pithy quote. "Topics upon which you have carefully reflected" refers to the instructions regarding the nine stages of śamatha training, a subject Tsongkhapa explains in detail later. It is most fruitful to cultivate this state of mind in a solitary place where your practice will not be interrupted. There you can internalize the nine stages of the development of śamatha. This is done by maintaining the focus and attention of your mind on its object. When your mind gets distracted, you simply bring your attention back to the object. You do not just let your mind wander.

The object of your śamatha meditation can be any of a number of topics discussed in the scriptures, such as impermanence, the four noble truths, and so forth. However, this is not an analytical form of meditation. If for example, the truth of suffering is your object, you do not analyze every aspect of suffering one by one; you just keep your mind attentive to the general suffering of existence in samsara. Whatever your object of concentration, you maintain that object in your mind without interruption. This is what is meant by "continuously attending inwardly." You set your mind on the object and leave it there.

When you engage in this practice, try to maintain your attention for as long as you can. At first your mind may only be able to remain focused briefly because you will become distracted or sink into dullness or sleepiness. However, if you keep trying, eventually you will achieve a stabilized mind and be able to remain focused on your object for as long as you like. If you sit down for a meditation session intending to stay focused on your object for two hours and you are successful, that indicates a significant degree of mental stability.

When you achieve śamatha, one result is incredible mental pliancy. Your mind follows your wishes and focuses wherever you like for as long as you like. Physical pliancy also increases in the sense that your body does not interfere with this mental pliancy. Once śamatha is achieved, there is no physical pain or discomfort to distract your concentration. A yogi who is well trained can control the subtle wind; this makes his or her body feel light. The mental power is so strong it almost feels like there is no body at all. This is the physical pliancy that accompanies the mental pliancy. These two pliancies produce a subtle feeling of bliss. The state of single-pointed meditative concentration that has the bliss of mental and physical pliancy is śamatha.

Bodhisattvas strive to achieve śamatha because it has a special benefit. Once you have that mental power, the senses follow the mind. Usually it is the other way around: the mind chases after whatever information is supplied to it by the senses. Under such circumstances the mind is always distracted. This is the common state of the mind in the desire realm. But when śamatha is achieved, your mental power is so strong that the senses' power to disturb your mind is eliminated. Therefore Tsongkhapa calls this meditative state a "mental king" because with it you can rule your mind. All the accompanying mental factors are like subjects of the primary mind that is king. Thus, when you have śamatha, you can achieve many yogic skills. That is why the sutra says, "bodhisattvas strive to achieve śamatha."

Introspection, or vigilance, is the main method for cultivating śamatha. It has two aspects. It introspectively examines the mind again and again, and it vigilantly checks to see whether the mind is still placed on the chosen object of meditation. I often refer to this as a spy who is watching the mind to see if it is still focused on its object. If it is not, then you must bring the mind back. Just as a spy uses various instruments like cameras and hidden microphones to track what his target is up to, you use vigilant introspection to keep tabs on your mind. Eventually, after enough training, the mind remains on its object without effort. It is a spiritual strength of mind.

Mental control is one of the key practices for a Buddhist practitioner. If your mind is not controlled, you create all sorts of problems that bring you misery and suffering. Everlasting peace comes from a mind that is able to free itself from ignorance and mental afflictions, and this requires mental control. When your mind is purified and free from all the obscurations and mental afflictions, you achieve the highest happiness or peace. Vigilant introspection is the basis for developing this mental control.

It is important to note that a person does not need to realize emptiness to attain śamatha. Someone who has developed śamatha has not necessarily cultivated insight and obtained high realizations. That is a separate matter. Non-Buddhists as well as Buddhists achieve śamatha. The achievement of śamatha simply indicates having a mind that is able to remain focused on its object without distraction. It does not depend upon or entail a realization of the ultimate truth. But this does not mean that śamatha is not an important and excellent quality. All Buddhist yogis and yoginis must strive to have it. Without śamatha nothing much can be achieved. But śamatha alone is not enough either. It alone does not lead to freedom from the mental afflictions, nor does it cut the root of ignorance.

(d) Why it is necessary to cultivate both

The mental control that can remove all ignorance is divided into two: śamatha and vipaśyanā. As Tsongkhapa has said, śamatha—the stabilization of the mind—alone cannot remove all the obstacles because it does not know the nature of reality. To cut the root of the afflictions you must use a stabilized mind to cultivate the wisdom that truly, directly knows the way in which phenomena exist. This vipaśyanā, or insight, begins with analytical meditation that enables you to develop a valid conceptual understanding of reality. Analytical meditation is discursive; it involves thinking about a topic in many ways. When this wisdom is joined to śamatha, which is nondiscursive concentration, the mind becomes especially sharp. It is similar to drilling a hole in something; you endeavor to keep the drill precisely on the spot where you want the hole. Likewise, when śamatha keeps its focus on insight into the nature of reality, you can remove ignorance and mental afflictions. Vipaśyanā and śamatha have great power when combined together.

Mere śamatha is not sufficient for achieving either individual liberation from samsara or the Mahayana goal of perfect enlightenment for the benefit of others. Nor can those final goals be achieved by vipaśyanā alone. Tsongkhapa says that if it is dark and you want to see a painting clearly, then you need a butter lamp that both shines brightly and is undisturbed by wind. If the lamp is bright but flickers in the wind, then you will not be able to see the painting clearly. If there is no wind, but the light from the lamp is weak, then you will not be able to see the painting clearly. In the same way, you can cultivate an understanding of emptiness—the ultimate nature of reality—using inference and logic, but the profound truth of emptiness is much clearer when seen through meditation. To have a direct realization of emptiness, you must have the very deep and profound meditation where all your other senses, sense consciousnesses, and thoughts stop, so that only one consciousness—the wisdom penetrating to the depths of the truth—remains. Only if you have the unshakable stabilization of śamatha combined with the penetrating insight of vipaśyanā can you see reality clearly.

If you want mere temporary peace, śamatha alone can provide it. The cessation of all distracting and troubling thoughts is achieved by developing śamatha. But even if you have this deeply concentrated mind where all thoughts are suspended, it will not mean much and will not help much. The root of our problems is ignorance, and thus the antidote to our problems must be wisdom. You need to remove from its root your mistaken understanding and grasping at the true existence of self and phenomena. The reality of all phenomena is emptiness—the lack of true existence. You use the mind that abides undistracted by other objects to focus on an understanding of emptiness, the ultimate truth. Only a direct realization of emptiness will eliminate the source of your problems and give you true peace.

Dharmakīrti makes a similar point in the second chapter of *Commentary on the "Compendium of Valid Cognition"* (2:222):

> Without disbelief in the object,
> One will not be able to abandon it.

Dharmakīrti says that all our mental afflictions are rooted in misunderstanding. There is no way to remove the afflictions other than to realize the lack of inherent existence in objects, which we ignorantly grasp as real. For example, you may become very fearful if you mistake a rope coiled in the corner of a room to be a poisonous snake. It is ignorance, or a lack of proper understanding, that causes the fear since there is no real snake there. As long as you cling strongly to the conception that the rope is a snake, you are frightened. The only way to alleviate your fear is to correct your misconception. When you see the truth of the matter, that there is no snake, you are completely free from fear. In the same way, as long as you grasp at the true or essential reality of phenomena, you will have the other mental afflictions.

In order to remove that ignorance, you must cultivate a direct understanding of the true nature of reality—emptiness. Because emptiness is very subtle and difficult to understand, you must begin by understanding it inferentially. Inferential understanding is an excellent starting point, but it is not clear enough to completely remove ignorance. By contemplating emptiness in combination with śamatha, you attain a direct realization of emptiness that penetrates more deeply. In brief, you first understand emptiness inferentially and then apply the stable mind of śamatha to that understanding. If you do not have the wisdom knowing reality, you are like a person who sees the rope and thinks it is a poisonous snake. Even with a correct inferential understanding of emptiness, you are unable to see reality clearly enough to remove all your fear without the stabilization of śamatha.

Grasping the self of persons and phenomena is not immediately removed even with a direct realization of emptiness. Self-grasping is removed gradually as you get more familiar, through repeated meditation on emptiness. On the path of seeing, the accumulation of wisdom is accrued during meditation on emptiness, and in the postmeditation sessions the accumulation of merit is cultivated. If there is no śamatha accompanying your direct realization, later reflection when you attempt to integrate that insight will not be very clear. Thus you need both śamatha and vipaśyanā to gather the two accumulations of wisdom and merit and remove the afflictions and the self-grasping upon which they are based. Tsongkhapa cites many sources to support this point. For example, Kamalaśīla says in his second *Stages of Meditation*:

> With bare vipaśyanā that lacks śamatha, the yogi's mind is distracted by objects; like an oil lamp in the wind, it will not be stable. For this reason, what sublime wisdom sees will not be very clear. As this is so, rely equally on both. Therefore the *Great Final Nirvāṇa Sutra* (*Mahā-parinirvāṇa-sūtra*) says:
>
>> Śrāvakas do not see the essence[2] of the tathāgatas because their concentration is greater than their wisdom; bodhisattvas see it, but unclearly, because their wisdom is greater than their concentration. The tathāgatas see everything because they have śamatha and vipaśyanā in equal measure.

The most common Sanskrit term used to indicate the nature of the tathāgatas is *tathāgatagarbha*, or *buddha nature*. But here, the Tibetan translation of the sutra uses the word *rigs*. Usually this word has the sense of "lineage," but here it refers to the essential nature of Buddha's mind—emptiness. The essence of the tathāgatas is that a buddha's mind is empty of inherent existence. The naturally pure mind is buddha nature. The emptiness of inherent existence of that mind is also buddha nature. There is no difference between buddha nature and emptiness. Therefore "the essence of the tathāgatas" means empti-ness. Thus to not see the essence of the tathāgatas is to not see emptiness.

Sentient beings' minds are also empty of inherent existence. Their empty nature entails the potential to transform into enlightened buddhas, whose nature is also empty. In other words, although sentient beings' minds are pres-ently obscured by afflictions, because the nature of their minds is emptiness, their minds can be transformed into the mind of a buddha. It is in this sense that all sentient beings are said to have buddha nature.

Some people say everybody is a buddha, but that is not accurate. We are not all buddhas at present, but we do all have the potential to become buddhas. In order to become buddhas, we have to purify our minds of the ignorance and other afflictions that currently cloud our understanding of reality. When we achieve buddhahood, we are free of all obstacles, but until then our vision is obscured, like when clouds obscure a clear sky. Just as cloudiness is not the final nature of the sky, the state of being obscured by ignorance is not the final nature of the mind. Clouds exist dependent upon causes and conditions; they change, they are not inherently and permanently part of the sky. If the mind inherently existed as obscured, then there would be nothing that could be done about it. The impurities of ignorance and the mental afflictions could not be separated from it. But that is not the case. The obscurations are impermanent; they are not the ultimate nature of the mind. The mind can be separated from its present ignorance and delusions. The mind is empty of any absolute nature. It is dependent, relative, and changeable. Only in this sense, because the mind has the potential to transform into the mind of a buddha, are we said to have buddha nature.

It is important to note that there are many philosophical perspectives on these issues. I am explaining Kamalaśīla's use of this quote from the *Great Final Nirvāṇa Sutra* from a Prāsaṅgika Madhyamaka perspective. The Prāsaṅgika system holds that in order for any of the three types of practitioners—śrāvakas, pratyekabuddhas, or bodhisattvas—to reach the goal of arhatship, they must have a direct realization of emptiness. Even śrāvaka āryas must see the essence of the tathāgatas, which is emptiness. Some other Buddhist schools disagree. However, from the point of view of Tsongkhapa, if anyone is to achieve the goal of enlightenment or arhatship, by definition they must realize emptiness. In *Engaging in the Bodhisattva Deeds* when a hypothetical Hinayana opponent asks why it is necessary to realize emptiness if liberation comes from understanding the four noble truths, Śāntideva responds on behalf of the Madhyamaka proponents:

> According to scripture, without this path, there will be no
> enlightenment.[3]

"This path" refers to the realization of emptiness. "Enlightenment" means the achievement of arhatship—the freedom from samsara that is achieved by abandoning all mental afflictions from the root.

Both Hinayana and Mahayana practitioners must see emptiness, but the bodhisattva's way of seeing it is superior. Some people are satisfied with only one or two reasons explaining why phenomena are empty. Śrāvakas are more interested in dedicating themselves to the cultivation of śamatha; because their understanding of emptiness is based on just one or two logical proofs, it is a little weaker and lacks depth. Other people, such as bodhisattvas, require many reasons. Bodhisattvas are said to use limitless proofs: they examine truth claims from many angles, such as from the perspective of function, from the perspective of time, from the perspective of causes, from the perspective of results, from the perspective of actions, and so forth, all of which are presented in Nāgārjuna's *Fundamental Verses of the Middle Way* (*Mūla-madhyamaka-kārikā*). When you understand something from so many different perspectives, your understanding is deeper, stronger, and firmer.

Bodhisattvas who have attained the path of seeing have a clear realization of emptiness in meditation, but when they rise from meditation they see things in an illusory way—things appear to be real, but these ārya bodhisattvas know intellectually that they are empty. In the postmeditation period, a bodhisattva's wisdom of emptiness is not a direct realization on the conscious level; it becomes subconscious. In fact, until they remove all the afflictions, bodhisattvas still grasp at things as truly existent in their postmeditation sessions. When the mental afflictions are removed but knowledge obstacles are still present, bodhisattvas have a more subtle sense of things being real in the postmeditation session. When yogis on the śrāvaka path rise from their meditation on emptiness, they also see things in an illusory way as real, but they have fewer logical or intellectual reasons to help them know things are empty in their postmeditation periods.

Buddhas realize emptiness clearly all the time. They have removed all mental obscurations—the afflictions and knowledge obstacles—from the root. Buddhas do not need to sit and meditate to realize emptiness. They are in constant realization of emptiness. In this sense their minds are continually in a meditative state. Even when they are engaged in activities such as teaching or giving charity, they have a deep realization of emptiness. They know all the reasons clearly and simultaneously. They possess śamatha and vipaśyanā equally at all times.

Those who have vipaśyanā supported by śamatha cannot be led astray by arguments in support of wrong views; as firm as Mount Meru, their insight cannot be blown about by the winds of misguided thought. Kamalaśīla quotes the *Moon Lamp Sutra* (*Candra-pradīpa-sūtra*) on this point:

> The power of śamatha makes your mind steady;
> Vipaśyanā makes it like a mountain.

Tsongkhapa elaborates on the meaning of this. When you can focus effortlessly on a particular object for as long as you like, it is a sign that your śamatha practice has been successful. Combining śamatha with the practice of vipaśyanā makes the latter stronger and more powerful. In contrast, when you engage in analytical meditation without a stable mind, you easily become distracted. Your mind wanders here and there, and you do not get very far. When you meditate on emptiness with śamatha, your mind is steady and can remain on its object—emptiness. Due to that stabilized state, you are able to see the depth and details of that object. This second quality, seeing the object clearly, is actually a function of vipaśyanā. The result of vipaśyanā practice supported by śamatha is the direct realization of ultimate truth—the emptiness of self. When you achieve this direct understanding of reality, your insight will be as solid as a mountain.

Let's look at this a little more closely. When you first meditate on emptiness, your object of concentration will be a concept, a *universal*, what we sometimes call a *generic image*. Before achieving śamatha, you will not be able to visualize that image clearly. As your mind becomes more stable through the cultivation of śamatha, the object of your meditation becomes clearer. Later, as you get more and more familiar with that concept, your understanding of it strengthens. Eventually, with the aid of the stability of śamatha, your conceptual understanding of emptiness will fade and a direct realization of emptiness will begin to emerge. The image or concept lessens as the direct realization becomes clearer and clearer. Finally you will clearly see the object, emptiness, without using concepts, ideas, or thought. It becomes a direct perception.

To see the truth of emptiness, śamatha and vipaśyanā must be joined; a stable mind must engage in analytical investigation to produce wisdom. When your analytical meditation has this concentrated quality of meditative stability and goes on to examine the self, you will realize the truth of selflessness. The *Compendium of Teachings Sutra* (*Dharma-saṃgīti-sūtra*) says:

> When your mind is in meditative equipoise, you will understand reality
> just as it is.

"Meditative equipoise" refers to the mind of śamatha, which is completely free from excitement and laxity. These are the two key obstacles to śamatha. *Laxity*, or sinking, is when the mind becomes heavy and dull. *Excitement* is when the mind is racing here and there, distracted due to the power of attachment. Because volatile mental states like aversion and jealousy also distract the mind from its object, they are included in the discussion of excitement. When the mind is under the power of laxity or excitement, it is not in the state of śamatha. Kamalaśīla also cites the Buddha to support his claim in his first *Stages of Meditation*.

Because your mind moves like water, it does not rest without the foundation of meditative stabilization; a mind that is not in meditative equipoise cannot understand reality just as it is. Also, the Bhagavan says, "With meditative equipoise, you know reality just as it is."

Śamatha is like a vessel. To have the wisdom that realizes ultimate truth you need a vessel to hold it. If you do not have the vessel of śamatha, when you do analytical meditation with the aim of realizing ultimate truth, your mind will get distracted. Without śamatha, you will not be able to see the ultimate truth as it is. But with a stabilized mind, you do not get distracted and will be able to understand the ultimate truth directly. Tsongkhapa used the analogy of a butter lamp that can clearly illuminate an object because light naturally shines from a flame. But if the flame flickers in the wind, the light is not steady and strong. If you put up a windscreen to protect the flame, the butter lamp will illuminate its object more clearly. This does not mean that the windscreen is the nature of illumination; it is a supporting condition, albeit a very important one. In the same way, the state of śamatha is a supporting condition for the insight that knows reality. Although wisdom that is undistracted and undisturbed depends upon the cultivation of śamatha, it does not arise from śamatha. An understanding of emptiness comes from analytical meditation. It is not accomplished from mere mental stabilization.

At first it may seem contradictory that you engage in analytical meditation while simultaneously having single-pointed concentration. And further, you may wonder, "Isn't the blissful physical experience that accompanies śamatha distracting?" We'll deal with the second question first. The sensation of physical and mental pleasure that comes with śamatha does not disturb concentration. It is a subtle peacefulness and calmness. To answer the first question, let's use the analogy of a large bowl of water with a little fish swimming in it. The fish may be swimming up, down, and all around, but it does not disturb the main body of water. In the same way, after śamatha is achieved, mental stabilization is not disturbed by analytic wisdom looking around and investigating the nature of reality. In fact, the wisdom becomes sharper and, of course, more stable. That stability comes from the practice of śamatha.

When you have achieved śamatha, all the virtuous practices you do—such as reciting meditational liturgies (sādhanas), performing rituals, engaging in analytical meditation, or meditating on a maṇḍala—become much stronger and the meditations become much clearer. This will be the case not only when concentrating on ultimate reality but also when meditating on the impermanence of phenomena, on karma and its results, or on any of a number of other topics.

When you engage in analytical meditation, say for example on impermanence,

you ask and attempt to answer various questions: "How are things impermanent?" "Why are they impermanent?" "What is the nature of change?" and so
on. On their own, merely stabilizing the mind or merely analyzing a topic will
not produce powerful insights. If you lack śamatha, even if you engage in the
appropriate forms of analysis for generating bodhicitta, for example, it will not
be very powerful. And conversely, if you do not investigate the necessary topics and only succeed in single-pointed meditation, you also will not generate
bodhicitta. You need the two in combination. When śamatha and vipaśyanā
are joined together in equal proportions, they become incredibly powerful and
strong.

Śāntideva explains it in this way in the opening verse of his chapter on meditative stability:

> The person whose mind is distracted
> Lives between the fangs of the afflictions.

If you are constantly distracted and have no control over your mind, you are
under the sway of the afflictions and at the mercy of the disturbing emotions.
Śāntideva goes on to say that the same is true even for practitioners who
engage in various meritorious activities and live austerely for a long time. If
their minds are distracted when they engage in these practices, the practices
become virtually pointless. It is important that your mind is not distracted
when you recite prayers or mantras if they are to have any transformative
power.

So you must ask yourself, "What is the purpose of achieving śamatha?" Is
it to feel good by calming the mind? Is it just to be able to sit and focus on a
single object without doing anything else? No. The purpose is to turn a concentrated mind toward virtuous objects and virtuous attitudes in order to become
familiar with them, integrate them into your mind, and to create merit. You
cultivate śamatha so that you can effectively use your mind in virtuous ways
that lead to liberation for yourself and others. More specifically, the purpose
of accomplishing śamatha is to have a mind with enough pliancy that it is able
to direct itself from one virtuous object to another at will and is able to remain
on the chosen object for as long as it wishes. With śamatha you can investigate
your object as deeply as you like and hold the mind there peacefully. When
you wish to move to the next virtuous object of investigation, you are able to
redirect your mind naturally and with complete ease.

When you attain śamatha, you will have mental strength and power. This
includes the ability of your mind to avoid any interruption of meditative focus
on virtuous objects. For example, if you have achieved śamatha and are engaged

in the practice of generosity—giving your belongings, providing services, or offering your merits or virtues to others—your mind will be continuously directed toward such activities. You will not be distracted by any mental affliction and find yourself engaging in nonvirtuous activities of body, speech, or mind. The same is true with patience, renunciation, perseverance, and faith. Śamatha is the strong and powerful mind that, through attention to virtue, is a key component for achieving liberation from samsara.

All virtues are developed through wisdom. For example, in order to properly practice generosity, you must know the nature of many things: the person to whom you are giving, what you are giving, how you are giving, the result of giving, the purpose of giving, and so on. Thus the real perfection of generosity is understanding these in light of the wisdom that knows reality as it truly is. Thus the ultimate benefit from analytical cultivation of any virtue occurs when the practice of vipaśyanā is grounded in a mind of śamatha. You must have both. Likewise, when practicing the various vows—such as individual liberation vows, bodhisattva vows, and tantric vows—you need both vipaśyanā and śamatha. It is not necessary to go into the details of each here; suffice it to say that the merit accrued by practice of the six perfections increases exponentially when accompanied by śamatha and vipaśyanā.

Sometimes it looks like a particular teaching's emphasis is all on vipaśyanā. Sometimes it looks like a teaching's emphasis is all on śamatha. Final emancipation, everlasting freedom, requires both. Tsongkhapa offers many quotations to support this argument. The first is from the great Indian paṇḍita Kamalaśīla, who said in his second *Stages of Meditation*:

> Cultivating just śamatha alone does not get rid of a practitioner's obscurations; it only suppresses the afflictions for a while. Unless you have the light of wisdom, you do not destroy the dormant tendencies.

Without the wisdom that directly realizes emptiness, the obscurations and afflictions will remain in your subconscious, just hidden for a while. Even if on the surface your meditation is calm and virtuous, the afflictions remain. Ordinary people are dominated by powerful grasping at the self—the egotistic view. All our emotions, all our thoughts, all our activities are centered on our selfish purpose and our mistaken notion of "I." Anxiety and worry arise from desire for this self to be happy and free from misery. Negative attitudes such as anger, hatred, pride, jealousy, and so forth arise from self-cherishing, self-clinging, and self-attachment. Once these negative attitudes and wrong views emerge, we become further immersed in the samsaric pain of sickness, old age, unhappiness, confusion, sorrow, birth, and death. It is true that through developing single-pointed concentration we can experience peace. But śamatha alone only provides a temporary peace because it does not destroy the ignorance that is the seed or root of the afflictions that keep us bound in samsara. Each of the negative emotions—desire, hatred, pride, and so forth—can easily become manifest when its seeds remain in our mind and external conditions support them. They are like a poison tree. If we merely cut a branch without killing the root, it will simply grow another branch again in the future. No matter how much śamatha practice you do, if it is not accompanied by insight—first cultivated with analysis—it will not help you to achieve liberation.

Kamalaśīla continues by quoting the *Sutra Unraveling the Intended Meaning*:

> Meditative stabilization suppresses afflictions;
> Wisdom destroys dormant tendencies.

Likewise, the *King of Samādhi Sutra* says:

> Although worldly persons cultivate concentration,
> They do not destroy the notion of self.
> Their afflictions return and disturb them
> As they did Udraka, who cultivated concentration in this way.

When the Buddha was alive, there was a non-Buddhist yogi named Udraka. He was one of the Buddha's teachers before his enlightenment. Udraka attained śamatha and was able to temporarily subdue his mental afflictions. His path led to the peak of cyclic existence, the highest level of the formless realm, but because he did not have the highest wisdom, he was unable to remove his afflictions from the root, and they continued to manifest and disturb him.

The stanza that follows this one in the *King of Samādhi Sutra* says that if you understand the emptiness of self and phenomena through analytical examination and then integrate that conceptual understanding with meditation, you will attain a realization of selflessness. This initial realization of emptiness does not immediately result in the removal of all the obstacles. You must become thoroughly accustomed to emptiness through ongoing meditation on it for a long time. Gradually the various mental afflictions will lessen. They will become smaller and smaller, and eventually even the most subtle mental afflictions will be completely removed from the root. It is at that point that you attain liberation, or nirvāṇa. There is no other cause that leads to the result of the attainment of nirvāṇa.

The Buddha says in the *Scriptural Collection of Bodhisattvas* (*Bodhisattva-*

piṭaka) that the teachings on selflessness are the basis for getting rid of all the mental afflictions. In other words, you get rid of the mental afflictions by generating deep insight, a direct realization of selflessness, based on a combined cultivation of śamatha and vipaśyanā. In order to meditate properly on selflessness or emptiness, you must first study the teachings on this topic, then contemplate these teachings, and finally integrate them through meditation. By doing this successfully, you will free yourself from aging and death and repeated rebirth in samsara. In summary, if you wish to attain the perfect enlightenment or omniscience of a buddha, you must attain śamatha and cultivate vipaśyanā.

There is another dimension to successful practice that needs to be mentioned here: ethical discipline. Ethical discipline is the first of the three trainings— ethical discipline, concentration, and wisdom—which incorporate all the practices needed to attain liberation and enlightenment. Ethical discipline is necessary for the cultivation of a stable mind, and a stable mind is needed for the cultivation of insight. This is the case because external distractions can easily dominate an untrained mind. Your body's sensory organs are formed to gather external data. As soon as your sense organs encounter their respective objects, you label them as attractive or unattractive. Based on those evaluations, your mind is pulled in various directions. It is incapable of remaining peacefully in one place. Therefore, in the beginning of your practice, you need to lessen the power of external influences on your mind. The way to do that is to keep your physical, verbal, and mental actions under control. The way to do that is to keep the vows of ethical discipline. Just as good soil is the foundation for good crops, ethical conduct is the ground for śamatha, insight, and other realizations. This is what is meant in the *Pile of Precious Things Collection* (*Ratna-kūṭa-grantha*) when it says:

> Keeping ethical discipline, you will attain meditative concentration;
> Attaining concentration, you cultivate wisdom;
> With wisdom you attain pure wisdom;
> As your sublime wisdom is pure, your ethical discipline is perfect.

The importance of wisdom is also stressed in the *Sutra of Cultivating Faith in the Mahayana* when the Buddha says:

> Child of good lineage, if you did not have wisdom, I would not say that you had faith in the Mahayana of bodhisattvas, nor would I say you knew the real nature of the Mahayana.

Having "faith in the Mahayana" means to trust in the goals of the Mahayana and the methods taught to achieve those goals. Trusting the practices of the Mahayana depends on some degree of understanding the nature of causality, how and why the goal of the Mahayana is achievable, the nature of the two types of obscurations—the mental afflictions and knowledge obstacles—and that these obstacles can be removed. Thus the faith discussed here is not blind faith; it is irreversible faith in that it arises from wisdom. Understanding arises from analytical meditation. On the basis of understanding you can engage in practice with confidence and trust.

It is interesting to briefly contrast this point with the teachings of Hva Shang Mahayana. According to traditional Tibetan histories, this Chinese master came to Tibet during the earliest spread of the Dharma. He taught that we just need to meditate and clear the mind of all thought; study, analysis, and ethical discipline are not only unimportant, they are actually obstacles. Why? Because all thought, even the study of Buddhism, muddies the clarity of the mind. In his view, a mind that is free of thought is naturally clear, like a crystal. So clearing the mind of thought is to realize the mind's true nature—emptiness. For example, a glass is clear, but when you fill it with colored liquid, the glass itself seems to take on that color. If you put ketchup in a crystal bowl, then the crystal bowl looks red. But that is not the nature of the crystal itself; the red color of the ketchup conceals the true nature of the crystal. According to Hva Shang, the thoughts in our minds are like these colors; they taint the natural clarity of the mind. Because all thoughts, even virtuous ones, color the naturally clear mind, we should attempt to cease all thought. This can seem very attractive. It is relatively easy and gives us temporary relief from worry.[4]

In contrast, Tsongkhapa and the Indian masters of the Prāsaṅgika Madhyamaka school stress that both śamatha and vipaśyanā are necessary. Neither alone can remove the mental afflictions, but when they are combined, they get rid of the afflictions from the root. It is a mistake to think, as some people do, that they do not need śamatha because wisdom will remove the afflictions. Likewise, it is a mistake to think, "If I just calm my mind so that it does not move and does not have any thoughts, that is enlightenment." Śamatha and vipaśyanā must be brought to fruition in union.

(e) How to be certain about their order

So if both śamatha and vipaśyanā are essential, and if they are most effective when practiced together, should you train in them simultaneously from the very beginning? Or, if they should be learned in a particular order, which should be cultivated first? Śāntideva said in *Engaging in the Bodhisattva Deeds*:

Vipaśyanā possessed of śamatha
Destroys the afflictions. Knowing this,
Seek śamatha at the outset.

This clearly indicates that first you train in śamatha. Then, based on that training, you cultivate vipaśyanā. Once the mental power of śamatha is achieved, you can develop the wisdom that knows reality. That wisdom, grounded in the stabilization of śamatha, is able to uproot the afflictions like greed, hatred, anger, and so forth.

Tsongkhapa goes on to address a hypothetical opponent who refers to Kamalaśīla's first *Stages of Meditation*. According to this opponent's understanding of that text, the object of śamatha meditation is indefinite; any sort of object can be chosen. In other words, the object of śamatha can be either a conventional phenomenon, such as a person, or that object's true nature, emptiness. The disputant therefore raises the following question, "If a person understands selflessness through inferential knowledge and uses that conceptual understanding of emptiness as the focal object of meditation in śamatha practice, why can't a direct realization of emptiness arise at the same time as perfect śamatha?" In other words, why can't we use this inferential understanding of emptiness as the object of our training in single-pointed concentration and thus transform it into a direct realization simultaneously with the cultivation of śamatha? Why must śamatha come first? Why can't we cultivate them simultaneously? Even nowadays, people often ask if they should meditate on śamatha and vipaśyanā simultaneously.

Tsongkhapa replies by explaining the way śamatha precedes vipaśyanā. Generally people think understanding the view of selflessness is vipaśyanā. But understanding selflessness conceptually is not actual vipaśyanā. To understand selflessness conceptually does not require śamatha. Before śamatha is attained you can generate the view of emptiness through inferential knowledge, such as with Madhyamaka logical proofs, by listening to teachings, with reasoning, and so forth. When Tsongkhapa says that we need to achieve śamatha before vipaśyanā, he is not referring to an inferential understanding of emptiness. He is referring to the direct realization of emptiness.

The opponent here worries that if we claim śamatha precedes vipaśyanā, then no mental transformation is possible without śamatha. This depends upon what the opponent means by mental transformation. If by mental transformation the opponent means that the mind is emotionally or experientially changed, then this does not require the achievement of śamatha. For example, if we go to a lecture and hear a very moving speech, it can effect a mental transformation in us. Or when we read or hear teachings about the suffering of sentient beings in samsara, we may experience an emotional transformation that stimulates us to feel real love and compassion for other living creatures. This sort of mental transformation is certainly possible without the achievement of śamatha. But if the opponent is referring to the permanent removal of the mental afflictions, then that does require the achievement of śamatha, which necessarily precedes a direct realization of vipaśyanā.

An analytical meditation or an inferential discernment of the ultimate cannot generate the special mental dexterity that is real vipaśyanā. Not until the physical and mental pliancy of śamatha is generated can this special mental dexterity develop. When the mind goes to and remains on your chosen object with ease, and when your body easily and spontaneously cooperates with the mind, you have attained the mental and physical pliancy that characterizes śamatha. With this you can engage in the subtle analysis of the ultimate. It is from this that the special mental dexterity of vipaśyanā arises. Until then, your insight only simulates or approximates actual vipaśyanā. Because it was taught this way in the *Sutra Unraveling the Intended Meaning*, Tsongkhapa says that if you do not have śamatha, no matter how much you engage in analytical meditation on the nature of reality, this special mental pliancy and bliss will not arise. Only when you have achieved śamatha and combine it with analytical wisdom examining the depths of reality will your practice generate the mental dexterity of vipaśyanā.

Although the two are combined later in practice, śamatha and vipaśyanā each have their own unique, complementary effects. It is only when you combine śamatha with meditation on emptiness using the power of analytical wisdom that this unique mental dexterity is obtained. If your meditation on emptiness is simply taking "emptiness" as an object of concentration without any analytical dimension to it, the resulting mental dexterity will still be a part of śamatha. This is true even after you achieve śamatha: vipaśyanā is meditation analyzing the nature of reality. And it is also the case that no matter how much logical analysis you do, if you have not cultivated stability first, this mental dexterity will not be achieved. Thus śamatha comes first and then vipaśyanā is cultivated. To support this point, Tsongkhapa refers back to a passage from the *Sutra Unraveling the Intended Meaning* that he quoted earlier.[5]

Many of the great and famous Indian scholars explain in their texts on meditation that you must first cultivate śamatha and on that basis cultivate vipaśyanā. Some of the sources Tsongkhapa draws from to support this position are Asaṅga's *Bodhisattva Grounds* (*Bodhisattva-bhūmi*) and his *Śrāvaka Grounds* (*Śrāvaka-bhūmi*), Bhāviveka's *Heart of the Middle Way* (*Madhyamaka-hṛdaya*), Śāntideva's *Engaging in the Bodhisattva Deeds*, and Kamalaśīla's three *Stages of Meditation*.

In fact, expanding upon the issue of the order of developing śamatha and vipaśyanā, Tsongkhapa reminds us that all of the six perfections ought to be cultivated in order. Here Tsongkhapa relies upon Maitreya's *Ornament for the Mahayana Sutras* (*Mahāyāna-sūtra-alaṃkāra*), which says, "the latter develop based on the former." On the basis of generosity, ethics is achieved. On the basis of ethics, patience is achieved, and so forth. It follows from this that it is only on the basis of cultivating meditative stabilization—śamatha—that insight—vipaśyanā—can be achieved.

Some Indian scholars have claimed that you can attain vipaśyanā by doing analytical meditation without separately practicing śamatha first. Tsongkhapa says that such a position is untenable and is contradicted by all the great masters and texts mentioned above. Intelligent people should not rely on this view. If you are beginning your training of śamatha and vipaśyanā and have not attained either, you should train in the proper order. Later, after you have attained śamatha and vipaśyanā, the order of further practice can change.

Tsongkhapa continues to address the order of these two practices by having his hypothetical opponent ask how he would respond to a statement in Asaṅga's *Compendium of Knowledge* (*Abhidharma-samuccaya*):

> Some attain insight but do not attain śamatha; they strive for śamatha on the basis of insight.

Asaṅga's text seems to present the opposite view here, doesn't it? This is a complicated point, and you need some background information to understand it. So I will begin, seemingly digressing, to provide you with the necessary context.

Buddhism categorizes the realms of existence into three: the desire realm, the form realm, and the formless realm. The grossest or roughest is the realm in which we live, the desire realm. The form realm is a little higher and subtler, and the formless realm is the subtlest. In the higher realms, life is a lot more peaceful. Generally speaking, we say that the form and formless realms are states of meditative concentration. These states of concentration are attained after achieving śamatha. In the desire realm our experience is so rough that in many ways it is characterized as the opposite of śamatha. Absorbed by attachment, we are constantly distracted and excited on the one hand, and fall to dullness and sleepiness on the other. In the form and formless realms the distracted quality of the desire realm is not present.

From the point of view of levels of meditative concentration, we define different stages. There is one in the desire realm, four in the form realm, and four in the formless realm. The single concentration that takes place in the desire realm is subdivided into the nine stages of the development of śamatha. After the ninth stage, śamatha is achieved. The achievement of śamatha marks the beginning point of the preparatory part of the first concentration, or meditative absorption, of the form realm. This can occur during a life in the desire realm; once śamatha is achieved your mental state will be that preparatory part of the first meditative absorption of the form realm. In other words, although you may still physically be in this human body, after you achieve actual śamatha your mind is part of, or associated with, a higher realm.

When describing each of the four levels of meditative absorption in the form realm and the four concentrations in the formless realms, we distinguish two parts: the preparatory part and the actualized part. Here the term *preparatory* does not mean that this mental state is separate from, or not a part of, that meditative absorption. Because it is only after you achieve śamatha that your mind has entered the preparatory part of the first absorption. The term *preparatory* is used to indicate it is the first part—it is where you use that particular level of meditative absorption to deal with the specific afflictions associated with that level; when those have been dealt with, you have entered the actualized part of that level of meditative absorption.

There are nine general types of afflictions of the desire realm, such as hatred, jealousy, attachment, and so forth. These nine are divided up into three groups: three rough or big, three medium, and three subtle or small. The time starting from the attainment of śamatha through the entire period you are working to subdue or remove all nine desire-realm afflictions is called the preparatory level of the first meditative absorption. When all the desire-realm afflictions are completely subdued or removed, you are on the actualized part of first meditative absorption.

Here we need to differentiate between the mundane path and the supramundane path. The mundane-path practices are very effective for subduing the afflictions that belong to the desire realm, the form realm, and the first three levels of the formless realm. The supramundane path eliminates the afflictions of all three realms totally and completely. This requires a realization of emptiness. Even though the supramundane path is superior, it is much harder at first. So you may want to pursue the mundane path initially to temporarily suppress the afflictions. Later, when you reach a point where your mind is more settled and controlled, you engage in the supramundane path. This can be a very good option for many people. The most intelligent practitioners use the supramundane path from the beginning, but you choose depending on your aptitude and predispositions.

So what do you do on the mundane preparatory part of the first meditative absorption of the form realm? You use śamatha and in your meditation compare the excellence of the first meditative absorption to the disadvantageous qualities of the desire realm. The first meditative absorption, while not perfect, is immensely better than the desire realm, which is characterized by misery, ugliness, impurity, and so forth. On the first meditative absorption you have a long life, a more subtle body, freedom from physical misery, purity, relative peacefulness, and so forth. As you contemplate these differences, your attachment to the desire realm will gradually lessen.

The mundane path continues in a similar way through all the other levels of the form and formless realms. On the preparatory part of the next level, you compare the advantages of the next higher level to the coarseness and misery of the one below it. This comparison suppresses the afflictions associated with the former level, and you enter the actual part of that next level. Gradually you subdue afflictions until you attain the highest level of the formless realm, the peak of cyclic existence. The mundane path can take you no further. It is not possible to suppress the afflictions of the highest level of the formless realm because there is nothing more subtle or peaceful within samsara with which to compare it.

Thus, even if you have attained the highest level of the formless realm through the mundane path, if you want to attain liberation from samsara, you must enter the supramundane path and eliminate the afflictions from the root, not just suppress them temporarily. To do that, you must cultivate a direct realization of emptiness. The supramundane path is entered when a yogi or yogini applies śamatha in a meditation on emptiness and achieves the state of a superior one; in other words, he or she becomes an ārya—a person with a direct realization of emptiness. When a practitioner has eliminated the nine desire-realm afflictions from the root through this meditation on emptiness, he or she has achieved the actual first meditative absorption of the supramundane path. Although this practitioner is an ārya, she or he is still not an arhat because the afflictions of the upper realms are not yet removed. Removing these on the supramundane path requires a deepened, further meditation of vipaśyanā in conjunction with śamatha.

It is easy for people to be confused about the order of cultivation of śamatha and insight because on the supramundane path, progression to the actual first meditative absorption does in fact depend upon a realization of emptiness. On the preparatory level of the first meditative absorption of the supramundane path, a portion of śamatha is achieved, and then it is conjoined with vipaśyanā. Only when the desire-realm afflictions are completely removed through a direct realization of emptiness is the actual part of the first meditative absorption achieved. And, as we've seen, a direct realization of emptiness depends upon śamatha.

To fully understand this point, the difference between the mundane and supramundane paths needs a bit more clarification. The preparatory stage of the first meditative absorption of the form realm has a mundane path and a corollary supramundane path. In other words, the preparatory stage for the first absorption is suitable for both the mundane and supramundane paths. The defining difference between them is whether the practitioner takes a mundane object of meditation—the comparative approach described above—or a supramundane object of meditation—emptiness. Thus we speak of this preparatory level as having two divisions: contaminated and uncontaminated. It is only the preparatory part of the first absorption that can be utilized to transition from the mundane to the supramundane path. As the practitioner suppresses all the afflictions of the desire realm on the preparatory level of the first meditative absorption, they can also employ vipaśyanā to remove these afflictions from the root. This transition cannot be done on any of the later stages of the mundane path.

From this perspective, the preparatory part of the meditative concentrations of all the other levels of the form and formless realms are only contaminated. They have only mundane paths where the practitioners are doing comparisons to realize that one level of samsara is superior to the preceding one. The object of their meditation is contaminated; it is not emptiness. In contrast, when the meditator on the preparatory part of the first meditative absorption uses emptiness as his or her object of meditation, he or she attains a direct realization of the nature of reality and removes the desire-realm afflictions from the root. After this, the ārya practitioner progresses from one actual stage to the next, from the actual first absorption of the form realm to the actual second absorption of the form realm, and so forth, on up to the highest point of the formless realm. There is no supramundane preparatory stage from the second absorption of the form realm on upward. Why? Because an ārya's realization of emptiness does not change. The object of an ārya's meditation on emptiness changes, but the realization does not.

Only on the mundane path are there preparatory stages on the higher levels. Non-āryas must practice this way because their comparative meditations only temporarily subdue their corresponding afflictions. From this point of view, the preparatory stage of the first absorption is superior to all the other preparatory stages. It is the only one that has a supramundane aspect; all the other preparatory stages of the higher meditative absorptions are purely mundane.

The Buddha taught that desire-realm afflictions are so sharp, so rough, and so powerful that achieving freedom from them is quite difficult. Therefore he spoke of the results of removing these afflictions in terms of four fruits: stream winner, once-returner, nonreturner, and arhat. In brief, when a person enters the supramundane path he or she becomes a stream winner. When that person has removed six of the nine desire-realm afflictions, he or she is called a *once-returner* because that being will remove the final three afflictions after only one more rebirth. When an ārya has removed all nine desire-realm afflictions on the supramundane path, that yogi becomes a nonreturner. Such yogis are called *nonreturners* because they are no longer compelled by karma and the afflictions to be reborn in the desire realm. To rephrase, at this point on the path, all the afflictions associated with the desire realm—those that lead us to produce karma that compels rebirth in the desire realm—are removed from the root. This is the case for all practitioners, including those on the Hīnāyāna path. If a nonreturner ārya is on the śrāvaka or pratyekabuddha path, then she or he will be born in one of the upper realms.

The sharpest ārya yogis can remove all the deluded afflictions of the desire, form, and formless realms at once. They are called "the ones who abandon all afflictions simultaneously." To understand this we need to look at the types of mental afflictions. The desire realm and the four levels each of the form and formless realms have nine mental afflictions. So there are eighty-one afflictions altogether. Each group of nine is divided into subgroups of big, medium, and small. The big or gross ones are further divided as big-big, big-medium, and big-small. The medium and small afflictions are similarly subdivided into three: medium-big, medium-medium, medium-small, and so forth. When we say that sharp yogis abandon all afflictions simultaneously, it means that they begin by removing all the big-big afflictions from the desire realm, the four levels of the form realms, and the four levels of the formless realm simultaneously. They remove all nine rough big-big afflictions at once. Then they remove all nine big-medium ones simultaneously. In this way they remove the eighty-one afflictions in nine steps beginning with the grossest of each of the nine levels of the three realms. On each step of the path they remove progressively more subtle afflictions from each of the realms simultaneously. This way of uprooting the afflictions is much faster than the alternative method, which is to eliminate the desire-realm afflictions one at a time, then the form-realm afflictions one at a time, and finally the formless-realm afflictions one at a time.

When yogis engage in the quicker method, they obtain all the actual first meditative concentrations of the form and formless realms simultaneously. This is the case because the most subtle of the desire-realm afflictions are removed at the same time that the most subtle afflictions from the two higher realms. And, by definition, one attains the first meditative absorption of the supramundane path when all the desire-realm afflictions are removed from the root.

The mundane path, which utilizes the comparative meditations, always takes the gradual approach. If a yogi or yogini begins with the mundane path, first temporarily suppressing the grossest manifestations of the afflictions before beginning the supramundane path, he or she will proceed in the same gradual way through each of the afflictions when engaging in the supramundane path. Such a yogi progresses through the desire-realm afflictions, then the form-realm afflictions, and finally the formless-realm afflictions, removing each one from the root as he or she goes. If a practitioner skips the mundane path and goes directly to the supramundane path, he or she will engage in the quicker route. The quicker route of "one who abandons all the deluded afflictions simultaneously" is, of course, preferable for those who are capable of it.

This is a complicated point, and the distinctive natures of the mundane and supramundane paths are revisited and elaborated further in chapter 6 below.

·2·

Preparing for Śamatha Meditation

(f) How to train in each
  (i) How to train in śamatha
    (a') Relying on the preconditions for śamatha
      (1') Dwelling in an appropriate area
      (2') Having little desire
      (3') Being content
      (4') Completely giving up many activities
      (5') Practicing pure ethical discipline
      (6') Completely ridding yourself of thoughts of desire and so on
    (b') How to cultivate śamatha on that basis
      (1') Preparation
      (2') Actual practice
        (a") Meditative posture
        (b") The meditative process
          (1") How to develop flawless concentration
            (a)) What to do prior to focusing the attention on an object of meditation
            (b)) What to do while focusing on an object of meditation
              (1)) Identifying the object of meditation upon which your attention is set
              (a')) A general presentation of the objects of meditation
                (1')) The objects of meditation themselves
                  (a")) Universal objects of meditation
                    (1")) Discursive images
                    (2")) Nondiscursive images
                    (3")) The limits of existence
                    (4")) Achievement of your purpose

(b")) Objects of meditation for
purifying your behavior
(1")) Ugliness
(2")) Love
(3")) Dependent arising
(4")) Differentiation of
constituents
(5")) Inhalation and exhalation
(c")) Objects of meditation for
cultivating expertise
(1")) The aggregates
(2")) The constituents
(3")) The sources
(4")) Dependent arising
(5")) What is and is not possible
(d")) Objects of meditation for purifying the afflictions
(2')) Who should meditate on which
object
(3')) Synonyms of the object of meditation
(b')) Identifying objects of meditation for this
context

(f) HOW TO TRAIN IN EACH

TSONGKHAPA NOW ADDRESSES how to train in śamatha: how to prepare
and then do the practice (the current chapter), methods of practice (chapter 3), pitfalls and how to deal with them (chapter 4), knowing when śamatha
has been achieved (chapter 5), and last, how to practice the rest of the path on
the basis of śamatha (chapter 6). Subsequently, volume 5 of this series explains
how to train in vipaśyanā and how to then unite śamatha with vipaśyanā.

The outline of the *Lamrim Chenmo* has three subtopics for the section of
how you prepare and then train in śamatha:

(a') Relying on the preconditions for śamatha
(b') How to cultivate śamatha on that basis
(c') The measure of successful cultivation śamatha

(a′) Relying on the Preconditions for Śamatha

A number of external and internal conditions make the development of śamatha easier. Yogis depend on six specific favorable conditions for śamatha practice. Try to ensure that you have these favorable conditions at the outset of your practice:

(1′) Dwelling in an appropriate area
(2′) Having little desire
(3′) Being content
(4′) Completely giving up many activities
(5′) Practicing pure ethical discipline
(6′) Completely ridding yourself of thoughts of desire and so on

(1′) Dwelling in an Appropriate Area

If you are serious about developing śamatha, you need to find a harmonious place for practice. What does *harmonious* mean here? This term refers to five specific qualities explained in the *Ornament for the Mahayana Sutras*:

> The intelligent practice in a place
> That is accessible, is a good place to live,
> Offers good ground and good companions,
> And has the requisites for comfortable yogic practices.

An "accessible" place is a locale where food, shelter, and other basic necessities are easy to obtain. Without that, instead of meditating, you will constantly have to go looking for food and other necessities. It is easy to get physically and mentally consumed with the need to obtain these things and lose sight of your practice. Moreover, these necessities must be acquired in a virtuous way, not by stealing, cheating, lying, and so forth.

"A good place to live" is a place that facilitates a serene meditative practice; it is free of every sort of problem that may disturb your mind. There shouldn't be any wild animals, thieves, or any other sort of hostile people or creatures who want to harm you. There also should be few people who engage in wild or non-virtuous conduct; living in close proximity or spending too much time with such people can influence your behavior and cause your practice to degenerate. This is why yogis often go to secluded and quiet places like caves so external factors do not disturb them.

The third, a "good ground," refers to the environmental qualities of a place, such as the climate, the prevalence of disease, the ease of physically adapting to that environment, and so forth. When all of the environmental factors of a place are suitable for long-term practice it is said to be a good ground.

The fourth, "good companions," refers to the benefit of having the company of one, two, or even more friends who are virtuous in their conduct and have a religious view that is harmonious with your own. The presence of such friends can be a great support to your practice.

Last, Tsongkhapa says that your place of practice must not be too busy or crowded with people during the day and should be quiet at night.

(2') HAVING LITTLE DESIRE

This is discussed simultaneously with the next topic.

(3') BEING CONTENT

It is best to be happy and satisfied with simple things and to refrain from attachment to fancy and expensive things. With regard to sustained meditation practice, Vasubandhu says in *Treasury of Knowledge* (*Abhidharmakośa*) that it is easy to practice if you do not desire more than what you have, and it is difficult if you have many unsatisfied desires.[6] Here "desire" means excessive attachment to the possessions you already have, and "unsatisfied desires" is attachment to things you do not possess. Thus Vasubandhu encourages us to minimize our desire to obtain more things and to be content with what we have. Tsongkhapa gives the example of a monk who should be content with his old, worn-out robes and not desire better ones.

(4') COMPLETELY GIVING UP MANY ACTIVITIES

Success in a meditative practice aimed at the development of śamatha requires you to give up certain worldly activities, such as commerce or excessive socializing. Even certain activities that are generally considered virtuous, such as practicing medicine, can be hindrances to the cultivation of the state of śamatha. The focus of this practice is single-pointed concentration, developing it requires periods of intensive meditation practice, and these sorts of activities function as distractions.

(5') PRACTICING PURE ETHICAL DISCIPLINE

The section presents advice on maintaining pure conduct of body, speech, and mind during this time of training. Tsongkhapa advises us to strictly maintain all the vows we have already taken. Those who have the lay vows, any of the types of monastic vows—such as novice vows or full ordination vows—bodhisattva vows, or tantric vows should do their best to keep them purely. Even if you have not formally taken vows, try to guide your activities in a virtuous direction and guard against the ten nonvirtues of body, speech, and mind.[7]

There are two categories of nonvirtuous actions: those that are naturally nonvirtuous and those that are only nonvirtuous if you have taken a vow to refrain from them for a higher purpose. For example, monks are not supposed to cut grass or let their hair grow beyond a certain length. Cutting grass is non-virtuous only if you have taken a vow promising that you will not do it. The guidelines for this category of action have some flexibility depending on the circumstances. There may be instances where for an even higher purpose it is better to violate a vow. Naturally nonvirtuous actions should be avoided by everybody.

Keeping the ethical commitments of body, speech, and mind purely and properly is an important component in training the mind in mental stabiliza-tion. If your sense organs are not controlled, it is difficult to tame your mind. Therefore, try not to break your vows of conduct. If you do happen to break a vow, even accidentally, you should quickly recognize this, feel regret, and try to purify the deed with confession and so forth. On this topic Vasubandhu's *Treasury of Knowledge* says:

> By hearing and contemplating the teachings and living in accord with
>   ethics,
> One can fully engage in the practice of meditation.[8]

The basis of meditative stability and wisdom is pure ethical conduct. Just as good nutrient-rich soil is the foundation for good crops, pure ethical disci-pline is the foundation of spiritual development for practitioners. This is what Tsongkhapa means when he speaks of the importance of having pure ethical discipline.

(6') COMPLETELY RIDDING YOURSELF OF THOUGHTS OF DESIRE AND SO ON

Desiring objects of the five senses, longing for worldly goals, dwelling on anxi-eties or wishes, and so forth should be avoided as much as possible when train-ing in śamatha. It is difficult to have a peaceful and calm meditation with these types of thoughts, even when positive environmental circumstances such as a quiet place to practice are present.

The desire for worldly things like wealth, praise, and fame must be countered by considering their faults. If you do not recognize their disadvantages and instead see them as desirable, you may become mentally and physically trapped in the pursuit of them. This can cause many problems: you may harm others to get what you want; you may create enemies; or you may even get tossed into jail. And paradoxically, although a human lifetime is short, our thoughts and actions are geared toward accumulating things, even though at the time of death these things are of no benefit. Even worse, the negative karma you have accumulated in pursuit of those things will surely follow you after death as you go to your next life. You should meditate on how attachment and the negative karmic activities it propels can lead you to fall into a lower rebirth. Another antidote to thoughts of desire is to meditate on impermanence. All samsaric things, whether attractive or unattractive, are transitory. Recognizing the impermanent nature of those things and the impermanent nature of ourselves will reduce desire.

Of course, these six prerequisites do not alone entail attainment of śamatha. But śamatha depends on these six conditions in that they facilitate the generation of good concentration for those who have not yet done so. And for those who have already generated concentration, these six prerequisites help maintain and strengthen it. Tsongkhapa said that his explanation of the prerequisites is based primarily on Kamalaśīla's middle *Stages of Meditation* and Asaṅga's *Śrāvaka Levels* (*Śrāvaka-bhūmi*). He encourages us to study these texts to learn more about them.

Among these six, the most important are maintaining pure ethics, ridding ourselves of thoughts of desire, and dwelling in an appropriate place. Geshe Dromtönpa, Atiśa's disciple and the founder of the Kadam tradition, said:

> We think that the fault lies only in our personal instructions. As we then seek only personal instruction, we are unable to attain concentration. This is the result of not abiding under its conditions.

Often people think that if they get some special instructions it would eliminate their difficulties in generating perfect śamatha. They blame the difficulties in their cultivation of śamatha on not having been taught some secret technique. But śamatha does not arise merely from receiving certain special instructions. You must have the prerequisite conditions. Without these six conditions, it does not matter how many special instructions you receive; śamatha will not arise. When you do have the prerequisites, the special instructions will work perfectly.

The Buddha taught that the practices of the first four of the six perfections— generosity, ethical discipline, patience, and perseverance—are also preconditions for achieving śamatha. For example, when you perfect generosity you do not seek things for your own benefit. Part of the perfection of patience is the ability to take on hardship for a wholesome purpose. Being well trained in pure conduct is the perfection of ethical discipline. It is not only knowing and taking vows but also living in accordance with ethical guidelines. The perfection of perseverance is a genuine enthusiasm for practicing the path and cultivating virtue. If you have these four perfections, the distractions and mental obscurations that hinder the cultivation of śamatha are subdued, your environment and mental state become much more conducive to successful practice, and you are able to achieve śamatha far more quickly. For these reasons, in the first *Stages of Meditation*, Kamalaśīla taught that the first four perfections are causes for cultivating the higher ones, and he cites the *Sutra Unraveling the Intended Meaning* as scriptural support for his claim:

> You will quickly accomplish śamatha when you disregard the desire for possessions and such, keep good ethical conduct, have a disposition to readily tolerate suffering, and persevere diligently. That being the case, sources such as the *Sutra Unraveling the Intended Meaning* teach that generosity and the other perfections are causes of the successively higher perfections.

Therefore do not neglect cultivation of the first four perfections.

(b') How to cultivate śamatha on that basis

The next topic concerns the way to cultivate śamatha. It has two subtopics: preparation and the actual practice.

(1') Preparation

Śamatha is not limited to people who have trained in the first four perfections. In fact, it is practiced and achieved by both Buddhists and non-Buddhists, āryas and ordinary individuals. The practice of śamatha does not require a deep realization of emptiness or actualization of the method side of the path. It is common to many different paths, but the way of approaching it for bodhisattvas is unique. Tsongkhapa explains the unique qualities of śamatha practice in relation to the bodhisattva path at this point in *Lamrim Chenmo*.

The six preparatory conditions are important, he says. But Mahayana practitioners should in addition meditate for a long time on bodhicitta. Although śamatha does not require bodhicitta, it is important for Mahayana practitioners to set their motivation for the development of śamatha to be for the benefit of all sentient beings. As they contemplate the best way to help sentient beings, bodhisattvas see that cultivating śamatha can be of tremendous assistance. They begin serious practice of śamatha for that reason.

To meditate on bodhicitta, first engage in the meditations and practices that are in common with beings of small and medium scopes.[9] These set the foundation upon which practice grows. Like beings of the small scope, you should meditate on the impermanence of life: this life has leisure and great qualities, but it is impermanent and can be lost very easily and quickly. Your next life could be filled with acute suffering and contain fewer opportunities to progress on the path. Medium-scope beings meditate on the pervasive nature of samsaric suffering. Here you contemplate the way all sentient beings are subject to the truth of suffering and think about the true cause of suffering. Finally you consider the way you can be of greatest benefit to all beings. These contemplations help to develop our bodhicitta. These are all excellent preparations for śamatha practice.

(2') ACTUAL PRACTICE

There are two subtopics under the general subject of the actual practice: meditative posture and the meditative process itself.

(a") MEDITATIVE POSTURE

Your mind depends, in part, on your body. So many things related to your physical form can disturb your mind and pull it away from its object. Therefore both the place you train and the way you position your body are important. Kamalaśīla describes the best posture for śamatha practice in the second and third *Stages of Meditation*. Before explaining the way to sit, I should mention that in addition to residing in a quiet and harmonious place for meditation, you should also have a comfortable, soft seat. You do not want to sit on a pile of rocks; that will needlessly make it difficult to practice. But your cushion should not be so comfortable that you will fall asleep; it should be just soft enough so that you can remain reasonably comfortable for a long time. The point is that it should be conducive to meditation.

The recommended posture is referred to as the seven-point posture of Buddha Vairochana. If you look at paintings of Buddha Vairochana, he is depicted in the full-lotus position; his legs are crossed with the tops of his feet resting on opposite thighs. The half-lotus position is also good. Sitting cross-legged, without the tops of your feet resting on opposite thighs, is also fine. If you cannot get into these positions due to physical limitations, it does not mean that you cannot achieve śamatha. This is simply a description of the ideal position. Later, if you are engaged in tantric meditation, there are particular advantages to the full-lotus position with regard to the subtle physiology of the channels. This is the case both symbolically and in actuality. But merely for the development of śamatha, you should find a position that is suitable and comfortable.

The second aspect of the posture is with respect to your eyes. In śamatha practice, your eyes should be slightly open and gaze downward toward the tip of your nose. Avoid having your eyes open too wide or completely closed. If they are open too wide, your mind can become distracted easily. If they are closed too tightly, you are much more susceptible to falling asleep.

The third aspect regards your back. Avoid slouching too far back or slumping over forward. Try to keep your spine straight; this will help you breathe and assist the circulation of blood. But avoid pulling your spine up too high and rigidly holding it that way; this can lead to conceit. The main point is that your body should be straight so that the mind can focus internally.

The fourth point of the ideal meditation posture is that your shoulders should be straight and even. One shoulder should not be higher than the other. If your body is uneven congenitally or due to an injury, that is okay. But generally you try to keep your shoulders even and balanced.

Fifth, the position of your head should also be straight. Like the back, it should not lean too far forward or too far back. If possible, your nose and navel should be aligned; in other words, your head should be tilted forward just a little bit. Avoid letting your head lean to one side or the other. The proper position helps circulation and keeps you alert.

The sixth point regards your teeth and lips. They should not be clenched too tightly; they should be normal and at ease.

The seventh point of the Vairochana posture is that the tip of the tongue should rest against the upper teeth in the front of your mouth. If you stay in meditation for a long time, this helps prevent drooling and also keeps your mouth from getting dry and you becoming thirsty too quickly.

The last point Kamalaśīla mentions is the breath. Your breathing should not be noisy or forceful. It should not be quick, as if you are frightened. Let it be natural, with no effort exerted to control it or slow it down. Just breathe normally. It is often helpful at the beginning to count your breaths up to twenty-one, repeatedly if necessary, until your mind is settled and internalized. When counting your breath, an inhalation and its exhalation count as one. If you have trouble keeping count properly, it indicates that your mind is not yet settled enough to begin to practice. If this happens, just start counting over again at one. This is a good technique for beginners to use in any type of meditation practice. When your mind settles down you do not need to count your breaths any longer.

The first seven points comprise the seven-point posture of Vairochana. The eighth, regarding breathing, is not traditionally included among descriptions of the seven-point posture, but it is included in Kamalaśīla's *Stages of Meditation*, which Tsongkhapa cites. It is good advice to follow.

In *Śrāvaka Levels*, Asaṅga explains the practice of śamatha extensively. He says that the Buddha taught practitioners to sit on a comfortable seat with a cushion or mat of grass when doing śamatha practice. Asaṅga gave five reasons for sitting cross-legged in this seven-point posture on such a padded seat. The first is that this position is conducive to the cultivation of the physical and mental pliancy that comes as a result of training properly. If you sit in odd positions or lay down, this pliancy will not arise. The second reason is that you will be able to sit in this position for a long time without getting tired. There are a number of other positions for which this is not the case. The third reason is that this seven-limb posture, which exactly imitates the perfect form and posture of Vairochana, is not common to non-Buddhist ways of sitting in meditation. The fourth reason is that when others see you sitting calmly and peacefully for a long time in this way they will be moved to faith. The final reason is that this is the posture Buddha taught to his disciples. They achieved high realizations by practicing in this way and went on to teach this as a proper and effective posture.

Tsongkhapa adds that keeping your back straight helps you to avoid lethargy and sleepiness. If you slump forward or backward, your circulation can be affected. As a result your mind will tend to sink into mental dullness. It is true. When I lean backward, I tend to fall asleep. So if you are planning to do long-term training in śamatha, it is best to use this posture from the beginning.

(b'') THE MEDITATIVE PROCESS

The essence of these teachings on śamatha came from the Buddha and the many great teachers and yogis who had extensive experience. They explain that at each stage of practice, there is a specific order in which to do things, certain obstacles that arise, and specific antidotes to counter those obstacles. Tsongkhapa compiled the best of these instructions in the *Lamrim Chenmo*. Most teachings on the accomplishment of śamatha discuss five obstacles that hinder practice and eight antidotes that counteract the five obstacles. These were taught in Maitreya's *Separation of the Middle from the Extremes* (*Madhyānta-vibhāga*). One of the famous Kadampa masters, Geshe Laksorwa (Dge shes Lag sor ba), and the great scholar Yönten Drak (Yon tan grags) taught that we must additionally utilize three preconditions—the four types of attention, the six powers, and the eight applications, which comprise the methods for progressing through the nine mental stages in the development of śamatha. This advice is based on Asaṅga's *Śrāvaka Levels*. I will discuss each of these below.

If you train in the preconditions and practice with perseverance by following these instructions, there is no doubt that you will achieve śamatha. If you do not know, or fail to utilize, the method taught by great masters, you will not achieve śamatha. According to Yönten Drak, the sources for the lamrim literature all say that those who lack the three preconditions will not achieve śamatha no matter how long they practice or how hard they try. He laments that by his time many oral traditions on how to practice śamatha no longer mention this important fact or even record the names of these techniques.

What are the sources for the lamrim literature? Generally speaking, an explanation of the stages of the path of the three vehicles is found in Asaṅga's five treatises, which follow the teachings of Maitreya regarding the method side of practice. Asaṅga's most extensive explanation of how to practice śamatha and vipaśyanā is in *Śrāvaka Levels*. Maitreya's *Ornament for the Mahayana Sutras* and *Separation of the Middle from the Extremes* are also great sources on the topic of śamatha. Based on those explanations, the great Indian teacher Haribhadra wrote extensively about the nine stages of śamatha training and the eight antidotes in his commentary on the *Ornament for Clear Knowledge* (*Abhisamaya-alaṃkāra*), as did Kamalaśīla in his three *Stages of Meditation* texts. The latter two masters were disciples of the great Śāntarakṣita, who was instrumental in bringing Buddhism to Tibet. Ratnākaraśānti also wrote excellent explanations about how to practice and achieve śamatha.

These great teachers explained the method of practice from the perspective of the sutra path, but their explanations are helpful for tantric meditation as well. Different objects of meditation are utilized in tantric practice because they emphasize divine forms, winds, drops, mantras, and so forth. Nevertheless, when trying to achieve śamatha, in either sutra or tantra practice, there are five faults or obstacles that must be overcome. The eight antidotes that combat these are the same in both sutra and tantra, and the general goal of practicing śamatha is the same in sutra and tantra—attainment of a spontaneous stabilized mind with mental and physical pliancy. In tantra, the ultimate goal may include the achievement of extraordinary powers known as *siddhi*, but when first trying to achieve mental stabilization, a yogi on the tantric path must accomplish the same basic things that a beginner on the sutra path must accomplish.

During the time of Tsongkhapa, there were very few people in Tibet who were familiar with the great Indian texts on śamatha and few who knew how to practice śamatha properly. Tsongkhapa said that qualified masters were as rare as stars visible during the daytime. Some of his contemporaries made wild claims about their personal accomplishments but did not actually know how to meditate, practice, and achieve mental stabilization. Only when a practice is grounded on teachings and detailed explanations of both sutra and tantra will it actually be effective and overcome any obstacles that arise.

There were many people during Tsongkhapa's time who argued that all thinking and analytical processes are bad. Such people often blamed books and intellectual thought for all their mental problems. They avoided the great teachings because it was too much work to study them. They hoped that there was some small and easy-to-follow instruction manual that would be more effective. Such misguided people said that from the very beginning you should just meditate and not study, think, contemplate, or use logic. This is not the case. The truth is that śamatha will never be achieved if you follow that kind of approach. It is an attractive method for the lazy; it may give you some transitory serenity, but it is based on a partial understanding and will not be effective. Successful śamatha practice requires preparation. You must familiarize yourself with the teachings of the great masters on this practice.

Tsongkhapa's explanation on the meditative process itself has two topics: how to develop flawless concentration (chapters 2–4), and the stages in which mental states are thereby developed (chapter 5).

(1") How to develop flawless concentration

There are three subtopics here:

> (a)) What to do prior to focusing the attention on an object of meditation
> (b)) What to do while focusing on an object of meditation (chapters 2–3)
> (c)) What to do after you focus on an object of meditation (chapter 4)

(a)) What to do prior to focusing the attention on an object of meditation

In order to produce faultless śamatha, you need to be free of the five obstacles to its achievement. Any spiritual practice requires you to train your mind over long periods of time. Laziness, or not wanting to exert effort in practice, is the first obstacle. Having the motivation to practice but forgetting the instructions is the second. During the actual meditation practice, the main obstacles are mental laxity and its opposite, excitement; they comprise the third obstacle to achieving śamatha. The fourth obstacle is failing to apply the antidote when needed. When one of the obstacles arises, such as distraction, you need to immediately apply the proper antidote to free yourself from it. The fifth obstacle is unnecessary application of antidotes. When the mind is perfectly engaged in single-pointed meditation, no antidotes are needed.

Before trying to develop śamatha, it is important to study and receive teachings on the practice. If you do not know what problems or obstacles may arise, there is little chance you will be able to apply the appropriate antidote. When you are practicing and realize an obstacle is present, it is important to know how to apply the antidotes to get free of it. Maitreya's *Separation of the Middle from the Extremes* teaches extensively about the eight antidotes that counteract the five obstacles. Four of the antidotes address laziness specifically. The remaining four obstacles each have one prescribed antidote.

Before you begin to meditate, it is very important to reduce or remove laziness. Laziness has many forms. In general, a lazy mind is not overtly attracted to unwholesome actions, but neither is it enthusiastic about virtue. One type of laziness is not wanting to do a particular practice. Someone may have an interest in it, but laziness takes over, and they do not make any effort in their practice. Still others are so enthralled with worldly distractions that they have no strong wish to achieve śamatha or meditative stabilization.

Laziness has four antidotes: faith, aspiration, perseverance, and mental pliancy. The fourth, mental pliancy, is actually the result of the first three. In brief, the opposite of laziness is perseverance, or joyous effort (*vīrya*). A persevering mind, in the Buddhist context, is one that is enthusiastic about virtue. The real antidote to laziness is the perseverance that takes joy in practicing meditation. When you are able to eliminate laziness through the application of perseverance, your body and mind spontaneously begin to express enthusiasm for practice. The fatigue of laziness ceases, and your body becomes subtly joyful about this state. This physical pliancy is most helpful in meditation.

In order to generate perseverance, you need aspiration. A strong aspiration to engage in śamatha comes from contemplating the benefits of the practice. If you see the many benefits of śamatha, then you will have strong faith or trust in that practice. So I am not talking about blind faith here; you must actually understand the benefits. When you see the benefits, from the smallest to the greatest, you will be attracted to practice. As this attraction becomes stronger, the aspiration to practice will come. When you have aspiration, you will have the perseverance to practice with commitment. This is yet another reason why it is important to study and learn about a practice rather than just jumping in and doing it right away. You will not be interested in doing something if you do not trust that doing it will be helpful. If you do not know all the benefits of the practice, you will not be inspired to do it. Without aspiration, you will not persevere in your practice. In short, it is important to understand why śamatha is valuable, what its benefits are, what you need to do to attain it, how long it may take to develop, what types of hardships and sacrifices may be involved, and how to address these.

So what are the great benefits of achieving śamatha? First, it counteracts the wild, distracted mind that hampers you on the spiritual path. Normally you do not have control over your mind. Your mind gets distracted; it goes this way and that, utterly out of your control. When your mind is uncontrolled, the result will be negative actions of body, speech, and mind. When your mind is fully controlled, you will have the desire and ability to engage in virtuous actions and refrain from nonvirtuous activities. Second, śamatha is the basis for a peaceful and enlightened mind. When you achieve śamatha, your mind will be happy, content, and filled with delight. Your body also experiences a type of bliss. With this physical and mental pliancy, your mind is suitable for work to achieve the higher goal of enlightenment. Only on the basis of śamatha can you cultivate real insight into the nature of reality. The union of śamatha and vipaśyanā is the true antidote to all your suffering and problems. It is the foundation for achieving liberation from samsara. Another benefit derived from the cultivation of śamatha is supranormal powers that facilitate your ability to help other sentient beings.

Usually we speak of five common or mundane supranormal powers or knowledges that result from śamatha: miraculous acts, the divine eye, clairaudience, the knowledge of others' thoughts, recollection of former states, and knowledge of death and rebirth. Miraculous acts are feats like the ability to turn one body into many, to transform large into small, to fly, to dive into the ground, and to walk on water. These knowledges and powers result from the śamatha practice that is common to Buddhists and non-Buddhists. Even though none of these powers are essential for the attainment of enlightenment, bodhisattvas can use these abilities to work for the benefit of all sentient beings. However, if a practitioner attains these powers but does not have love, compassion, and the realization of emptiness, they may engage in strange activities that have interesting, or even harmful, results.

If right away, as a beginner, you seek out a cave to meditate in but you are without much background knowledge, you may give up your practice quite quickly. However, if you first build zeal for practice through contemplation of its benefits, your enthusiasm will keep you committed to your practice. You will not want it to degenerate, so you will focus on its cultivation, and it will increase. Once you have strong faith in the benefits of śamatha, laziness will subside. You will not want to delay practice even one moment. In addition, the things that once distracted you will hold less appeal—sometimes yogis forget to eat because they are so engrossed in their meditation practice. Once you are inspired to practice, hardships seem small compared to the great fruits of cultivating śamatha. When you achieve the special joy that accompanies mental pliancy, encouragement to meditate will come from within. You will need no encouragement from others. You will be self-motivated. And yet you will still need to cultivate your enthusiasm for the practice. Even after attaining śamatha, you should urge yourself again and again to remember these teachings so that your motivation does not wane. This is how you produce and maintain faith.

Once you have this strong wish to meditate, what do you do then?

(b)) What to do while focusing on an object of meditation

(1)) Identifying the object of meditation upon which your attention is set

(2)) How to focus your mind on the object of meditation (chapter 3)

(1)) Identifying the object of meditation upon which your attention is set

This topic includes:

(a')) A general presentation of the objects of meditation

(b')) Identifying objects of meditation for this context

(a')) A general presentation of the objects of meditation

This has three further subtopics:

(1')) The objects of meditation themselves

(2')) Who should meditate on which object

(3')) Synonyms of the object of meditation

(1')) The objects of meditation themselves

The Buddha taught four types of objects of meditation: universal objects of meditation, objects of meditation for purifying your behavior, objects of meditation for cultivating expertise, and objects of meditation for purifying afflictions.

(a")) Universal objects of meditation

There are four types of universal objects of meditation: discursive images, nondiscursive images, the limits of existence, and achievement of your purpose. All objects of meditation fit into these four categories. The first two, discursive and nondiscursive images, are generated by the meditator. They are mental images or reflections of thought in the mind. Discursive images, or you could say, concepts, are byproducts of analytical thought and thus are objects of vipaśyanā. When we engage in analytical meditation, we first mentally construct a discursive image by thinking about it. When we meditate on the four noble truths, for example, the image is not a physical object with particular characteristics that exists in the world. Rather, such an object belongs to the mind. The mind analyzes the topic by delving into its qualities and details and in this way creates a concept. In contrast, nondiscursive images are byproducts of nonanalytical thought and are objects of śamatha. Śamatha is a single-pointed meditation without analysis. The mind is merely focusing on an object. The mind becomes stabilized, and the image of the object that appears to the mind is like a reflection.

The third object of meditation is called the *limits of existence*. Rather than being posited by the meditator like discursive and nondiscursive images, the limits of existence are posited in reference to an observed object. The limit of existence can mean two things with regard to objects: the first kind of limit completely encompasses what exists, and the second completely encompasses the way in which things exist. There is nothing outside these limits.

Vasubandhu presents a clear example of the first type of limit of existence in his *Treasury of Knowledge*. He categorizes all composite phenomena in three ways: by way of the framework of the five aggregates, by way of the framework of the twelve sources, and by way of the framework of the eighteen constituents. The five aggregates—form, feeling, discrimination, compositional factors, and consciousness—are well known. The twelve sources divide all composite phenomena into two groups of six: the six sensory objects—form, sound, smell, taste, touch, and objects of mind—and the six corresponding sensory organs. This manner of categorization combines each organ and its corresponding consciousness—for example, the eye organ and visual consciousness—into a single category as opposed to the eighteen constituents, which presents them separately. Thus, when compounded phenomena are described in terms of the eighteen constituents, there are the six types of objects, the six organs that perceive them, and in addition the six consciousnesses that receive the sense data. Everything that exists in the world can be included in these three frameworks.

In a special sense, we say that the four noble truths include all things that are to be known. This is not literally true because there are objects of knowledge that are not part of the four noble truths. However, the four noble truths include everything necessary to attain liberation: from the perspective of samsara, you need to know the truth of suffering and the truth of its cause; from the perspective of what leads to liberation, you need to know the truth of cessation and truth of the path. That is enough; nothing more needed. In that sense the four noble truths are a limit of existence. The final conclusion of knowledge of the four noble truths is the understanding that there is nothing that is not empty of essence. Emptiness completely encompasses the way in which all things exist. So this is an example of the second type of limit of existence—the way things exist. Another example is the fact that all compounded phenomena are impermanent.

The fourth object of meditation is called *achievement of your purpose.* In this, the object is observed from the standpoint of final achievement. These objects of śamatha meditation are visualized. You become accustomed to them through repeated meditation in which you direct your focus on the object. By the power of doing that repeatedly, mental obstacles such as laziness, excitement, lethargy, and so forth get removed as you get closer to your goal of śamatha. Eventually you become completely transformed and realize or accomplish your goal.

(b")) OBJECTS OF MEDITATION FOR PURIFYING YOUR BEHAVIOR

When you have a disease, a doctor will prescribe medicine for you. If you have only one ailment, you will only need one medication. If you have multiple problems or your illness is complex, you may need more than one medication. Likewise, since we have more than one mental affliction, there are many types of meditation that serve as different cures for the different types of mental problems that afflict us. Śamatha meditation focuses on one object at a time. However, before we can successfully engage in śamatha practice, we need to reduce our gross afflictions. Only then can we begin to achieve mental stability.

Different people are dominated by different mental afflictions. Some people's minds are more dominated by hatred. Others are dominated by attachment, conceit, anger, or ignorance. Each of these five primary afflictions has a corresponding meditation practice designed to counteract it. Each practice takes a different object of meditation to purify its associated negative habit. Meditation on these objects purifies the negative behavior and inclinations, thereby allowing the mind to settle sufficiently to practice śamatha. The five objects are: ugliness, love, dependent arising, differentiation of constituents, and inhalation and exhalation.

In the desire realm, attachment is generally the most powerful affliction.

In particular, people are attached to bodies—their own and those of others. When we see bodies as lovely and pure, our minds become susceptible to excessive attachment. This can keep us from successful śamatha practice. The antidote to this attachment is to meditate on the ugliness, filth, and impurity of the body. Here you mentally dissect the body and meditate on its components—the intestines, blood, muscles, and so forth—and how these are unclean and unattractive. Many teachings suggest contemplating thirty-six different internal elements in terms of their color, shape, smell, make-up, and so forth. This is an analytical meditation. You consider whether each of these internal constituents is beautiful and pleasing or ugly and putrid. It is like taking an inner tour of the body, finding that it is not so attractive after all. Śāntideva says that when you cut open the body with the knife of wisdom, you will see its ugliness. You can also become accustomed to the repulsiveness of the body by meditating on a decaying corpse, a method taught extensively in the scriptures. Traditionally such a meditation is done at a cemetery. In meditation you consider how the color and shape of a corpse changes, how worms eat the flesh until only the bones remain. When you conclude that the object of your attachment is not really worthy of attachment, your mind begins to stabilize. If you meditate in this way, you become accustomed to seeing bodies as impure, and attachment to them diminishes as a result.

Meditation on love is an antidote to hatred and anger. Anger is one of the most powerful and destructive mental states; it is critically important to apply love to counter it. Generally we categorize people into three groups: friends whom we love, enemies whom we hate, and strangers toward whom we feel neutral. However, although you usually think of someone as being absolutely your friend or absolutely your enemy, there is actually no such thing. Enemies and friends are created in your mind due to fear, attachment, and so forth. An enemy at one point in time may be a friend at another. You can easily see that sometimes your enemies help you and your friends harm you. You have to train yourself to have the same loving attitude for all three groups.[10] You start by generating love for relatives and friends, proceed to neutral people, and last your enemies. Then you consider the three categories of people alongside one another, wishing for all of them to have happiness and not to have misery or suffering. This process makes it easy to understand that all people suffer in similar ways; they all want to have happiness and avoid misery. Ultimately, all the people in all three categories are equally worthy of being objects of your love. If you have love, generation of bodhicitta is not difficult. In many ways this meditation resembles the sevenfold cause-and-effect meditation for cultivating bodhicitta.

When speaking of love as an object of śamatha, it is love that has complete equanimity. Successful meditation on love means your consciousness becomes that attitude. Real love is when love equally for all arises spontaneously in your mind. There is no place for anger or hatred when you have this love. Therefore, love is the antidote to anger. Cultivation of spontaneous love that arises equally for everybody will dispel anger and hatred.

The next useful antidote is meditation on dependent arising. This serves to counter ignorance, especially the subtlest type of ignorance—ignorance of the nature of reality that grasps at the self as absolute and real. There are many varieties of ignorance, such as not knowing what is virtuous and what is not virtuous, or not knowing about karma and its effects. But the egotistic view is the most powerful form of ignorance and is the root of all our problems. The egotistic view produces selfishness, anger toward others, conceit, pride, jealousy, and so on.

There are a variety of ways to understand dependent arising. For example, you can consider that everything that existed in the past, exists in present, and will exist in the future is dependent on various causes and conditions. There is nothing permanent, independent, absolute, or existent by itself. Everything is relative; when this thing arises, that thing happens, and when that happens something else occurs, and so forth. The Buddha taught that although a plant may look autonomous, it is not. First a seed must come in contact with soil, water, sunlight, warmth, air, and so forth for it to germinate and grow. Another approach to understanding dependent arising is to consider that things depend upon parts. A plant, once grown, is not one solid undifferentiated thing; it has many parts and different aspects such as shape, color, and so forth. Nothing there is independent. Meditation on how phenomena exist in dependence on causes and conditions, on parts, and so forth helps you to realize there is no absolute, independent, inherently existent self or soul. As you come to see this, your grasping at things as solid and independent begins to lessen and eventually disappear.

Meditation on the differentiation of the constituents is geared toward combating pride and conceit. This meditation deconstructs your belief in the substantiality of your identity through examining the way you are composed of parts. By asking "What am I made of?" you break down your concept of "me" into components, such as the five aggregates, the twelve sources, and the eighteen constituents. Many other configurations are presented in the sutras as well, such as the six elements that make up a person: air, water, fire, earth, space, and consciousness. Additionally you find descriptions of the person in terms of eighteen elements, sixty-two elements, and so forth. Through meditating on any of these you come to see that you, the person in whom you have so much pride and conceit, does not exist as an independent, absolute, substantial person. You are a combination of elements and dependent upon parts. This collection of parts and elements is functional. It differs from other collections and their particular functions. It is fine to label this particular collection "me." But usually we go on from here and mistakenly project onto this collection some objective, independent, truly existent self. We grasp at that and get attached to what we take to be "me" and "mine." This mistaken belief dominates us completely. When we understand that what you label "I" is actually a mere aggregation of constituent parts, conceit and pride is greatly reduced.

Meditation on the breath is prescribed for those whose minds are constantly distracted and seemingly cannot settle down. Here you take the inhalation and exhalation of your breath as the object of your meditation. When attempting to stabilize your mind in this way, you can add detail to your observation of the breath. For example, it may be useful to supplement your observation by counting: "one" in and out, "two" in and out, and so forth. When your mind gets distracted, you lose your count. When you realize that has happened, just start your counting over again at "one." This type of meditation is common to both Buddhists and non-Buddhists. Meditation on the breath is simple to explain, but it is not so easy as it may seem.

(c")) Objects of meditation for cultivating expertise

These objects of meditation are for the cultivation of mastery, or expertise, in your understanding of reality. The Tibetan word translated here as "expertise" (*mkhas pa*) can mean "master," "scholar," or "wise." Here it has all of these senses and primarily refers to the opposite of being ignorant. The five objects of meditation for expertise—the five aggregates, the eighteen constituents, twelve sources, dependent origination, and what is appropriate and not appropriate—help you to intellectually understand the nature of reality more clearly.

The first object for expertise is the five aggregates: form, feeling, discrimination, compositional factors, and consciousness. Briefly, *form* is any kind of physical or material thing. The other four aggregates are all nonmaterial, or mental. The second aggregate, *feeling*, refers to the sensations perceived by the five senses and the mental consciousness. The third is *discrimination*. When we have a sensation or feeling, we make a judgment about it—we decide this is good, or this is bad, and so forth. Let us jump to the fifth aggregate before returning to the fourth. The fifth aggregate is called *consciousness* and refers to the six primary consciousnesses—the five primary sense consciousnesses and the mental consciousness. The fourth aggregate, called *compositional factors*, is comprised of things that arise from causes and conditions that are not encompassed by the other four aggregates. Included here are both virtuous and nonvirtuous mental states: the virtues of equanimity, dexterity, humility, wisdom, faith, perseverance, and so forth; the nonvirtues of desire, hatred, jealousy, pride, conceit, ignorance, and so forth; and karma, which can be either virtuous or nonvirtuous. All these are conditioned phenomena; they are combinations, or composites, that exist in dependence upon causes and conditions. And anything that is the result of causes and conditions has the potential to produce something else.

You may wonder why the Buddha singled out these particular five categories as a comprehensive description of a person. The reason is explained in the early Indian Abhidharma commentarial texts. As we saw above, all material phenomena fit into the category of form, while the other four aggregates deal with the mind, or consciousness. Consciousness can be divided into six primary consciousnesses (the fifth aggregate) and fifty-one secondary consciousnesses. At any moment, each of the primary consciousnesses is accompanied by at least five of the secondary consciousnesses. These are called the five omnipresent secondary consciousnesses, or mental states. Included among the five omnipresent secondary consciousnesses are feeling (the second aggregate) and discrimination (the third aggregate). All other secondary mental states are included in the fourth aggregate, compositional factors. Feeling and discrimination are singled out from the other fifty-one secondary consciousnesses and given the status of being aggregates because they play such a dominant role in our experience.

The purpose for this way of categorizing things is to undermine the ignorant view of the self. It provides you with a clear outline to follow in meditation when investigating what you truly are. As you meditate on the aggregates one by one, you see that not a single one is "me" or "I." Form is not the "I," feeling is not the "I," discrimination is not the "I," and so forth. Then you look through the compositional factors and see that none of these is the "I" either. You come to see that there is no independent person or "I" in any of the aggregates individually or collectively; nor is there an "I" completely separate and outside of the aggregates. Finally you realize the selflessness of the person: you see that there is no absolute or independent self—the person, or "I," is merely relative, merely dependent in nature. In other words, the person exists, but the way it exists is completely dependent; it is simply designated upon the dependent arising of a composite of material (form) and nonmaterial (mental) parts. When you realize this you are said to be skillful. Thus, this is a teaching for the skillful ones, for masters, for those with expertise.

The second object of meditation for expertise is the eighteen constituents. These function as another framework for categorizing the elements that make up living beings and the world. The eighteen constituents, as mentioned, can be divided into three groups of six: objects, organs, and consciousnesses. The first six constituents present the elements of existence from the perspective of objects: forms, sounds, smells, tastes, tactile objects, and the concepts, ideas, mental images, and so on that are the objects of the mental organ. Corresponding to each of these six objects are six organs and six consciousnesses, thus totaling eighteen. The organs perceive the sense objects, and the consciousnesses cognize the data perceived by the sense organs. For example, the ear organ perceives sounds, and that perception is cognized by the auditory consciousness. The six consciousnesses arise and function differently because they have different corresponding organs. The sense consciousness associated with the eye organ will perceive colors and shapes but not tastes, the sense consciousness associated with the ear organ will perceive sound but not color, and so forth.

The purpose of attaining mastery of the eighteen constituents is to gain understanding of the dependent nature of phenomena. When you examine the eighteen constituents, you come to see that there is no real, independent, or absolute consciousness, object, or organ. For eye consciousness to arise, there must be at least three conditions: an eye organ, a visual object, and an immediately preceding visual consciousness. The object and the organ also depend on causes and conditions. When this is understood properly, you recognize the dependent nature of the eighteen constituents. You know that there is no independent or absolute thing there. This is a way to develop a masterful understanding of the nature of phenomena.

The third object for expertise is the twelve sources. The presentation of the twelve sources is very similar to the presentation of the eighteen constituents. The reason for this presentation is also similar: it is another way to understand the dependent nature of phenomena. In brief, the difference between the presentation of the twelve sources and the eighteen constituents is that here each of the six organs and their respective consciousnesses are counted together as one. The twelve sources were taught in great detail in sutras and treatises like Vasubandhu's *Treasury of Knowledge* for the purpose of identifying the three conditions necessary for the arising of any particular moment of consciousness. What are these three conditions? First, the internal elements, meaning the organs, are the dominant condition for the arising of their respective consciousness. For example, there are many causes and conditions for visual consciousness to arise, but the eye organ is the primary condition. A shape or form is referred to as an object-condition, and an immediately preceding visual consciousness is known as the immediately preceding similar condition. All the other consciousnesses can be discussed using the same framework. When we understand each cause and condition, it becomes easier to understand the truth of the self and truth of phenomena.

The next object of meditation for expertise is dependent arising as presented in the twelve links of dependent origination. The purpose of knowing this is to understand how the suffering lives of sentient beings arise. It says in the sutras that those who understand these links of dependent arising know the Dharma. This means that they know the supreme Dharma—nirvana—and that they will be able to reach it. Those who clearly see the twelvefold chain of dependent origination will also be able to realize buddhahood. This topic was explained in detail in volume 2 of this series, so I will go over it only briefly here.

The first link is ignorance. Because of ignorance we create the second link in the chain, karma. Here *karma* refers to intentional physical, verbal, and mental actions that are the causes for any type of life in samsara. Every karmic action plants a potential—a seed—in the mind. So the third link is the consciousness that receives and holds that potential. This is a particular definition of consciousness in a specific context. Some commentaries discuss this consciousness as two: causal consciousness and resultant consciousness. In this twofold schema, causal consciousness is the third link of the twelve factors of dependent origination. The continuum of the causal consciousness continues during this life and into future lives when the body that created it has ceased to exist. When the karmic seeds deposited in the causal consciousness meet the particular conditions appropriate for ripening, they will come to fruition. The resultant consciousness is an effect caused by the maturation of the causal consciousness. It is the first moment of consciousness in the next life. The Buddha explained this using the analogy of a farmer planting a seed. Until the seed meets with moisture, warmth, and so forth, the seed will not sprout. It remains dormant in the ground, held there until the appropriate conditions are met. The seed is analogous to the causal consciousness; it is the primary consciousness just before entering a mother's womb. The germination of the seed is analogous to the resultant consciousness, the first moment of a new life. It is only the causal consciousness that is the third link in the chain of causation.

The fourth link is name and form. This begins at conception, when a consciousness enters the mother's womb and joins with the sperm and egg. There are two components necessary for successful conception: physical and mental. The physical part is the zygote—the egg received from the mother fertilized by the sperm from the father. This physical component is called *form*. *Name* refers to the primary causal consciousness from the former life, along with the five omnipresent secondary mental factors that accompany it. In other words, name is resultant consciousness and comprises aspects of all four mental aggregates. Some types of rebirth have no physical component; they have no form, only name. An example of this would be a rebirth in the formless realm.

Name and form develop into the fifth link in the chain of causation, the six sources. In this context, the six sources are the six types of organs—the five sense organs and the mental organ—as they develop in the womb. The sixth link is contact. After the organs have completely developed, they are the primary conditions for the production of their respective consciousnesses. *Contact* refers to the meeting between the organ, its object, and consciousness. During our lives, contact is constantly occurring in a variety of ways. The seventh link is feeling, which refers to the entire host of feelings, from misery to happiness to neutral feelings. Feelings, both physical and emotional, arise when our organs come into contact with objects. All our feelings, whether pleasant or unpleasant, are the results of contact and our past karma.

These feelings create causes for future results because they lead directly to the next link, attachment. Attachment here can be understood as positive or negative depending upon whether a pleasant or unpleasant feeling is its basis. When we feel good, we want more, we don't want it to end. When we feel unhappy or uncomfortable, we are attached to the idea of getting rid of it and avoiding it in future. This is attachment in the context of the eighth link in the chain of dependent origination.

Attachment goes on to create an even stronger, more powerful grasping that is the seed for the next life. It is a particular type of grasping, just before your death, that awakens the karma that determines where you are to be born next. If, for example, you are going to be born as a hungry ghost with a miserable life of hunger and thirst, at the time of death you have a strong aversion to food and drink. This powerful grasping will cause the ripening of a seed from a prior karma to be born as a hungry ghost. This, of course, also works for positive karma too. This powerful grasping just before death is the ninth link.

Existence, which is the result of that grasping, is the tenth link. It is the last moment of consciousness of a life, right at the moment of death. It is a mental karma, either virtuous or nonvirtuous, which along with attachment and grasping is the immediately preceding cause for the next life. This karma, the last moment of consciousness, is called *existence* because it is so close to and is the main cause of the next life.

Canonical texts have a grouping known as "the three: desire, grasping, and existence" (*sred len srid pa gsum*). There are two levels of attachment distinguished by degree: desire and grasping. Desire is the earlier, less intense attachment, which becomes increasingly more powerful until it is called *grasping*. At the time of death, a powerful virtuous or nonvirtuous karma arises that in connection with the grasping will yield the next life. Therefore that karma is given the name of the result that it produces: existence. Existence is like a seed, moistened by grasping in the soil of attachment. From the seed of existence comes birth into another life. Birth is the eleventh link in the chain of causation. After birth comes the twelfth link, aging and death.

The twelve factors of the chain of dependent arising can be understood to occur over the course of three lives: a prior life, the present life, and a future life. The way to understand how beings migrate from life to life, and what type of life they will have, is to develop expertise in this set of twelve. You should do analytical meditation on each of the links individually, thoroughly examining and analyzing each one, as well as the way they connect to form a whole.

The fifth object of meditation for the expertise of masters is meditation on what is and what is not possible in relation to the karmic actions we take. It is possible for a pleasant experience to arise as the result of a virtuous karma, but it is not possible for a pleasant experience to be the result of a nonvirtuous karma. For example, if you are very generous, the result will be that you will have wealth in the future. If you do the opposite, and act in a miserly, stingy way, you will find yourself in poverty. The result of negative actions can only be misery and suffering. A maturation of a negative cause will not be a long life that is full of happiness.

Generally the objects of meditation for the cultivation of expertise are objects of analytical meditation, not the nondiscursive meditation of śamatha. However, here Tsongkhapa shows that they can be objects of both śamatha and vipaśyanā. At this point in the *Lamrim Chenmo*, Tsongkhapa explains how to use these as the objects of śamatha meditation; later he will explain how to use them as objects of vipaśyanā meditation.

When you meditate with śamatha there can only be one object. So how do you use these varied topics as objects of śamatha meditation? Let's use the example of the five aggregates to outline this method. First you engage in analytical meditation; you examine the details of each of the aggregates in an in-depth analysis of their true nature. Ideally you will see that all of them are a mere composite. When you see them all in this way through analysis, you bring them together into one unitary comprehension. This conclusion becomes your singular object of śamatha meditation. You focus on this without excitement or laxity. Similarly, the eighteen constituents can be summarized into one object, a relatively existent constituent. The twelve sources also can be summarized into one. Whatever the object, your mind will eventually focus on that object as a single category. It is like when you are meditating on emptiness, and you begin by examining some basic things about a particular phenomenon. Eventually, through a process of reasoning, you recognize that not only is the specific object of your analysis empty but all phenomena are empty. Then you can meditate single-pointedly on the conclusion, emptiness. Simply put, this is how to use the objects of mastery as objects of śamatha meditation.

(d")) OBJECTS OF MEDITATION FOR PURIFYING THE AFFLICTIONS

This is the fourth and final subdivision of the objects of meditation themselves. There are two connotations of *purifying*. The first relates to temporarily subduing a present affliction, whether it is desire, hatred, or any other one, by meditating on a specific antidote. The other sense of *purifying* refers to the permanent cessation of the affliction. The difference between temporarily suppressing a present manifestation of an affliction and its permanent cessation can be illuminated with an analogy. When an invasive weed is spreading throughout your yard, there are two ways to deal with it. One way is to cut the weeds off at ground level to remove them for the time being. The other way is to dig them out from the root to completely get rid of them.

In the same way, there are two methods to deal with your mental afflictions. One method is to practice the various kinds of meditation that subdue the afflictions, pushing them to a subconscious level. The purpose of this type of meditation is to prevent that affliction from having the conditions it needs to manifest. The seed of the affliction remains, but it has less ability to become grossly problematic for the time being. The method to do this is the progressive meditations of the mundane path. Remember, this is comparing the coarseness of a lower stage with the advantageous qualities of the next higher level, progressing from the desire realm up through the levels of the form and formless realms.

The other method is to get rid of the afflictions themselves. Tsongkhapa says that to do this you should meditate on the sixteen aspects of the four noble truths. The Buddha taught that each of the four truths—the truth of suffering, the truth of the cause of suffering, the truth of cessation, and the truth of path—has four aspects. The meditations that you employ to realize and understand the sixteen aspects of the four noble truths are referred to as *supramundane* because they lead to complete liberation from samsara. In other words, they lead to a direct realization of emptiness. As with the objects for expertise, the objects for purifying the afflictions can be both objects of single-pointed śamatha meditation and objects of vipaśyanā meditation using the scrutiny of analysis. For śamatha meditation, here again, you keep your attention on a single point of focus.

Kamalaśīla says in his second *Stages of Meditation* that all objects of meditation can be summarized into three categories: reality, the aggregates (including phenomena), and the form of the Buddha. The first is the category of emptiness. For this you consider the teachings of all twelve limbs of scripture and realize that they all lead to the wisdom understanding the true nature of reality:

emptiness. Śāntideva put this quite succinctly in the first stanza of the "Wisdom" chapter of *Engaging in the Bodhisattva Deeds*:

> All of these limbs were taught by the Sage
> In order to develop wisdom.[11]

Some of the scriptures lead directly to the realization of emptiness; others approach this reality more indirectly. Once you have studied the scriptures and see how they can be summarized into the single topic of emptiness, you meditate on the category of emptiness with single-pointed focus.

The second object mentioned by Kamalaśīla for stabilizing the mind is the aggregates, including phenomena. The categories of the five aggregates, eighteen constituents, and twelve sources are tools to use in analysis so that you can come to see that nothing is unproduced or independent; all phenomena are merely dependent aggregations. This is insight meditation: you take an object and investigate and analyze its aspects in great detail. Then with wisdom you take the many details and summarize them into one core conclusion. As noted before, this single conclusion can then be utilized as an object for śamatha. For example, after some analysis you can see that all produced things are included among the five aggregates. Here, because your focus is to use these as objects of śamatha meditation, you concentrate on the conclusion of your analysis—that all five aggregates fit into the single category of "aggregate." In short, once you have summarized your analysis of the aggregates into a single category, you meditate on that category with single-pointed focus. You do the same for the eighteen constituents, the twelve sources, and so forth.

The third object for stabilizing the mind is the physical form of the Buddha. The body of the Buddha can be imagined after you have been told what it looks like. Or, if you have a representation of the Buddha in a statue or painting, prior to meditating you observe it from the bottom to the top and from the top to the bottom. Then, in meditation, you recollect this image of the body of the Buddha as the object of observation.

Tsongkhapa points out that when choosing an object of meditation for the development of śamatha, you should pick one that has a useful purpose. Each of the four objects of meditation explained above—universal, those for purifying behavior, those for expertise, and those for purifying the afflictions—is taught in the scriptures to have a special purpose. For example, the varied objects of meditation for purifying the afflictions are useful because different individuals have different habits, propensities, and minds dominated by different afflictions. Some people are primarily influenced by desire; others by anger or hatred; others by jealousy; still others have more ignorance. Some people have an equal distribution of the afflictions with no particular affliction standing out more than the others; some people have less manifest forms of all of them. There are degrees to all of this. When a particular affliction, be it anger, desire, or something else, dominates your mind, you are incapable of any effective practice. So you should first apply the antidote to that most powerful affliction and do so in a single-pointed śamatha practice. When you use specific objects in this way, it is easier to turn away attachment and the other negative emotional states that afflict you and inhibit your progress on the path. If you are able to subdue the gross problems, it is easier to obtain real śamatha and progress from there.

Taking another example, the five objects of meditation for expertise—the five aggregates, eighteen constituents, and twelve sources, and so forth—are critically important for development of insight. In this context *insight* means a direct realization of selflessness or emptiness. You come to understand the emptiness of the self of persons by investigating the make-up of the person in detail. You mentally take the self apart piece by piece, and then you pick each of the pieces apart. As you come to see that all the internal and external parts of the person depend on each other, that consciousness, the various organs, and so forth are part of chains of dependent arising, it is easier to see the lack of an inherent nature in that self and its parts. This is the way to gain an insight realizing selflessness. It is through a proper understanding of these objects of meditation for expertise that you gain an understanding that there is no permanent, independent, absolute soul or self. This leads to understanding that the self is empty of any inherent existence. Conclusions that accord with this reasoning are excellent objects of śamatha.

Tsongkhapa stresses that people who use twigs or rocks as objects for their śamatha meditation are unaware or do not understand the teachings on the objects of meditation. They are not taking full advantage of the opportunity present in their practice. Some people have a different misunderstanding; they think that stabilizing the mind without an object is what is meant by meditation on emptiness. They use an analogy that likens the mind to a clear, unclouded crystal or glass. Just as when you view an object through clear glass, the glass seems to take on the characteristics—the color, shape, and so forth—of the object, so too does the mind take the form of object that appears to it. Therefore, when emptiness is the object of meditation, no object of any sort should appear in the mind; there should be no consciousness at all. Tsongkhapa says this is a mistake. He asks the holders of such a view, "If there is no consciousness in your meditation on emptiness, how can that be a consciousness realizing emptiness?" And if they insist that there is consciousness, then Tsongkhapa says they would have to accept that their method perceives characteristics or apprehends signs. In other words, their consciousness does have an object.

This argument is difficult, so some explanation may be useful. Tibetan has several words related to consciousness: mind or intellect (*blo*); awareness (*rig pa*); cognition, knowing, or cognizing consciousness (*shes pa*); mind (*sems*); and there are others. Sometimes these Tibetan words are difficult to translate, because the English words *cognition, knowledge,* and so forth do not necessarily refer to consciousness. The English terms can refer to the object alone, the act of knowing, or the knower. But in the Buddhist context, *cognition* refers to a consciousness that cognizes an object. Consciousness itself is not a physical thing; a consciousness arises after an organ meets with an object of a corresponding kind. For example, an eye consciousness arises after the eye organ comes in contact with a visual object. If there is no object, no consciousness will arise. When all the conditions are presents—an organ, a corresponding object, and a prior moment of consciousness—the consciousness that arises is called *cognition.* This consciousness can be correct or incorrect in its perception. But either way, correct or incorrect, something is perceived; something is cognized; something is manifest to that consciousness. If there were no object, then it would not be a cognition or consciousness. Just as the flame of a candle cannot arise without a wick, so consciousness cannot arise without an object. Therefore the following technical terms *object, object of meditation,* and *object of consciousness* all have the same referent.

So if you are meditating on emptiness, emptiness is the object of a consciousness. If there is no consciousness, there cannot be a single-pointed concentration that meditates on emptiness. According to the Prāsaṅgika Madhyamaka, everything lacks an inherent nature. There is nothing that is completely independent; there is nothing that has intrinsic existence. This emptiness, or lack, is the ultimate mode of being. It is ultimate reality; it is the way things actually exist. A mind concentrating upon that reality is a mind meditating on emptiness. Thus meditating on emptiness does not mean thinking nothing at all. It is incorrect to say that a mind that is completely blank, with no object and no thought at all, is a meditation on emptiness. It would be much easier to meditate on emptiness if that were the case, but it is totally wrong.

In fact, those who say that in meditation on emptiness there is no object contradict themselves. When they attempt to meditate on emptiness in this way, they think, "I will not put any object in my mind. I will keep my mind free of any appearing object." What they are doing is taking their mind to be the object of their meditation. True, there is no external object or particular thought as an object of meditation, but there is still an object of meditation: the clear and knowing nature of the mind. The mind is the focus of their attention in meditation. If the person asserting this position does not agree, then what is he or she doing? There would be no purpose for not having any object at all.

These issues are often misunderstood. That is why Tsongkhapa advises us to study the great scriptures, their commentaries, and other great texts that have detailed explanations of these matters. They explain how to do śamatha meditation, the varieties of objects that can be utilized to cultivate śamatha, and the purposes for each type of object, and they clarify many issues related to these topics. If you want to attain śamatha, then you should become knowledgeable about how to do it. After gaining a degree of familiarity with the material, then you can meditate.

(2')) Who should meditate on which objects

Thus far we have discussed the various types of objects of meditation. But which object should you meditate on? Atiśa explained in *Lamp for the Path to Enlightenment* that you meditate on whatever object is most suitable for you. In other words, the answer to this question depends upon your karma and predispositions. You may be someone whose mind is powerfully dominated by attachment, conceit, anger, or hatred. Or you may be someone whose primary problem is that your mind constantly wanders; you are distracted and unable to focus. So don't meditate on the first object you hear about; choose an object that is beneficial for your practice. This is another reason why studying texts on śamatha is important: it will help you determine which object is most suitable for you.

Tsongkhapa quotes from Asaṅga's *Śrāvaka Levels*, where the Buddha advises his disciple Revata on how to choose the most appropriate object.

> Revata, if attachment uniquely dominates the behavior of a monk-yogi, a practitioner of yoga, he focuses his mind on the object of meditation of ugliness. If hatred dominates his behavior, he meditates on love; if ignorance dominates his behavior, then he meditates on the dependent arising of this condition; if pride dominates his behavior, he focuses his mind on the differentiation of the aggregates.

Tsongkhapa goes on to present several other passages from this text that give advice about the objects to be used by individuals plagued by specific types of afflictions.

> If discursiveness uniquely dominates his behavior, then he focuses his mind on an awareness of the exhalation and inhalation of the breath. In this way, he focuses his mind on an appropriate object of meditation.

And:

> In this regard, persons whose behavior is dominated by attachment, hatred, ignorance, pride, or discursiveness should, for a while at the outset, just purify those behaviors by contemplating objects of meditation for purifying behavior. After this they will see the stability of their minds, and they will ascertain only their objects of meditation. So they should definitely persevere at using their objects of meditation.

As mentioned above, if you are dominated by attachment, then you use the impurity and impermanence of the body as your meditation object. The Buddha taught that people who are dominated by anger toward others should utilize love as an object of meditation. For others, ignorance is their dominant problem and so they should meditate on the Buddha's teaching of the twelve-fold chain of dependent arising. If pride is your dominant affliction, you have an exaggerated opinion of yourself and think you are superior to others. In this case, a useful object of meditation would be the eighteen constituents as presented in Vasubandhu's *Treasury of Knowledge*. When you look at the details of these teachings, you will realize how little you actually know. Your conceit will diminish as a result of seeing how much more you have to learn. Some people are always distracted, their minds constantly wander. An effective antidote to this problem is to use your breath as the object of meditation.

If any of the five major afflictions—attachment, anger, ignorance, pride, and a distracted mind—dominate your mind, you will not be able to develop single-pointed concentration. Śāntideva uses the analogy of blood poisoning in *Engaging in the Bodhisattva Deeds* to illustrate how the afflictions pervade the mind once they gain entry. The afflictions spread, and the mind is in no position to engage in successful śamatha meditation:

> Just as poison spreads throughout the body
> Once it has reached the blood,
> So does a fault spread throughout the mind
> Once it has reached a vulnerable spot.[12]

Along the same lines, Śāntideva says:

> This band of thieves, the mental afflictions,
> Look for an entrance.
> Upon finding an entrance, it steals my virtues
> And destroys life in fortunate realms of existence.[13]

Just as robbers lie in wait for an opportunity to steal other people's belongings, the mental afflictions are always waiting for the proper conditions to harm your otherwise virtuous mind. Which of the five major afflictions dominates your mind depends upon how habituated you were to that affliction in prior lives. If in the past you were repeatedly engrossed in a mental affliction, it left an impression or predisposition in your mind for you to react similarly in the future. These potentialities from past lives can be so strong that in this life you react in disproportionately powerful ways to insignificant situations. For example, if in your past lives your prevailing attitude was attachment, now when you encounter even a small attractive thing, you react with strong desire that lasts for a long time.

So the first thing to do is to attempt to reduce whichever affliction is most dominant by applying the antidotes. Of course, in addition to these five major afflictions there are many others, such as envy. The point is to focus your mind on the object that can most effectively serve as an antidote to your most dominant affliction. It is important to apply the antidotes as needed in order to prevent those afflictions from spreading and strengthening. When the afflictions are lessened, you can focus more specifically on śamatha practice.

Some people are already quite balanced or even-minded; the afflictions of anger, attachment, ignorance, and so forth are not too strong, and no single one of them is dominant. It is not that their minds are pure and without afflictions; it is just that the afflictions currently manifest to a lesser degree. This occurs because they had not been frequently engrossed in any of the major afflictions in their previous lives. When these people encounter desirable objects and so forth, an affliction arises in a weak way for a brief period of time. Their minds are simply more accustomed to having a less powerful response to such situations. They are fortunate in this sense. Because their faults are not so coarse and obstructive, they do not need a specific object of meditation to serve as an antidote to a particular affliction. Asaṅga explains in *Bodhisattva Levels* (*Bodhisattva-bhūmi*) that practitioners whose afflictions are relatively balanced do not need to specifically reduce any particular affliction, such as attachment or anger. The purpose of meditation for them at this point is to stabilize their minds and cultivate concentration. Therefore they choose whatever object they like from among those described earlier. Asaṅga explains this in the same way in *Śrāvaka Levels*:

> Those whose behavior is balanced should work at whichever object they like so as to attain just mental stability; this is not for the purpose of purifying behavior. Understand that the same applies to those with slight afflictions.

There are other people who have still smaller degrees of these afflictions. Not only were they not habituated to these dysfunctional tendencies in their past lives, but also when they did look at the afflictions, they realized that they were mental obstacles. They practiced applying the antidotes to attachment, hatred, and the like. As a result of these past efforts, in this life the mental afflictions arise very slowly and with less intensity. This gives the practitioner an opportunity to apply the antidotes.

Right now, as a human, you can use your mental abilities to investigate attachment, anger, jealousy, pride, and the like. You can see all the negative results that come from such disturbing emotional states. In addition, you have the capability to fight against these negative mental states and tendencies. You can apply antidotes to remedy your situation. Even if you are not yet able to destroy the mental afflictions from the root, the effort you make now toward reducing these dysfunctional tendencies will have a very beneficial effect during this life or the next. When you become accustomed to the antidotes through repeated practice, you create the potential to lessen your inclination toward attachment, hatred, and the other disturbing emotions. You create a more stable basis upon which you can engage in effective practice.

When you have no training in applying the antidotes, whenever an afflictive mental state arises, you just let it occur. You do not know how to do otherwise. Your actions may even cause the negative mental states to increase, making them stronger and more persistent. In the future your mind will be dominated by these negative mental states as a result. In your future lives you will naturally have strong negative inclinations that you cannot control. This is the unfortunate situation for many.

It takes much longer to achieve meditative stabilization for those who are dominated by any of the five strong negative mental inclinations. The second type of person, those described as balanced or even-minded, is fortunate in that it will not take too long to generate śamatha. The third type of person, those who have very small afflictions, will easily and quickly obtain a calm, peaceful, stable mind.

Now Tsongkhapa turns to the question of which disciple should work with the objects of meditation for expertise. Again he quotes the *Śrāvaka Levels*. At this point in the text, Asaṅga is again drawing from a sutra that is no longer extant in which the Buddha responds to questions from his disciple named Revata.

> Revata, if a monk-yogi, a practitioner of yoga, is confused about the characteristic nature of all composite things, or confused about the thing called person, self, living being, life, that which is reborn, or the nourisher, he should focus his mind on the objects of meditation for expertise in the aggregates. If he is confused about causes, he should

focus on the objects of meditation for expertise in the constituents. If he is confused about conditions, he should focus on the objects of meditation for expertise in the sources. If he is confused about impermanence, suffering, and selflessness, he should focus on the objects of meditation for expertise in dependent arising, and on what is and is not possible.

The objects of expertise pertain to the cultivation of wisdom in that the more you understand and practice with these objects of meditation, the more ignorance is removed. These objects were discussed above, so I will not go into detail here. In brief, if a practitioner is ignorant about the characteristics of all phenomenal things or the nature of the person, he or she should use the objects of meditation for expertise as their objects. It is important to study these subjects. When you are a beginner, how can you know that everything is empty of an inherent nature? If you do not understand what it means to say, "Everything is empty," how could you see that in meditation? First you need to learn some of the details about what is meant by "everything." Then you need to learn the reasons behind the Prāsaṅgika Madhyamaka assertion that "everything is empty." Finally, you need to learn how to contemplate those reasons and be able to come to conclusions based upon them. It is at that point that you can direct your single-pointed meditation on that conclusion.

The same is true for cultivating a realization like the selflessness of persons. If you want to meditate on selflessness, first you must master the object of expertise of the five aggregates. You need to learn what the five aggregates are. Then you can reason that there is no self that is either identical with or separate from the aggregates. There are specific ways to think this through. Likewise, if you choose the topic of the eighteen sources, you need to understand that this framework is presented mainly from the perspective of the mind. The teachings on the eighteen sources explain how consciousness arises, its types, and its causes.

The same sutra discusses what type of person should focus on the objects of meditation for dispelling the afflictions. Above Tsongkhapa discussed the objects of meditation that address the five most dominant afflictions. Here he is concerned with the general afflictions of the desire realm, form realm, and formless realm:

> If you wish to be free from the attachment of the desire realm, focus your mind on the coarseness of the desire realm and the calmness of the form realm; if you wish to be free from the attachment of the form realm, focus your mind on the coarseness of the form realm and calm-

ness of the formless realm. If you wish to become disenchanted with all of the perishing aggregates and wish to be free from them, focus your mind on the truth of suffering, the truth of the origins, the truth of cessation, and the truth of the path.

You will recall that the mundane path uses comparative meditations to suppress the afflictions temporarily. The mundane path can only take you to the highest level of the formless realm; it does not end with liberation from the samsara. Through a direct realization of the ultimate truth, attained by practice on the supramundane path, you completely remove the afflictions from the root and eventually attain liberation.

Why are some of the most complex topics regarding insight into the nature of reality presented here, in the śamatha section of the *Lamrim Chenmo*? It may seem counterintuitive for such complicated analytic meditations to be inserted into an explanation of single-pointed concentration. Tsongkhapa explains that the very same objects used to reduce and eliminate the mental afflictions can be used for the development of śamatha. For that reason they are explained briefly here. At a later point in your practice, after you have perfected śamatha, the same object may be used in analytic meditation for the cultivation of vipaśyanā. Śamatha is a powerful stable mind. With it you can look at reality much more effectively. It is important to be able to clearly see what is negative and what is positive. Wisdom distinguishes these. But intellectual understanding of causality, the nature of reality, and so forth is not enough. Sometimes even though you know something, you have no power to act upon it. True insight relies on śamatha. The power of śamatha combined with vipaśyanā is the only thing that can totally destroy the mental enemy. Thus, it is critical that practitioners develop them both. Objects such as the ultimate nature of reality used to cultivate insight will be explained in depth in the vipaśyanā section of the *Lamrim Chenmo*. But because the same objects can be used to develop śamatha, they are briefly introduced here.

(3')) SYNONYMS OF THE OBJECT OF MEDITATION

When you find the proper object, you begin to analyze and examine it, in order to construct a representation, or image, of it in your mind. This is the process of developing a visualization. The resulting mental image, the visualized object, is referred to by a number of different names in sutras and commentaries. Tsongkhapa quotes from Asaṅga's *Śrāvaka Levels* to illustrate some of the many synonyms that are used to refer to the mental image held in śamatha meditation.

Also, that image is called "image"; it is also called "sign of concentration," "object in the domain of concentration," "technique of concentration," "door to concentration," "basis of attention," "body of internal conceptualization," and "appearing image." Know these as synonyms of the image that accords with the object that is known.

All of these are basically synonymous; they all indicate the same thing in different ways. Tsongkhapa mentions this here so that you will not get confused if you come across a variety of technical terms in your study of this subject. One phrase that is often used is "sign of concentration." The term "sign" indicates a particular feature, or focal point, of the mind in meditative concentration. Two other synonyms are "object of śamatha" and "object of concentration." These simply refer to the object utilized as the focal point of your attention in meditative stabilization. Another phrase found in canonical texts is "technique of concentration." In order to develop perfect śamatha, you have to utilize the proper technique, or method. Thus "method" is another name. Another commonly utilized synonym is "door to concentration." This refers to how the mental image is like the entryway to meditative stabilization. Still another phrase is "basis of attention." That refers to the basis upon which you fix your attention or concentration. Asaṅga also mentions the phrase "body of internal conceptualization," which refers to your image of internal thought.

(b')) Identifying objects of meditation for this context

There are hundreds of different meditations. There are sutra-type meditations, tantric meditations, and so forth. Each of these has a specific purpose and if done properly will yield a specific result. The goal that Tsongkhapa is discussing here is the achievement of śamatha—a mind that is able to stay on a particular object for as long as you wish without any kind of distraction. Therefore Tsongkhapa reiterates that you should choose an object of meditation based on your own situation; you examine which mental affliction is dominant in your mind and meditate on the antidote to that affliction. Do not think that this is unnecessary. You must first subdue your grossest mental afflictions before you can successfully cultivate śamatha. It takes quite a long time to achieve śamatha even for those who specifically address their most powerful mental afflictions. It should be obvious that those who have strong mental afflictions but do not apply the antidotes will not achieve actual śamatha even if they engage in concentration meditation. Such people may attain a concentration that provides some serenity, but it is not actual śamatha. So if your mind is dominated by a specific affliction like anger, the object of meditation that you should begin with is definite.

The ensuing explanation is a bit more specific about the object of meditation than what was presented above in the preceding section. Tsongkhapa draws upon a number of texts that explain Mahayana meditation theory and practice. Among Buddha's discourses, there are two sutras in particular: the *Sutra on the Samādhi That Perceives the Buddha of the Present Face to Face* (*Pratyutpanna-buddha-saṃmukhāvasthita-samādhi-sūtra*) and the *King of Samādhi Sutra*. Kamalaśīla composed three texts called *Stages of Meditation* in accordance with these sutras. First Tsongkhapa elaborates on the use of various objects for śamatha by quoting the Indian master Bodhibhadra:

> Here, śamatha is twofold: that attained by looking inward and that based on an object of meditation viewed outwardly. Of those, looking inward is twofold: focusing on the body and focusing on what is based on the body. Of those, focusing on the body is threefold: focusing on the body itself in the aspect of a deity; focusing on ugliness, such as skeletons; and focusing on special insignia such as a *khaṭvāṅga*.
>
> Focusing on what is based on the body is fivefold: focusing on the breath, focusing on subtle divine insignia, focusing on the drops, focusing on the aspects of light rays, and focusing on delight and bliss.
>
> Śamatha based on an object of meditation viewed outwardly is twofold: special and common. Of those, the special is twofold: focusing on a deity's body and focusing on a deity's speech.

According to Bodhibhadra, the objects of śamatha meditation are categorized in two ways: those found by looking inward, which are known as internal objects; and those found by looking outward, which are known as external objects. Atiśa affirms this way of categorizing objects in his autocommentary on *Lamp for the Path to Enlightenment*.

Bodhibhadra further divides these categories of objects. He starts by saying that among the internal objects there are those that use the body itself as the object and those that use objects that depend upon or are related to the body. He then subcategorizes the objects that use the body into three further categories: focusing on the body itself in the aspect of a deity; focusing on ugliness, such as skeletons; and focusing on special insignia such as a *khaṭvāṅga*. The first is a tantric method. The second is the antidote to attachment involving recognizing that the body is ugly and impure; when you use your own body as the meditation object in this context, your practice takes on an entirely different tone. In the third, you focus on a special implement or symbol that has religious or iconographic significance. For example the meditational deity Cakrasaṃvara holds a *khaṭvāṅga*, a type of trident. There are special occasions in meditation when you use this object as a symbol for your own body.

Bodhibhadra goes on to present five categories for explaining the topic of objects that are based on the body. The first of these is quite simple—your breath. The second is called *subtle insignia*. These are subtle internal signs. The third is the drops utilized in tantric practice. Various sorts of things can be used in this context, like the tip of fire or special letters. The next is light rays. The final object based on the body is a certain kind of mental delight and physical bliss.

With regard to the external objects of meditation, there are those that are special and those that are more ordinary. Ordinary external objects can be anything from a painting to a piece of stone; they really can be any commonplace material object. The special external objects are the body and speech of a buddha but can also be holy objects like stupas.

One of the most special objects for śamatha meditation is the body of the Buddha. This is typically Śākyamuni, but it can be any buddha. Of course, the main focus of this practice is to cultivate meditative stabilization, but because the perfect body of a buddha is an extremely virtuous object, you create a tremendous amount of merit by focusing upon it. Some sutras say that if you see a buddha directly, great merit is generated. But even seeing representations of buddhas in statues or paintings can be the cause for accumulating virtue and merit.

When a perfect representation of the Buddha's body, with its major and minor marks, is held clearly in your mind, it becomes a "field" of merit. This is an agricultural analogy. A farmer needs a good, fertile field to produce a great harvest; an ordinary or inferior field will yield only mediocre crops. Commentaries often refer to upper fields and lower fields for creation of merit. The upper field includes the Buddha, Dharma, and Sangha, the last of which includes bodhisattvas and so forth. When the Buddha is the focus of your practice, and you recollect his excellent qualities, accomplishments, and activities with faithful respect, you are doing a kind of prayer. Making prayers, prostrations, offerings, and so forth to honor the Buddha, or any of the Three Jewels, creates incredible merit. The lower field is sentient beings who are in unfortunate circumstances. When you think of these poor beings' misery, suffering, and problems, you should feel strong love and compassion for them. Even one moment of genuine love and compassion will create tremendous merit. In turn, this becomes the cause for more virtuous actions in the future. Thus the lower field is the object of your compassion, love, charity, support, and help. Not only do these two fields of merit provide amazing opportunities for the creation of merit, they also provide an opportunity for purification. In this vein, you visualize the Buddha, before whom you acknowledge your previous nonvirtuous actions.

You can see that there are great differences between meditations using ordinary objects and special objects. Any object, even a piece of animal horn or a rock, can be used as an object for the cultivation of single-pointed meditative stability. The point is just to remain focused. But if you are concentrating anyway, why not concentrate on something virtuous? If you use an image of the Buddha with some knowledge of the Buddha and what his qualities are, then when you joyfully meditate on that object with faith, it is so much more beneficial. You contemplate the qualities of the Buddha's body, speech, and mind and wish to attain that state of perfection yourself in the future. When you use an object of śamatha meditation in that way, a double purpose will be achieved. This is obviously so much better than using an object that does not have anything special about it.

There are additional benefits that come from using the Buddha as your object when practicing śamatha meditation. These are presented in detail in the two sutras mentioned above, *The King of Samādhi Sutra* and *The Sutra on the Samādhi That Perceives the Buddha of the Present Face to Face*. Tsongkhapa encourages his readers to study these and Kamalaśīla's explanation of these sutras in the three *Stages of Meditation* texts. Tsongkhapa just gives two examples. First, if you are very familiar with your object, at the time of death you can recollect the qualities of the Buddha and take refuge. And if you practice visualizing an image of the Buddha now, doing tantric practices later will be much easier. In tantric practices such as deity yoga, there are times when you need to clearly visualize the deity in front of you and there are times when you need to imagine yourself as that deity. The main point here is that by using a virtuous object in śamatha meditation, you can achieve śamatha and in the process accomplish other beneficial purposes. This is a skillful way to practice.

The next question that arises is, "What kind of Buddha image should you use?" Tsongkhapa draws from Kamalaśīla's third *Stages of Meditation* to respond to this question.

> In that regard, practitioners should first fix their attention on whatever they may have seen and whatever they may have heard about the physical form of the Tathāgata and then achieve śamatha. The physical form of the Tathāgata is a golden color like that of refined gold, adorned by the signs and exemplary features, dwells with its retinue, and affects the aims of living beings through various means. By continuously directing their minds toward it, yogis develop a wish for its good qualities and quell laxity, excitement, and so forth. They should continue meditative

stabilization for as long as they can see it clearly, as though the Buddha were sitting in front of them.

You may have read or heard teachings about the qualities of the Buddha's body, like its color, proportions, major and minor marks, and so forth. You should think again and again about what you have heard. Try to bring this description into your mind. You imagine what it is like and then focus on that image. This way of constructing an image may or may not produce the richness of detail that is ideal. It depends upon the abilities of the individual practitioner. In general, it is easier if you first look at a representation of the Buddha and then bring that image into your mind. In this case, try to find a statue or painting that is well made. Do not think of it as a piece of metal, stone, or canvas; rather think that this is representative of the Buddha. Look from the bottom up, then from the top down. Look at every aspect; take note of the color, the shape, the hand positions, the eyes, and so forth. Look at each of these again and again and try to fix them in your mind. Once you are thoroughly familiar with the object, become accustomed to it by cultivating its visualization in your mind again and again.

Once you get the basics down, proceed to more subtle qualities. The next part can be a little difficult to visualize clearly. The Buddha's body has thirty-two major marks and eighty minor marks, like elongated earlobes and an uṣṇīṣa protruding from the crown of his head. He is sitting amid a group of disciples. And even when the Buddha seems to be just sitting there, his mental powers are so incredible that he is actively engaged in creating tremendous benefit for sentient beings. You can visualize rays of light emanating out from him to help others. See the Buddha as a protector of sentient beings, engaging in activities, not just a solid stone sitting there. Contemplate his perfect qualities, like his perfect wisdom, compassion, generosity, and so forth. As much as possible, try to think of the Buddha as made of light. Although you do not need all of this detail, do the best that you can to visualize in this way. Eventually the image will become so vivid it is as if the Buddha is sitting right in front of you. Kamalaśīla says that until it becomes that clear, you should continue to meditate and practice. Over time the image will become a little clearer.

There are two ways to go about visualizing the Buddha. The first is to visualize the Buddha as an object that you have mentally constructed. The second is to think that the Buddha is actually there in front of you, not a mere byproduct of your imagination. The second method is better, especially for the beginners, because it helps generate trust and faith. Generally speaking, this is something that is common to both Mahayana and Hinayana.

It is useful at first to accustom yourself to the form of the Buddha with your visual consciousness, but when you are actually meditating, the image must appear to your mind. However, some people say that to do śamatha meditation you should put a statue or painting of the Buddha in front of you and meditate while gazing upon the image. They argue that it is not about bringing a visualized mental image to mind but becoming accustomed to it with open eyes—directly looking at the color, shape, and so forth. This idea is rejected by the great eighth-century Tibetan master Yeshe De, with whom Tsongkhapa is in agreement. They concur that śamatha is not completed on the basis of a sense consciousness but on the basis of the mental consciousness. Therefore holding the object merely with visual consciousness is not correct. In other words, just staring at the object to keep it in your visual consciousness is not the way to complete śamatha; you have to bring the image into your mind. Why? Because the achievement of śamatha is based upon mental consciousness, and an object of a mental consciousness appears to the mind, not to any of the sense consciousnesses. In this context, the object of a mental consciousness is a mental image or a concept.

When you visualize the object in your mind, you should focus upon it with stability, without distraction or mental dullness. It is also important when you are training in śamatha that you do not change your object of meditation frequently. If you get tired, it may seem useful to meditate on another object for a short time to combat the fatigue. However, changing your object too much in the beginning is not good. It will create an impediment to achieving your goal of a stable mind. Tsongkhapa says that eminent masters like Asaṅga in his *Levels of Yogic Deeds* (*Yoga-caryā-bhūmi*) and Kamalaśīla in his *Stages of Meditation* emphasize the importance of maintaining a single object for śamatha practice in the beginning. They strongly discourage beginning meditators from trying many different objects. Āryaśūra makes the same point in his *Compendium of the Perfections* (*Pāramitā-samāsa*):

> Solidify your mind's reflection
> By being firm on one object of meditation;
> Letting it flow to many objects
> Leads to a mind disturbed by afflictions.

If you do not follow this advice and let your focus shift to many different objects, your mind will become scattered or disturbed. As a result, various kinds of afflictions may arise. Likewise, in *Lamp for the Path to Enlightenment*, Atiśa says that practitioners should remain settled on a single suitable object.

> Settle your mind in virtue
> On any single object of meditation.

The teachings of all of these great masters emphasize the importance of concentrating on a single object. It is like this: if you rub two sticks together with persistence in the same place, you can generate heat and even start a fire. But if you rub one part of a stick, then move to another area of the stick, or keep switching sticks, you will not get the result you want. In the same way, your mind should remain on a single object of focus in śamatha training. So first search for the proper object, and after you find it, use it as the basis of your training in mental stabilization.

After your mind is fully controlled, you can change your focal object. Once you have achieved śamatha you can peacefully remain focused upon any object for as long as you like. Your mind is completely tamed with respect to distraction and mental dullness. At that point, you can successfully meditate on the variety of detailed and subtle aspects of the objects we discussed earlier—aggregates, constituents, sources, and so on. Kamalaśīla's first *Stages of Meditation* also says:

> Only when you have earned concentrated attention should you focus in detail on the particulars of objects, such as the aggregates and constituents. It is in light of the particulars of yogis' meditation on objects such as the eighteen emptinesses that the Buddha states in sutras such as the *Sutra Unraveling the Intended Meaning* that there are many aspects of objects of meditation.

The "eighteen emptinesses" is a categorization scheme that differentiates emptiness by way of its bases. Some other texts mention twenty divisions of emptiness. As you have seen, there are many aspects to many objects of śamatha. There are literally hundreds of types of objects of meditation. But until you actually attain śamatha, you should focus upon just one.

So if your choice of an object of meditation is the body of the Buddha, Tsongkhapa recommends that you first conjure a rough image in your mind of the general body of the Buddha, including color, shape, size, and so forth. Then as your mind becomes more stable and clear with respect to that gross image, you can add increasingly more subtle detail. The process is to begin by visualizing the head of the Buddha, then the main part of his body along with the arms, and finally move on to visualize the lower limbs. Do this several times, and then try to visualize the whole body together. At this point, be satisfied and focus upon the object that comes to your mind—even if it is not complete and not very clear or vivid. It is all right if your visualization is vague and the limbs, size, and color appear only in a rough way. At this point you do not need to clarify it or visualize more detail. Every detail does not have to be seen. You have found your object of mental focus. This is what you should meditate upon.

If you are not satisfied and at this early stage try to gain more clarity and see every detail, some problems can arise. Although you may be able to get a little bit of clarity by focusing on various details again and again, you will destroy the stability of your meditation. Clarity is beneficial, but not at the expense of the stabilized mind. Remember, the primary goal of śamatha training is to be able to focus on your desired object as long as you wish. If you are not satisfied with the appearance of your object and are always shifting your focus in order to clarify it, you will not develop meditative stability. You have to control that impulse and content yourself with a rough amount of clarity and detail at this point. Generally it is more useful to focus on the object that is there than on one that is not. So when you find the proper object, even if it is not too clear, try to train in stabilization. After your mind is stable, clarity is easily attained. Different practitioners begin with different abilities in regard to how easy or difficult it is for them to stabilize the mind and how easy or difficult it is to develop a clear image. But in the beginning of your training, when you are weighing the importance of stabilization versus clarity, first try to stabilize. Stability is much more important at this stage. Of course, with actual śamatha you will have both clarity and stabilization.

Generally speaking, the instructions on how to develop śamatha in the *Lamrim Chenmo* are in the context of the sutra vehicle, not the tantric vehicle. Tantric practitioners on the generation stage have different concerns. They may be trying to visualize a mandala or meditate on a deity; it is very important that their visualization be clear with regard to the details: the heads, eyes, color, number of hands, and the symbols and ritual implements in each hand. They work hard to bring each detail, one by one, into clear focus so that eventually the image looks like the actual deity is present. They do not have to look at an image with their eyes; the deity complete in all its splendid detail appears clearly to their mind. When every subtle detail is clearly visualized, they have perfected the generation stage. Until that happens, they should work on the clarity.

Since it is difficult for most of us to visualize all the complex detail of a tantric deity, it is quite permissible to use any of the more simple objects explained earlier. In other words, if you are unable visualize such an image in your mind, it is not advisable to try to develop śamatha using the body of a deity as your object of meditation. Again, the reason is that the main purpose at this point is merely to achieve śamatha rather than the tantric stages and so forth. You need the object to appear to some degree in order to hold on to it. If it does not appear to your mind, it will not serve to help you achieve śamatha.

Therefore this is what you should do. When you first focus on the body of the Buddha, if some part of his form appears clearly, hold that in your mind. If it becomes unclear, then renew your visualization of the body as a whole again. For example, you should meditate on the body of the Buddha as being gold in color. If in your visualization the color changes to red, or any uncertainty about the color arises, do not continue. Stop and go back to where you started with the correct color. The same is true with respect to the size, shape, or posture of the image. If any of these qualities become uncertain, in terms of not reflecting your desired visualization, then you should stop.

The mind often does this sort of thing. It begins with a particular visualization as an object of focus but then it starts to wander. For example, if you are meditating on the Buddha in the seated posture, it may after some time appear to be standing up. This is what Tsongkhapa means by "uncertainty of shape or posture." The same kind of thing can happen with regard to number. You may start to meditate on a single buddha, but slowly it becomes two or three. This is called "uncertainty of number." And again, you should stop right away. It is not good when you start meditating on one thing and your mind pursues something else. As soon as you recognize that has happened, that you are no longer focusing on the object you initially intended, stop and go back to what you planned earlier. Do not follow the changes or uncertainties.

⚜ 3 ⚜

Focusing Your Mind

(2)) How to focus your mind on the object of meditation
    (a')) The flawless method
    (b')) Eliminating flawed methods
    (c')) The length of sessions

———◈———

(2)) HOW TO FOCUS YOUR MIND ON THE OBJECT OF MEDITATION

WE ARE NOW beginning the second major topic of the śamatha section of the *Lamrim Chenmo*: how to focus your mind on the object of meditation. We have discussed in some detail the various objects of meditation and how to go about choosing one. But now the issue is how to actually focus on the object. This subject is further divided into three: the flawless method, eliminating flawed methods, and the length of your meditation sessions.

(a')) THE FLAWLESS METHOD

Let's begin with the first topic: the flawless method to train in śamatha meditation. To determine the perfect method, we first need to define the goal of this practice. Actual śamatha has two qualities that are of primary importance: vivid mental clarity and single-pointed concentration. Mental clarity is an awareness that is absolutely precise and lucid with regard to its object. Single-pointed concentration is the strength to maintain nondiscursive mental stability with regard to its object. It is not a mind that is partially on its object and partially somewhere else. Its focus is directed. Some people say that the physical and mental bliss that is experienced when you achieve śamatha should also be considered among the primary qualities of śamatha. However, that bliss does not accompany all of the concentrations that access the first level of the form realm, the first meditative absorption. In addition, the meditative absorption of the fourth level of the form realm does not have any associated mental or physical bliss, and this stage is said to be the optimal place for achievements on the path of any of the three vehicles. Moreover, on certain higher formless concentrations, the feeling of your meditation should be neutral, neither too unpleasant nor too pleasant. Therefore adding bliss to this list of the principal qualities of śamatha is incorrect.

There is an obstacle that corresponds to each of these two principal qualities of śamatha. It is difficult to summarize these two obstacles in two words, but *laxity* and *excitement* will be used here. Vivid mental clarity is blocked by laxity, or mental sinking, and single-pointed concentration is threatened by excitement. Both of these obstacles have coarse and subtle forms. It is critically important to be able to recognize these two obstacles in both their subtle and coarse manifestations. A good place to read about them is Śāntideva's "Guarding Introspection" chapter of *Engaging in the Bodhisattva's Deeds*. Without the knowledge and ability to recognize these obstacles, you will not be able to stop them when they arise. If you do not eliminate these obstacles, you cannot achieve real śamatha. If you do not achieve śamatha, you will be unable to cultivate vipaśyanā and achieve liberation. Therefore you should strive to understand the nature of the obstacles, their subtle and coarse qualities, how they arise, and how to stop them.

How to identify and actually stop these obstacles will be explained in chapter 4, but I will give a very brief description of what they are here. *Coarse excitement* is when your mind becomes distracted and leaves its intended object. *Subtle excitement* is when the mind remains focused on its object but there is a temptation or inclination to move toward another object. *Laxity* is a loosening of the mental clarity of your object. The mind becomes weak, just as it is right before you fall asleep. This can be very subtle. Subtle mental laxity can look like deep meditation with no distraction, but there is a slight loosening. Your mind may be firmly single-pointed on its object, but it becomes too internalized. As you sink more and more into dullness, darkness and a lack of clarity become more apparent. At this point some people even fall asleep.

Perfect śamatha is the ability to naturally remain on your meditation object, without interruption, and abide for as long as you wish with perfect clarity. There are two things needed in order to achieve this: a method that keeps your mind from getting distracted from its object of focus, and an accurate way to know whether your mind is distracted or lax or becoming distracted or lax. The first of these necessary conditions is often referred to as *mindfulness*, a technique that prevents your mind from forgetting the object of meditation.

The second is *introspection*, or *vigilance*, a method to constantly and consistently assess your mental situation. It is a way of knowing whether your mind is getting distracted or dull—tending toward excitement or laxity—and so forth. Vasubandhu's *Commentary on the "Ornament for the Mahayana Sutras"* (*Sūtra-alaṃkāra-bhāṣya*) says:

> Mindfulness and introspection bring about close mental focus because the former prevents your attention from wandering from the object of meditation and the latter clearly recognizes that your attention is wandering.

Mindfulness prevents excitement by not letting the mind stray from its object. Introspection is cognizant of the mind being excited or becoming excited. When you use both mindfulness and introspection, your mind remains properly focused.

Mindfulness is simply to hold and stabilize the object appearing to your visualization. This is not analytical meditation; you are not looking for more clarity or new qualities. A lack of mindfulness means that you have forgotten your object of meditation; your mind has gone to something else. Once you have visualized whatever object you have chosen in the manner described above, hold your attention on it with stability and strength. You do not want your mental grip of the object to be too weak; you don't want to feel as if you are ready to lose it and fall asleep. Conversely, your apprehension of the object should not be too tight. Find an appropriate middle. Your mind should be alert and delighted in its practice. Do not get discouraged; keep your spirits high. When you actually do this practice, these teachings will make more sense. They are a bit difficult and abstract until you have some experience.

In his *Compendium of Knowledge*, Asaṅga explains mindfulness as follows:

> What is mindfulness? In regard to a familiar object, your mind is not forgetful and operates without distraction.

Mindfulness, then, has three features. The first feature is that the object of mindfulness is one you already know: it is something that is familiar to you, something with which you have experience, something to which you are already accustomed. Mindfulness does not attempt to accrue new knowledge or focus on a new, unfamiliar object. The object of mindfulness is something that has come to your mind before. The Tibetan word translated as "mindfulness" (*dran pa*) is sometimes translated as "recollect" or "remember."

The second key feature is that mindfulness is free of forgetfulness. In this context, "not forgetful" does not mean that you remember what your teacher told you about your meditation object—for example, how your teacher described the body of the Buddha. It also does not mean that you know the answer if someone asks you something about your object, for example, "What is the Buddha holding in his hands?" That is not enough. With regard to mindfulness, "not forgetful" means being able to hold the image of your object in your mind with clarity and without the slightest bit of distraction. If there is any distraction, then mindfulness of your object is lost. Mindfulness involves the power to hold on to an object. It means that once your attention is fixed on the object of meditation, you hold it there without new examination. It holds its object firmly; your awareness and clarity are continuous.

The third feature of mindfulness is its function. Its purpose is to keep the mind focused on its object. The intent is to hold the object and keep your attention from straying. In this sense, it is both the maintenance of concentration and the elimination of distraction. In short, the function of mindfulness is to control your mind; it ties your mind to your chosen object for as long as you wish. It is naturally free of the two hindrances of excitement and laxity. This is important. How do you practice mindfulness when you concentrate on something? First you focus your mind on your chosen object. Then one aspect of your mind recognizes that it is focused on your desired object. From that point on, there is no more analyzing, examining, or thinking about the object. Your mind just maintains the strength of its attention without distraction.

To cultivate a tamed mind like this requires training. You must be vigilant every moment. As soon as you realize that you have lost your attention, you have to resume concentrating on your object. In fact, as soon as you realize you are leaning toward laxity or distraction, you have to bring your attention back. This is the function of introspection—it is like a spy in your mind that keeps watch on the mind itself. In a number of great treatises, the uncontrolled mind is likened to an untamed elephant, mindfulness is likened to the rope that binds the elephant to a sturdy pillar, and introspection is likened to the tools used to keep the elephant under control. Bhāvaviveka's *Heart of the Middle Way* says:

> The erring elephant of your mind
> Is securely bound by the rope of mindfulness
> To the sturdy pillar of the object of meditation
> And is gradually controlled with the iron hook of intelligence.

Kamalaśīla's second *Stages of Meditation* uses a similar analogy:

> With the ropes of mindfulness and introspection, tie the elephant of
> your mind to the tree trunk, the object of meditation.

If trained properly, elephants can become powerful tools that act according to
your directions. In order to tame an elephant, you need a special method: in
ancient India, trainers would tie a wild elephant to a pillar or a tree and poke
it with iron hooks if it did not do what it was supposed to do. The method
required specific tools: a strong pillar, a strong rope, a sharp hook, and an excellent trainer. Tsongkhapa says there is no contradiction between Bhāvaviveka's
use of the analogy that says introspection is like the hook and Kamalaśīla's
that says that both mindfulness and introspection are represented by the rope.
Either way, mindfulness is the tying of your mind to the object. Introspection
also binds your mind to the object; if you are not aware of what your mind is
doing, it can easily stray from its object. Introspection catches both the mental
sinking of laxity and the distracted mind of excitement. When it recognizes the
arising of either of these faults—or ideally, recognizes when they are about to
arise—introspection alerts the mind to return to the object; it does not let the
faults flourish. So in that sense you can say that introspection ties the mind to
the object. Vasubandhu also says that both mindfulness and introspection are
methods for focusing the mind on the object.

Mindfulness is the primary practice when we are doing śamatha meditation, but introspection is also critical, especially in the beginning. Tsongkhapa
advises you to keep this watchful eye on your mind even as your attention is
fixed on the object. He exhorts you to examine the mind with the wisdom of
introspection to see whether it is abiding on the object or not, whether it is
focusing properly or not, and so forth. In other words when you have set your
mind on an object and are abiding in concentration, in a very subtle way one
corner of your mind keeps watch to see if your focus remains on its object or
if there is any danger of laxity or excitement. You do not have to begin introspection immediately after you set your mind on the object. You can leave it
for a little while, but begin checking before too long. You want introspection in
place before your first burst of energy is exhausted. If you keep up that energy
by checking the mind again and again, it will help prevent falling into mental
dullness.

Mindfulness is definite and sure. It apprehends its object with certainty.
Some systems argue that your mind should be relaxed and not hold the object
too tightly. They encourage people to stay loose and relaxed, and they do not
encourage real power with regard to the way you focus on the object of meditation. If you follow that type of instruction it may seem like you have perfect
concentration because there is initially mental clarity and focus. But when your

focus is too relaxed, there will always be a subtle laxity. Your mind will have no strength, and subtle mental sinking will slowly increase, leading to dullness, cloudiness, and darkness. Your mind will be drawn in that way. Without this active power, your concentration will always be faulty. You can meditate for years and years with subtle laxity, and true śamatha will not arise.

Some other systems of meditation say that you should train the mind to stabilize by "not thinking about any object at all." They advise you to think, "I will not use any object. If any object comes to my mind, I will not follow it." They are trying to have the mind just abide in itself. But even this form of meditation requires mindfulness. The mind itself, without discursiveness, is the object of meditation. This meditation is simply the technique of maintaining mindfulness. To be successful in such a meditation, you still must have strong mindfulness and the mental spy of vigilant introspection. In a sense, introspection examines the mind, the subject side, while mindfulness holds the object with the force of certain knowledge. Without these two you cannot do this properly.

(b')) Eliminating flawed methods

Now that you understand what mindfulness and introspection are, you can discern whether a way of practicing śamatha is right or wrong. Tsongkhapa explains the flaws in other systems based upon quotations from sutras, the teachings of great masters, and by using logic. The structure he uses is to have imaginary opponents present critiques of his views, and then he presents his reply.

The first opponent takes issue with Tsongkhapa's assertion that mindfulness is the active way that the mind holds its object. The opponent says that this may prevent laxity but it will increase excitement. Therefore relaxing a mind that is too tight leads to stability. Tsongkhapa says that this person does not distinguish between laxity and meditation. He is concerned with only stability and not the other critical feature of śamatha—clarity. The flaws of following the advice that "Good relaxation is good meditation" were mentioned above.

The second opponent confuses laxity and lethargy. He says that laxity is the darkening and clouding of your mind. Further, without laxity the mind is limpid and clear, and this limpid clarity is flawless concentration. Tsongkhapa says that this too is incorrect and that he will elaborate the differences between laxity and lethargy later.

To summarize his reply to these two opponents, Tsongkhapa says that in meditation it is hard to find the right balance that is free from both excitement and laxity. If you hold your object too tightly, you may have clarity but excitement can arise that will prevent stability. If you sustain a stable meditation by becoming too relaxed, you may have stability, but laxity will prevent vivid clarity. Mental clarity does not refer merely to the clarity of the object; it also refers to the way of holding the object. Even if the object is vivid, if your mind has weakness, then there is no mental clarity. Faultless concentration must be both stable and have clarity. The Buddha uses an analogy to describe this. He says that the proper balance in śamatha practice is like a musician playing a stringed instrument. In order to hit the perfect note, a musician needs an instrument with strings that are neither too tight nor too loose. In the same way perfect śamatha requires a perfect focus that is neither too tight nor too loose. If you focus properly, with a perfect balance that is neither too loose nor too tight, you will eventually achieve a spontaneous and faultless state of śamatha.

Discussing the difficulty of finding the right balance, the great Indian master Candragomin said in his *Praise of Confession* (*Deśanā-stava*):

> If I use exertion, excitement arises;
> If I abandon it, slackness ensues.
> It is hard to find the right balance in this.
> What should I do with my troubled mind?

Finding and maintaining just the right balance is hard. Try to avoid going back and forth between the two extremes of trying so hard to focus that you get distracted and relaxing so much that you fall into the trap of laxity. The Buddha said that you would find the right measure through experience. It is difficult to understand this in the abstract. Talking about this prior to actual experience is like a beggar talking about the king's treasury. He has never seen it but he describes it.

Let's say that you are holding a measuring cup full to the brim with oil. You do not want to spill any of it. If your grip is too loose, the cup will wobble and oil will spill. If your grip is too tight, your hands will shake and the oil will spill. You need just the right balance to keep the oil from spilling. It will not work if you are either too relaxed or too tense. In addition to Candragomin, Tsongkhapa quotes from the Indian masters Buddhaśānti, Asaṅga, and Kamalaśīla to make this point.

So the next hypothetical opponent asks Tsongkhapa, "Is it right to monitor the way you are meditating at the same time that you fix your attention on the object of meditation? Can this even be done while your mind is fully concentrated on a single object?" Tsongkhapa replies, "Yes, you must do that." Introspection is a critical part of successful śamatha practice. You must check your mind often with the mental spy of introspection to evaluate whether your mind is abiding on your chosen object. You must also check if it is doing so properly. There are signs that your concentration on the object is beginning to lose strength or has lost its clarity. In just a short time, your mind can easily go to one of those extremes. For support of his opinion, he refers the questioner to a passage in Kamalaśīla's second *Stages of Meditation*:

> After you have thus set your attention on whatever your chosen object of meditation may be, fix it there continuously. While you stay right with the object, analyze and investigate your mind, thinking: "Is my mind apprehending the object of meditation well? Or is it lax? Or is it distracted by the appearance of external objects?"

Tsongkhapa, following Kamalaśīla, advises meditators to keep a watchful eye on their minds even while their attention is fixed on their object of meditation. You do not stop concentrating and then check your mind. You maintain your concentration and use introspection to see whether the mind is abiding on the object or not, whether it is falling into laxity or dullness, whether it is getting excited and moving to objects other than the chosen object.

It is like driving a car on the highway. You do not stop driving while you are keeping an eye on whether your car is going straight, whether another car is pulling in front of you, whether an oncoming vehicle is crossing the center line, whether your car is running properly, and so forth. If you do not pay attention to these sorts of things because you think, "My car is on the road so I do not need to worry about it," big problems may arise. In the same way, you examine your mind in meditation with mental introspection. It is as if you are watching from a corner of your mind while you continue to meditate. In the beginning your internal watchfulness may be a bit rough, but later introspection becomes a part of wisdom. When you go longer and deeper in meditation, introspection always acts. It watches without disturbing the mind's focus. Even if your mind has not yet become lax or distracted but is merely on the verge of those states, the introspective mental spy will know it and be able to stop it. Introspection has to be learned. So you should practice it from the very beginning.

The way to maintain continuous mindfulness is to remind yourself of the intended object of meditation. Asaṅga's *Śrāvaka Levels* encourages us to continually recollect or apply mindfulness to the object of meditation:

> In this regard, what is a one-pointed mind? Any continuum of attention that remembers again and again, focuses on a consistently similar object, and is continuous, free of misdeeds, and possessed of delight is called "concentration," as well as "a one-pointed virtuous mind."
>
> What does it remember again and again? You perceive the object of meditation—the characteristic of someone in equipoise—from the

viewpoint of any teaching that you have memorized or heard, and upon which you have received instructions and explications from your gurus. You engage and focus on this object with continuous mindfulness.

When Asaṅga describes the single-pointed mind as "free of misdeeds," he is referring to being free of the faults of laxity and excitement. Being "possessed of delight" means to having the mental joy of perfect śamatha. In the second paragraph, Asaṅga asks what should be remembered again and again? The answer is, you should recollect the instructions of your spiritual teacher regarding the object of meditation. You should hold that object precisely the way it was explained to you. Obviously, this means that when you meditate, your mind is not passive and not doing anything. Merely relaxing is not enough. You remind yourself again and again about the object based on what you have been taught.

Sthiramati makes a similar point in his *Explanation of "Separation of the Middle from the Extremes"*:

> The statement "Mindfulness means not forgetting the object of meditation" means that you mentally express the instructions on stabilizing your mind.

"Express the instructions on stabilizing your mind" is another way of saying that you set your mind on the object as a way of counteracting forgetfulness. It is a way to describe holding the object with tempered strength. The point Tsongkhapa is making here is that just because you once knew something from hearing teachings or holding an object in meditation, it does not mean that you can completely relax and have no worries about it fading away. You have to remind yourself of the object of meditation at intervals. You must place your mind on the object and then be vigilant. When mindfulness and introspection are strong, they not only recognize faults when they arise, they also detect the warning signs of the faults before they arise. Then you can prevent them. This is the function of mindfulness and introspection; it is precisely what all these great masters have been describing.

It is an error to think, "Mindfulness combined with introspection is incorrect because introspection is discursive thought." Such an error is based on the idea that pure śamatha meditation is without any thinking at all, that all thought is an obstacle, and the mind should just set on its object and relax. That is not only meditation without introspection, it is meditation without mindfulness. There is no effort involved, and as a result it will not prevent the two major faults.

(c')) THE LENGTH OF SESSIONS

How long should a session be when we do this kind of meditation practice? When you are sick, you may be prescribed medication that should be taken multiple times in small doses. In the same way you should apply antidotes in regular small doses in order to free yourself from mental diseases. With regard to training in śamatha, these doses are meditation sessions. There are a number of possible ways to approach mastering mindfulness meditation—with a long retreat, a short retreat, multiple sessions per day, and so forth. Generally all the Tibetan traditions recommend multiple short sessions per day, albeit for different reasons.

If you stop while your meditation session is going well, you will be enthusiastic about pursuing additional practice sessions. As a beginner, if you push yourself to go meditate until you are exhausted, you may look back on that session with less enthusiasm and not want to practice more. Tibetans often say that meditating is sort of like having a friend or relative visit. If they do not stay too long and leave on a happy note, you will feel strong friendship for them when they depart. You will look forward to seeing them again. But if they overstay their welcome or leave after you have had an argument, you may not want to invite them back again any time soon. The same is true at the beginning of śamatha training. It is good to end your meditation sessions while you are enjoying it and feel that you could continue much longer. This way you will be more eager for the next session.

So, you may ask, how long is a short session? The great Indian teachings on śamatha such as Asaṅga's *Śrāvaka Levels* are not explicit about the duration of meditative sessions. Kamalaśīla does address the length of a meditation session in his final *Stages of Meditation:*

> At this stage engage in meditative equipoise for twenty-four minutes, an hour-and-a-half, or as long as you can.

But Kamalaśīla made this statement in a discussion about the cultivation of vipaśyanā. In other words, he gave this advice to those who had already developed śamatha, not to those who were just beginning their training in śamatha. Nevertheless, Tsongkhapa says that this advice is applicable to śamatha training. Here Kamalaśīla recommends varying lengths of time but concludes by suggesting you meditate for "as long as you can." This means that your meditation should last as long as there are no signs of laxity or excitement. In other words, the length of a meditation session is not fixed: it may be a few minutes, an hour, or longer.

For this reason, some teachers have said that multiple short sessions are preferable because if your meditation session is too long, you become very susceptible to the extremes of excitement and laxity. A longer session is all right if you practice the techniques of mindfulness and introspection. If you do not identify any present or imminent laxity or excitement, you can relax a bit and continue. You proceed as if you were a sentry in a battle zone. A sentry's responsibility is to watchfully patrol a perimeter. Sentries vigilantly check to see if there is any danger, and if there is no sign of imminent danger, they can relax a bit and continue their patrol.

If you are a beginner, short sessions better allow you to stay fresh and strong. If you continue too long, forgetfulness, which is the opposite of mindfulness, will arise. When you fail to recollect your chosen object, your mind is wandering, and you have lost your focus on the object of meditation. It is also possible that your mind sinks into mental dullness. You may even fall asleep. It is not easy for beginners to quickly recognize when the faults of excitement and laxity occur, to say nothing about being aware of them before they emerge. In short, when you are sitting on your cushion, it is easy for your mind to drift into distraction or dullness. It is difficult for beginners to prevent this because blocking these faults requires powerful mindfulness and introspection.

You can fail to recognize laxity and excitement at two points in your meditation: after you have completely forgotten your object of meditation and while you still have some recollection of your object. The former situation is worse. But both situations reinforce the importance of vigilant practice of the antidotes to the major obstacles. In the first instance, you have fallen completely under the spell of excitement and entirely forgotten your object of meditation. Powerful mindfulness is the necessary antidote to this problem. In the latter case, your mind is not entirely separated from the object, but it is not equipped with a sharp mental spy. Introspection that quickly realizes that laxity and excitement are present or imminent is the more important corrective here. Both mindfulness and introspection are very important. If you do not practice and reinforce them, they will be weak and these obstacles will arise.

As you continue to do this practice, you will develop the ability to hold concentration for a longer time. You will quickly recognize even the slightest signs of laxity and excitement and be able stop them from arising. When you have reached that level, you can engage in a longer meditation session. Thus shorter sessions are recommended when you have less facility with the antidotes; but as your ability increases, so can the duration of your meditation session.

You need not be stubborn about the length of your sessions. The duration of your meditation session should accord with the state of your body and mind. If you get sick, you may have less energy, and in that case it makes sense for your

94 steps on the path to enlightenment

sessions to be shorter. You can take a break. Address your physical or mental problem, or at least alleviate it to some degree, and then you can begin another session. So long as you are aware of the dangers of longer sessions that we have discussed, once you have the ability, you may want to extend the length of your sessions.

$$\div 4 \div$$

Dealing with Laxity and Excitement

(c)) What to do after you focus on an object of meditation
  (1)) What to do when laxity and excitement occur
    (a')) Using the remedy for failing to recognize laxity and excitement
      (1')) The defining characteristics of laxity and excitement
      (2')) The method for developing introspection that recognizes laxity and excitement
    (b')) Using the remedy for failing to try to eliminate them even when they are recognized
      (1')) Intention and the way it stops laxity and excitement
      (2')) The underlying causes of laxity and excitement
  (2)) What to do when laxity and excitement are absent

(c)) WHAT TO DO AFTER YOU FOCUS ON AN OBJECT OF MEDITATION

THIS CHAPTER CONTAINS practical advice. It explains what to do when focusing on an object of meditation. It is important to recall that the instructions in this chapter are part of the discussion of the five primary obstacles to śamatha. The first obstacle is laziness; this is a problem because it can keep you from beginning and then maintaining your practice. Forgetting the instructions that enable you to practice properly is the second obstacle. Third, even if you engage in meditation and remember the instructions about what to do, excitement and laxity may arise. Excitement and laxity are two distinct obstacles, but they are counted together as one primary obstacle. The fourth obstacle is the failure to apply antidotes when those obstacles arise. The fifth obstacle is the application of antidotes when they are not needed. Just as it is detrimental to your meditation if you let obstacles arise and do nothing about them, it is also damaging to excessively apply antidotes when no obstacles are present. The third, fourth, and fifth primary obstacles are the topic of our current discussion.

There are two basic questions answered here: What to do when the two obstacles of laxity and excitement occur? And what to do when your meditation is free of these two?

(1)) WHAT TO DO WHEN LAXITY AND EXCITEMENT OCCUR

With regard to the first question, the initial step is learning to recognize these obstacles. In order to put a stop to them, you must know what they are and be able to recognize them, even before they arise, in your meditation. Some people may realize that laxity and excitement have arisen in their meditation, but they do not make an effort to get rid of them immediately. When they see a slight degree of laxity or excitement, they ignore it, thinking, "This is not a big deal; it won't affect me much." These people are wrong; it is very problematic if you do not make effort to get rid of the subtle manifestations of the obstacles.

(a')) USING THE REMEDY FOR FAILING TO RECOGNIZE LAXITY AND EXCITEMENT

We begin by learning to recognize these obstacles to meditation.

(1')) THE DEFINING CHARACTERISTICS OF LAXITY AND EXCITEMENT

If a gatekeeper does not know how to identify the characteristics of a thief, he may allow a thief to enter the building. In the same way, you need to be able to recognize the obstacles to the development of śamatha. The remedy for not recognizing them is to understand their defining characteristics. You need definitions of excitement and laxity. Tsongkhapa quotes a definition appearing in Asaṅga's *Compendium of Knowledge*:

> What is excitement? It is an unquiet state of mind, considered a derivative of attachment, that pursues pleasant objects and acts as an impediment to meditative serenity.

The English word *excitement* is often used to translate the Tibetan term *göpa* (*rgod pa*). In a general sense it means "distraction" or "mental scattering." There are many causes for excitement and distraction: anger, hatred, jealousy, ignorance, and various other deluded mental states can trigger it. Even a virtuous inclination can be a cause for your mind to become distracted.

Tsongkhapa explains that there are three components to Asaṅga's definition of excitement: its object is attractive, its subjective aspect is scattered, and it works to keep you from having a stable focus on your object of meditation. The first component of the definition concerns the object. The object of an excited mind is something that is attractive to you. Whether or not the thing is actually attractive does not matter; there is no such thing as objective attractiveness. It is a subjective attribution. The second component also has a subjective dimension to it; your mind is unsettled and willfully strays from the object upon which you had planned to focus. Excitement can be traced to a desire to pursue things that are enjoyable. You may find yourself indulging in a pleasurable memory, thinking about a potentially nice experience, or wishing to relax. It is easy for the mind to drift toward an object of attachment. When your mind does this, it is distracted from the internal object of meditation and is looking outward. This is why Asaṅga makes the point that all excitement derives from one form or another of attachment. The third component is the function of excitement. Excitement interrupts a mind that is abiding on its chosen object of meditative stabilization.

Your mind in meditation is like the metaphorical elephant tied to a pillar by the strong rope of mindfulness. Like the elephant, your mind may want to pull away. You may become attracted to a sensory object—a color or shape, a sound, and so forth. Your mind seems to be helplessly pulled toward some object that seems more pleasant than your object of meditation. Candragomin expresses this in *Praise of Confession*:

> Just as you are focused on meditative serenity,
> Directing your attention toward it again and again,
> The noose of the afflictions pulls your attention
> Helplessly with the rope of attachment to objects.

At the same time you are making an effort to stabilize your mind by repeatedly recollecting your object of meditation, the "noose of the afflictions" tries to pull you away with "the rope of attachment to objects." Now a hypothetical questioner asks Tsongkhapa, "Is it considered excitement when afflictions other than attachment distract you from your meditative object?" This interrogator also asks a related question, "Should a distraction that pulls you toward a virtuous object be considered excitement?"

To understand Tsongkhapa's response requires some background explanation. Abhidharma texts such as Vasubandhu's *Treasury of Knowledge* explain that the afflictions can be categorized into twenty general categories. Some afflictions are branches of attachment while others are branches of other major mental afflictions. One of these categories is called a wandering mind—a mind that is distracted from its object. All of the afflictions in this group are examples of a mind that is straying from its object; they differ only slightly in name and nature. When the mind wanders away from its object under the influence of attachment, it is called excitement. When the mind strays from its object under the influence of something other than attachment, it is said to be distracted, or scattered. There are many mental factors that can distract you from your object of concentration. They may not even be afflictions. Your mind might stray toward a virtuous object while you are trying to meditate. For example, when you are practicing śamatha, your mind may be pulled by a wish to practice generosity, patience, or some other virtuous activity. This is a distraction from your meditation because your mind strays from your chosen object. However, it is not called excitement in such a case. Although both virtuous and afflicted things may pull the mind away from its object of meditation, the most powerful and common interruption comes from attachment. And yet, it is often the most difficult to recognize. That is why excitement that derives from attachment is emphasized here.

Now we move on to the second major obstacle to śamatha, laxity. Tsongkhapa says that many Tibetans who translated Indian Buddhist texts into Tibetan used a term for this that can easily be misconstrued. Instead of *laxity (bying ba)*, some translators used a Tibetan word that usually means "discouragement" (*zhum pa*). You should not confuse a feeling of exhausted depression, where the mind has no energy or strength, with the technical definition of laxity in the context of practicing śamatha. When "discouragement" is used to indicate laxity, it is referring to weakening or slackness. It is a mind that is not firm or vivid. I often refer to this quality as "mental sinking."

Most Tibetan practitioners of Tsongkhapa's time seemed to define laxity as a lethargic state of mind; it stays on its object of meditation without being distracted, but it has no limpid clarity. According to Tsongkhapa, these yogis have mistakenly conflated laxity and lethargy. The two are not the same. Lethargy is a cause of laxity; if something is a cause of another thing, it cannot be identical with it. Because lethargy is the cause of laxity, it is not the same thing as laxity. This is attested to in Kamalaśīla's middle *Stages of Meditation*:

> If, being oppressed by lethargy and sleepiness, you see your mind become lax or in danger of laxity...

Lethargy is a kind of mental heaviness or darkness. It can be the cause of mental dullness and drowsiness. The *Sutra Unraveling the Intended Meaning* says:

> If there is laxity due to lethargy and sleepiness, or if you are afflicted by any secondary afflictions in meditative absorption, it is a case of internal mental distraction.

When lethargy causes laxity, the mind experiences distraction. But this type of distraction is different from the type discussed previously. This distraction is directed inward, not to external objects.

Asaṅga explains in his *Compendium of Knowledge* that lethargy is an aspect of ignorance because it assists the other afflictions:

> What is lethargy? An unserviceable state of mind classified as a derivative of delusion, it works to assist all root afflictions and secondary afflictions.

The mind can be disturbed in a variety of ways. Earlier we looked at a distracted or excited mind. Being too dull is another such way. In general, afflictions in the desire realm, like desire, hatred, jealousy, and so forth, are nonvirtuous. However, some subtle secondary mental factors that accompany the egotistic view are neither virtuous nor nonvirtuous; they are ethically neutral. Lethargy derives from ignorance and in its more coarse instances it is nonvirtuous. Subtle lethargy is sometimes an ethically neutral obstruction. Either way, lethargy is a combination of the body and mind that feels heavy. It has no flexibility or suppleness. Without suppleness, you may need to bend but find it to be extremely difficult. Lethargy creates a situation unsuitable for certain practices such as śamatha. Vasubhandu's *Treasury of Knowledge Autocommentary* (*Abhidharma-kośa-bhāṣya*) says:

> What is lethargy? The heaviness of the body and the heaviness of the mind that are the unserviceability of the body and unserviceability of the mind.

When the mind is heavy, it makes the body heavy. Drowsiness renders both the mind and body unserviceable for the aims of cultivating śamatha and other goals.

Now that Tsongkhapa has made clear what lethargy is, he moves on to discuss laxity. In the second *Stages of Meditation*, Kamalaśīla says:

> When your mind does not see the object vividly—like a person born blind, or a person entering a dark place, or like having one's eyes shut—then recognize that your mind has become lax.

Tsongkhapa says that this is the only clear definition of laxity he has found in any of the classic texts. Laxity can be much more difficult to identify than excitement. It is subtler. It can even be confused with proper concentration. There are times when your mind is focused on its object of meditation and is abiding properly; it is not distracted to external objects. But at the same time, it may have no clarity with respect to its object. It is stabilized, but its hold is weak; the apprehension of the object is not vivid. According to Tsongkhapa laxity can be either virtuous or neutral; it is never nonvirtuous. In contrast, lethargy can be either nonvirtuous or neutral.

The instructions on meditation in the classic texts say that when laxity arises, it is useful to bring to mind objects that are pleasant. The image of a buddha or light are antidotes to that dark, heavy feeling overcoming your mind. In addition, bringing to mind pleasant objects reinvigorates the mind so that its slack hold on the object is tightened once again. These antidotes help the mind awaken and cheer up. A cheerful, freshly invigorated mind is energetically attentive and clearly ascertains its object. From the point of view of the object, your visualization must appear clearly to your mind; from the point of view of the subject, your mind must have a tempered mental strength in the way it holds the object.

You need both clarity and inner strength. For that, you have to find just the right balance in terms of your energy. You do not want to be so energetic that your mind gets excited and scatters. But you need mental energy to have the precisely calibrated strength to hold on to your object without slackening. The laxity of mental sinking can creep up on you in a sneaky way. Without your realizing it, laxity is there, though you think that you are in deep concentration. Your focus is still on the object, but it has become weak, and the clarity of your visualization has dimmed. Such a fault will delay the attainment of perfect concentration for a long time.

Although these are general teachings based on scriptural sources, this is not some abstract theory. You need to put these teachings into practice in a very real sense. Until you meditate and examine your mind with introspection, it will be very difficult to understand the nature of laxity. Until you actually have some experience with this practice, all these teachings can seem strange.

(2')) THE METHOD FOR DEVELOPING INTROSPECTION THAT RECOGNIZES LAXITY AND EXCITEMENT

It is not enough to simply know the characteristics of laxity, excitement, and some related mental factors. You must develop introspection, the primary antidote to laxity and excitement, so that you recognize the presence of these two obstacles. As your skill in the technique of introspection increases, you will get better at identifying the obstacles as soon as they arise. Eventually you will be able to identify them when they are on the verge of arising.

Earlier I compared introspection to a mental spy that keeps watch on your mind. The mental spy continually checks your mind to see if it is under the influence of laxity or excitement. Introspection is a kind of wisdom that knows whether either of these obstacles is present or absent when you are meditating. Part of developing śamatha is to gain an aptitude in introspection. This takes practice.

You must train in introspection until you have the ability not only to recognize these faults when they arise but also to recognize their signs before they occur. In other words, a key component of introspection is an ability to recognize the subtle indications that excitement or laxity are about to arise. When you can do that, and you know the antidotes to the faults and how to apply them, then you will be able to stop them before they come to fruition. Both the middle and final *Stages of Meditation* by Kamalaśīla make this point.

Introspection is always present in strong meditation. If you lack powerful introspection, you will never be certain that your meditation is free from laxity and excitement. You could meditate for a long time and never know that you spent the entire meditation session under the influence of subtle laxity and excitement. That is why Maitreya's *Separation of the Middle from the Extremes* says that it is necessary to have introspection. Without it, it is entirely possible that you will not recognize if these two faults occur. That will certainly harm your meditation.

Now Tsongkhapa imagines someone asking, "How do I cultivate introspection? What is the best method to generate this sharp mind?" He replies that mindfulness is its most important cause. Mindfulness, as mentioned above, is the antidote to forgetfulness. Mindfulness means that your mind continuously keeps in mind its chosen object. In other words, you do not get distracted and forget the object. The function of introspection is to quickly and easily identify the obstacles. If you are mindful, you will not fail to sense the presence of laxity and excitement. In *Engaging in the Bodhisattva Deeds*, Śāntideva said:

When mindfulness dwells
At the gate of your mind for its protection,
Then introspection will appear.

Śāntideva says here that when mindfulness is present, introspection is not far behind. If a sentry is posted at the gate, it will be easy to tell who has gone in or out, and who is about to go in or out. Mindfulness at the door of your mind makes it easier for introspection so see whether laxity or excitement has arisen or is about to arise. Sthiramati's *Explanation of "Separation of the Middle from the Extremes"* (*Madhyānta-vibhāga-ṭīkā*) makes a similar point:

> The statement "There is recognition of laxity and excitement by intro-spection if mindfulness does not lapse" indicates that mindfulness, when fully present, is accompanied by introspection. That is why it says, "if mindfulness does not lapse..."

When you have mindfulness, you will recognize through introspection if either of the two obstacles arises. In other words, introspection is, in part, caused by or dependent upon mindfulness.

Tsongkhapa goes on to explain another method for generating and main-taining introspection. His advice follows that of Śāntideva, who says in *Engaging in the Bodhisattva Deeds*:

> Examining again and again
> The states of the body and the mind—
> Just that, in brief,
> Is what it means to preserve introspection.

While mindfulness is keeping your focus on your chosen object of meditation, the function of introspection is to constantly check whether excitement or laxity have arisen or are about to arise. This mental spy subtly examines your mental state again and again. "To preserve introspection" means to continually re-engage in examination; this is how you maintain introspection and rein-vigorate your mindfulness. These are two different but complementary skills. When you are trying to meditate, you maintain your focus on your chosen object with mindfulness while repeatedly checking for the two obstacles with the vigilant mental spy of introspection. These two techniques work together to keep your mind from coming under the control of excitement and laxity. You must gain facility in both of these skills if you want to be successful in your meditation practice.

Above, Śāntideva says that introspection examines the body in addition to the mind. Practices that incorporate physical action also require a kind of introspection. Just as introspection examines the mind to make sure your mental activity is within the guidelines of the practice, it also examines your body to make sure your physical actions remain ethical.

To develop the practices of mindfulness and introspection, you should rely on the authoritative teachings from the sutras and great commentaries. On that basis, you can gradually come to rely on your own wisdom. In other words, you will develop skill in mindfulness and introspection as they are explained in the great texts. Through this you will gain confidence. Confidence arises from the combination of intellectual learning with experience in practice. This is very important. Without both—first learning the essentials and then gaining experience by putting your study into practice—your practice cannot succeed. Sheer determination and enthusiasm alone will not bring your hoped-for goal. If you exert a lot of effort in practice without having much understanding of the practice, you will just wear yourself out. But if you combine practice with the wisdom of learning, you can achieve the great purpose of your practice. Tsongkhapa quotes from Āryaśūra's *Compendium of the Perfections* to make this point:

> Using only perseverance, you will end up exhausted.
> If you practice with the aid of wisdom, you will achieve the great goal.

Tsongkhapa says that many people in his day did not clearly understand these teachings on how to practice śamatha. They muddled the practices of mindfulness and introspection. Tsongkhapa implies that these practitioners are like drunks, wandering around without a clear idea of how to get where they want to go. Because they do not understand the practice, they stumble around, repeating the same mistakes. Although they practice for a long time, because they confuse śamatha with meditative stabilization mixed with subtle laxity, they fail to achieve śamatha.

Tsongkhapa urges us to avoid falling into the same trap. The way to avoid the problem is to understand the nature of the obstacles, the distinct functions of mindfulness and introspection, and how they work together against the obstacles of laxity and excitement. He advises us to rely upon the explanations in the great texts he has been citing here. By doing so, your understanding of the practice will become clear, and you will be able to avoid the common mistakes.

(b')) Using the remedy for failing to try to eliminate them even when they are recognized

This section is addressed to practitioners who recognize the obstacles but do not take immediate steps to stop them. It is easy to become habituated to a slight degree of laxity or excitement in your meditation. But complacency about these faults is dangerous. You should view even the subtlest instances of the faults as detrimental to your practice. It will be very difficult to cultivate perfect śamatha if you allow yourself to become accustomed to the presence of these two obstacles. As soon as you recognize with introspection that even slight laxity and excitement have arisen, you should apply the antidote right away.

Tsongkhapa divides his discussion of the remedy for failing to try to eliminate the obstacles even though you recognize them into two topics: intention and the way that it stops laxity and excitement, and the underlying cause of laxity and excitement.

(1')) Intention and the way it stops laxity and excitement

Asaṅga's *Compendium of Knowledge* defines intention as follows:

> What is intention? It is the mental activity of applying your mind, having the function of drawing your mind to virtue, nonvirtue, or the ethically neutral.

As mentioned earlier, the Prāsaṅgika school describes six primary consciousnesses: the five sense consciousnesses and the mental consciousness. Each primary consciousness is accompanied by five omnipresent secondary consciousnesses: feeling, discrimination, intention, attention, and contact. The primary and secondary consciousnesses have the same object, but they have slightly different functions. The function of intention, the third of these omnipresent secondary consciousnesses, is to direct the attention of the primary consciousness to its particular object. It works much like a magnet pulls metal shavings. When a primary consciousness encounters its corresponding object, it is intention that directs the mind to that particular area. It is as if the mind has a duty to follow intention. According to the upper schools, the essence of karma is intention. It is the mind that propels you to do a certain action, be it virtuous, nonvirtuous, or ethically neutral. Whenever you do something, whether it is a virtuous action like building a stupa or a nonvirtuous action like killing, the secondary mental consciousness of intention is there. When you do something physical, your body is obviously present and necessary, but intention is what drives the action.

When practicing śamatha, intention is what propels your mind to apply itself to the elimination of the obstacles. In other words, intention is the desire to initiate application of the appropriate antidotes to laxity and excitement. The actual antidote is the specific technique that restores the mind's proper hold and the clarity with which it holds its object. Intention, therefore, is sometimes referred to as "application." Intention, in the sense of application, is the antidote to the obstacle of "not applying the antidotes." To apply an antidote properly and at the right time, you first must be able to recognize the obstacles when they occur. The intention to eradicate them immediately is the next critical step. Intention is the antidote that collects other appropriate antidotes so that you can address the problem.

Tsongkhapa now has his hypothetical questioner ask, "If you have the intention to eliminate laxity and excitement, what do you do to stop them?" Let's consider how this works with regard to laxity first. When laxity arises, usually the mind is trying too hard to withdraw from external stimulation. Because the mind becomes excessively internalized, its hold on its object slowly loosens. At first this may be very slight; this is the arising of subtle laxity. Laxity at this point does not mean that you have completely lost your object of concentration and fallen asleep. Here it actually seems that you are still focusing properly on your object. However, from here momentum in the direction of laxity builds, and the situation gradually worsens. Your hold on the object lessens more and more. Eventually, if not countered, your hold is completely lost and you fall asleep.

What should you do when too much of your energy is drained by excessive internalization? What antidote should be applied when your intention is to wake up? It is helpful to direct your mind outward to joyful things that are pleasant. Usually when pleasurable things come to the mind, they cause afflicted excitement or distraction. Here you do not want to cause the afflictions to arise; you simply want to reinvigorate your mind. Therefore you pick an object that stimulates the joy of faith, rather than pleasure in attachment, to counteract laxity. A good object for this is a beautiful image of the Buddha, your spiritual teacher, or bright sunlight. Immediately after the antidote has cleared away the laxity, you return to your original object of meditation and hold it with a freshened, tightened concentration. As you can see, in times of extreme laxity, it is okay to briefly change your object of meditation. Kamalaśīla explained this in the first *Stages of Meditation:*

How? When you are overcome with lethargy and sleepiness, when there is a lack of clarity in your apprehension of the object of meditation and your mind has become lax, meditate on the idea of light or bring to mind the most delightful things, such as the qualities of the Buddha. Dispel laxity in this way and firmly hold on to the object of meditation.

Your intention here is to alleviate the darkness and sleepiness in your mind and then return it to its original object. Thus, intention is the part of the antidote; it brings you to choose an object to energize your mind. When your mind is sinking into laxity, do not pick an object that makes you sorrowful or sad. Do not meditate on the suffering of samsara, the impermanence of life, or on death. These are important topics for meditation, but you should not choose them as the antidote when you intend to reinvigorate a dull, sinking mind. Why? The reason is that these objects do not immediately generate joy. At the time of extreme internalization and mental laxity, you need something that can cheer you up and give your mind some energy.

Another method you can use to remedy laxity is to use analytical meditation to contemplate the nature of reality. In śamatha meditation you are trying to focus single-pointedly on an object; you are not analyzing it in detail. But when mental laxity and dullness arise, you must try to extend your mind outward and activate it. So analytical reasoning can be very helpful if done for a short time. It will wake you up and stop the mental sinking. That is why, according to Āryaśūra, the wisdom that analyzes emptiness is a beneficial object to halt laxity. He says in the *Compendium of the Perfections*:

> When slack, your mind is stimulated and inspired
> By virtue of the energy of striving for insight.

"Slack" emphasizes the aspect of laxity that is excessive withdrawal inward. It is part of the decline in the way you apprehend your object of meditation. You counteract this by temporarily shifting your object of meditation to something that stimulates and expands your mind. So when your mind becomes too internalized, discouraged, or weak, use the power of the analytical wisdom of vipaśyanā to restore your mental energy and positive attitude. Tsongkhapa quotes Bhāvaviveka's *Heart of the Middle Way* to support this point:

> In the case of slackness, expand your mind
> By meditating on an extensive object.

And:

Further, in the case of slackness, inspire yourself
By observing the benefits of perseverance.

Śāntideva's *Compendium of Trainings* (*Śikṣā-samuccaya*) explains this too:

If your mind becomes slack, inspire yourself by cultivating delight.

The many great scholars and yogis who have achieved high meditative accomplishments agree about this way of using intention to direct your mind to the antidotes.

Even in everyday life there are times when you get lethargic. Your fatigue begins to be noticeable even before it is fully present. You mind feels heavy and tends toward darkness. Lethargy causes you to become sleepy in ordinary situations, so it should be no surprise that it leads to laxity in meditation. When practicing meditation, Tsongkhapa says that the best antidote to laxity is to reflect upon the good qualities of such things as the Three Jewels—the Buddha, Dharma, and Sangha—or the benefits of bodhicitta, or your precious human rebirth. Contemplating these sorts of things will make you cheerful and increase your energy. These analytical meditations can all be used as antidotes to stop the sinking mind of laxity. However, for these analytical meditations to help you to wake up and reapply your mind to its object, you must have had some previous experience with them.

If you try this, but it does not seem to refresh you, Asaṅga suggests in *Śrā-vaka Levels* that you get up and go for a walk. While you are walking, you can contemplate the qualities of any of the six recollections: the Buddha, the Dharma, the Sangha, ethical discipline, generosity, and the celestial buddhas and bodhisattvas. Or, while you walk, you can recite passages from sutras or excerpts from the great masters' works that illuminate the faults of mental dullness and sleepiness. You could even just look up into the sky or splash your face with cold water!

There are times when laxity is very subtle and occurs infrequently for just a short time. If this is the case, when you realize that you are losing your concentration, try to strengthen your level of attention while continuing to focus on your original object. Do not apply one of the antidotes described above where you change your object for a short time. In short, if the laxity in your meditation is very slight, just reaffirm your attention on your chosen object of meditation. Simply apply yourself to make it stronger. In contrast, when the laxity is gross and occurs repeatedly, suspend your concentration on your object of meditation and clear away the laxity by using any of the remedies above. You should choose whichever of the antidotes is most suitable for your particular situation. When your energy returns, then return to your original object of śamatha meditation. If you have the intention to apply an antidote and then do one of these things, your response to laxity will soon become very strong.

Laxity can occur when you meditate on any sort of object. It doesn't matter if you are focusing outward on an external object, such as a statue or light, or inward on your mind. If you feel like darkness is descending on your mind or your meditation object is unclear, it will be difficult to avoid falling into laxity if you do not apply an antidote right away. Because the problem is darkness, the antidote is light. Meditate on any kind of light. Asaṅga's *Śrāvaka Levels* says:

> Cultivate śamatha and vipaśyanā correctly, with a mind that is bright and radiant, a mind of clear light, free of gloom. On the way to śamatha and vipaśyanā, meditate on a sense of brightness in this way. If you do, then even if at the outset your interest in an object of meditation is dull and brightness is fading, the cause and condition of having accustomed yourself to that meditation will clarify your interest in the object of meditation and lead to great brightness. If there is clarity and brightness at the outset, clarity and brightness will later become more vast.

A lack of brightness or light in your meditation means that your object is not clear. Your mental power is not strong, and the object appears weakly. Accustoming your mind to brightness creates the conditions for a clear image in both forms of meditation. It makes an unclear image become clear and sharpens an image that is already clear. This antidote counters the dullness and darkness that is a common obstacle to accomplishing the goals of the practice. Thus Asaṅga says you should use the antidote of light and brightness from the very beginning of your practices of śamatha and vipaśyanā.

What kind of light should you use? Asaṅga explains this in *Śrāvaka Levels*:

> Hold in meditation the sign of brightness from the light of an oil lamp, the light of a bonfire, or the orb of the sun.

You can use the antidote of light during practices other than śamatha or vipaśyanā meditation. For example, use it to wake up when fogginess seems to descend while you are reciting mantras, doing tantric sādhanas, or reading. You should have a strong intention to immediately apply whatever antidote is appropriate in just the right proportions. It requires a finely balanced energy for the mind to stay on its object effortlessly. You need to invigorate the dull, lax mind and also subdue the wild energy of the excited mind.

Tsongkhapa next deals with the other main obstacle to concentration and śamatha: excitement. As said above, excitement is a mental state where the mind is dominated by desire and pursues its object of attraction. In other words, when the mind is excited its focus has moved from the object of meditation to an object of desire of any of the consciousnesses. The challenge is to bring your focus back, to internalize and return your mind to the object of meditation.

In order to direct the mind inward, so that it no longer runs wildly to objects of desire, you need to develop an attitude of renunciation. You need to transform your thinking; you must become disillusioned with the ostensibly good qualities of those seemingly attractive objects. The mind has a distorted sense of the objects it pursues. You rush wildly from one thing to another because you think these objects are objectively and truly lovely and will bring you happiness. You need to understand that this is not the case. Once your mind is calmed and the excitement has been pacified, you can return to the original object and continue śamatha meditation. Kamalaśīla's first *Stages of Meditation* says:

> When you see that your mind is occasionally becoming excited as you recall previous excitement, play, and so forth, calm the excitement by bringing to mind disillusioning things, such as impermanence. Then strive to engage the object of meditation without your mind becoming involved in activity.

During meditation, it is common for the mind to recollect things, people, or situations that gave you enjoyment previously. Instead of staying on the object of meditation, your focus shifts to these remembered attractive objects. This is excitement. When the mind has already wandered, or there are signs that it is about to do so, you need to apply an antidote. Kamalaśīla recommends contemplating "disillusioning things" that help you to renounce or cut your attachment to the object of desire. He offers the example of meditating on impermanence. This can mean meditating on the impermanence of the particular attractive object, but it also refers to meditation on the impermanence of life, contemplating death and so forth. When you think about the misery of death and the general sufferings of samsara, you begin to see the futility of grasping these kinds of objects. Desire's grip on your mind slackens and excitement diminishes.

Bhāvaviveka reiterates the same sentiment in his *Heart of the Middle Way*:

> Calm excitement by bringing to mind
> Impermanence and so forth.

"And so forth," indicates the fundamental lamrim teachings that were discussed extensively in the earlier volumes in this series: the impermanence of life, karma and its effects, the misery and suffering of samsara, the impure nature of all of these phenomena, and so forth. Meditating on these subjects reduces excitement and makes the mind capable of returning to its original object of meditation. In the same text Bhāvaviveka said:

> Pull your mind back from distraction by noting
> The faults of the distracting objects.

Your mental focus can be moved back to your chosen object of meditation more easily when you think about the faults of the objects of distraction. Śāntideva gives the same advice in the *Compendium of Trainings*, "If excitement occurs, calm it by bringing impermanence to mind." Another antidote is to consider the disadvantages of being distracted. That too will help lessen the draw of the object of desire.

When you are attempting to practice śamatha but excitement is particularly strong or persistent, cultivating disenchantment with the objects of your attachment is essential. It is better to stop your śamatha meditation session for a short while and meditate on topics that make you disillusioned with the objects of your attachment. When excitement is particularly strong, just returning your mind to your object of concentration does not work; it will just run away again. So when you experience a powerful pull to an object of desire, find the contemplation that will be most powerful in your particular case. Once you have used it to subdue your mind, then you can return to your original meditation. When excitement is not so extreme, however, you can simply bring your mind back to its original object without any intervening meditation on a different object.

A key point to remember is that when excitement is the problem, you should not apply the antidote to laxity. Do not bring your mind to delightful or inspiring objects: that will only enhance the distraction. You need to properly distinguish between the problems and apply the appropriate antidotes. Asaṅga summarizes this point in *Śrāvaka Levels*:

> Thus, once your mind has become withdrawn inward and you note that there is slackness or the threat of slackness, maintain and gladden your mind by thinking of any inspiring things. This is maintaining your mind. How do you settle your mind? While maintaining your mind, when you note that your mind is excited or that there is the threat of excitement, withdraw your mind inward and settle in a calming stabilization.

(2')) THE UNDERLYING CAUSES OF LAXITY
AND EXCITEMENT

Tsongkhapa now identifies the causes that give rise to laxity and excitement. He begins with another quotation from Asaṅga, this time from the *Levels of Yogic Deeds*:

> What are the signs of laxity? Not restraining the sensory faculties; not eating in moderation; not making an effort to practice rather than sleeping during the early and later parts of the night; ongoing lack of introspection; deluded behavior; oversleeping; being unskillful; being lazy in one's aspiration, perseverance, intention, and analysis; giving only partial attention to śamatha without accustoming yourself to it and fully refining it; letting your mind stay as though in darkness; and not delighting in focusing on the object of meditation.

"Signs of laxity" here means the causes of laxity. Asaṅga addresses both the common and uncommon causes of laxity in the passage above. The first four are the common causes of laxity. They are called "common" causes because they are also causes of excitement.

In order to have success during your meditation sessions, you must conduct yourself in certain ways physically and mentally between sessions. If your senses are unguarded or your behavior is unethical, it will undermine your meditation. The mind picks up things and brings them into meditation. If you witness something discouraging or terrible, it may weaken your concentration and resolve. This can cause you to fall into laxity. Or say that, prior to meditating, you watch a fast-paced action movie. Instead of focusing on your object, the movie will come into your mind. Thus not restraining the sense faculties is one of the causes of laxity and excitement.

The second common cause of laxity mentioned by Asaṅga has to do with how much you eat. Leave a third of your stomach empty when you are going to begin a meditation session. If your stomach is full, it is difficult to meditate. Eating too much will make you sluggish and dull. It is easy for laxity and finally sleep to overcome you.

The third cause is an unhelpful sleep pattern. Night is generally divided into three parts: the evening (before midnight), the middle of the night, and the later part (or early morning). It is good to establish a routine for sleep and practice. Asaṅga advises us to sleep in the middle of the night and practice in the evening and the later part of the night. If you do not have a regular time for sleep, or if you sleep through the entire night, or if you do not sleep in the middle period of the night, it can cause obstacles to śamatha to arise.

A lack of ongoing introspection is the fourth cause common to laxity and excitement. You should always be aware of what is going on in your mind as well as what you are doing with your body and speech. If you are unaware, who knows what you will do? Introspection is on watch for the signs of laxity and excitement and their imminent arising. It is the first line of defense. So a lack of introspection is a cause for the arising of these obstacles.

As for the specific, or uncommon, causes of laxity, the first is laziness. This is not general indolence or idleness. Laziness in the context of śamatha is in regard to the four ideal qualities in the way of focusing on an object. Here, laziness is losing the strength of your hold on your object of meditation due to the weakening of your aspiration, perseverance, intention, or analysis. If any of these four areas become weak, your hold on the object lessens and it causes laxity. If you become accustomed to practicing with these four types of laziness, it will cause even more laxity to develop.

"Giving only partial attention to śamatha without accustoming yourself to it and fully refining it" is the next cause of laxity listed by Asaṅga. The cultivation of śamatha takes repeated practice in order to become so familiar that it becomes spontaneous. If you have real enthusiasm for the practice and follow the instructions given in the *Lamrim Chenmo*, it is possible to achieve śamatha in just a few months. But if you do the practice only half-heartedly, you will be unable to achieve śamatha even with years of practice. A half-hearted effort that lacks antidotes and includes many of the causes of laxity and excitement simply cannot bring the desired result.

The final cause of laxity specifically mentioned by Asaṅga is "not delighting in focusing on the object of meditation." It is similar to the previous cause in some ways. It refers to the fact that you are content with laziness and mostly want to go to sleep. This is sometimes a direct cause of laxity and sometimes an indirect cause of laxity. This kind of attitude should always be avoided.

Now Tsongkhapa cites the same text for a brief description of the signs of excitement. As before, "signs" refers to causes. Asaṅga says:

> What are the signs of excitement? The first four points listed above for the signs of laxity—not restraining the sensory faculties and so on; behaving with attachment; having an agitated manner; lacking a sense of disenchantment; being unskillful; having a great sense of grasping in your aspiration, [perseverance, intention, or analysis]; failing to accustom yourself to perseverance; meditating in an unbalanced way without refining your apprehension of the object of meditation; and being distracted by any sort of exciting topic, such as thoughts about relatives.

As mentioned, the first four causes of laxity—uncontrolled behavior, improper eating habits, improper sleep patterns, and a lack of introspection—are also causes of excitement. You should understand they cause excitement in the same way that they cause laxity. The rest of the causes listed in this passage are particular causes of excitement.

"Behaving with attachment" refers to any sort of behavior that is driven by strong desire. It can refer specifically to sexual desire, but the mind can become almost obsessive due to many other kinds of attachment. Attachment pulls the mind away from the object of meditation to the object of desire.

"Having an agitated manner" refers to when the mind gets too wild, excited, or rough. This is a borderline manic state in which the mind is so excited that you do not see the faulty and disadvantageous consequences of your actions. This type of mind does not have any sorrow, remorse, or other similar feelings. When your mind is so wound up, you do not listen to any guidance or take any precautions.

The primary factor of excitement is an extreme kind of grasping. This is excessive holding to a delightful object. Specifically, excessive grasping is in relation to the four ideal qualities in the way of focusing on your object. Whereas laziness is losing the strength of your hold on your object of meditation due to the weakening of your aspiration, perseverance, intention, or analysis, here you hold these four too tightly and excitement results. You need strength and energy to remain focused on your object, but the strength with which the mind holds the object of meditation must be in the right measure.

"Failing to accustom yourself to perseverance" means not making a regular effort in your practice. Śamatha practice requires effort. When you do not try to hold firmly to your practice and are drawn to other objects—even friends and relatives—this can be a cause of excitement as well.

If you understand the primary obstacles to successful śamatha practice and make an effort to cease the incorrect behaviors, it will be of great benefit to your practice. Therefore Tsongkhapa says that the four practices that keep your senses and your mind in check between meditation sessions are very important. Controlled behavior through guarding the doors of the senses, eating and sleeping properly, and maintaining introspection are critical for preventing both laxity and excitement. Tsongkhapa here reinforces his point that you should understand and overcome not only the gross obstacles but also the subtle ones. When these causes arise even in the most subtle manner, you should respond immediately and apply the antidote. Just because they are subtle or seem not to last for a long time does not mean that they will not disrupt your śamatha practice. Try to understand what the gross and subtle causes are, how they arise, and so forth. Learn to recognize the signs of subtle ones even before they arise and learn how to immediately apply their appropriate antidotes. Even if your meditation session is short, work on recognizing all these obstacles. It is better to have a brief session during which you cultivate good habits than a long meditation with many faults. With good practice, gradually the duration of your meditation practice will increase and your mind will become more stable; it will get better and better. Finally you will achieve perfect śamatha.

Sometimes people are too impatient. When laxity or excitement arise after just a couple of minutes, they quit. Or they continue, but out of frustration they do not apply the antidotes. Longer meditation sessions where you tolerate subtle excitement or laxity creates a negative pattern that causes the obstacles to become even greater in future sessions. You will develop bad habits. Then, no matter how long you meditate, you will not complete śamatha in the pure sense. If you follow the advice given by Tsongkhapa and the other great Indian masters, you will find that even though at first you can hardly stabilize your mind, soon you will be able to remain on your object for a few minutes. This will inspire you to further practice. It is an indication that the methods are working. So please follow the excellent advice given by these great masters.

In the beginning, excitement is typically the more frequent problem. Then, in your attempt to establish some degree of stability and calm, you may find yourself slipping into laxity. If you put too much energy into protecting against laxity and hold too tightly, you can swing back to excitement. It is not uncommon for beginners in śamatha practice to experience this kind of back and forth. This is why introspection is critical. Alternate, working back and forth, striving for the proper balance of tempered strength. Gradually, flawless concentration will arise.

(2)) What to do when laxity and excitement are absent

When you have completely removed the mental unevenness of subtle laxity and excitement, your mind will abide calmly and sharply on your chosen object. That is proper śamatha practice. Is there anything specific you should do when your mind enters real equipoise that is free from these obstacles? No. When your mind is properly concentrating on its object, it is incorrect to make further efforts to remove laxity and excitement. The obstacles are not there, so applying the antidotes to them is a fault in your concentration. When your mind is in equipoise, let it remain there. Strive to apply the antidotes only when the obstacles arise, or are about to arise, in your mind. This is the meaning of equanimity in meditation. Equanimity here refers to those periods of successful meditation when there is no need for extra effort. Kamalaśīla's second *Stages of Meditation* explains this as follows:

When laxity and excitement have gone and you see that your attention is calmly remaining on the object of meditation, relax your effort and abide in equanimity; remain this way for as long as you please.

A hypothetical opponent asks Tsongkhapa, "How can making an effort and applying the antidotes be considered a fault in śamatha practice? Previously you said that not making effort was a fault." Tsongkhapa responds by stating that when your mind is distracted from the object, you should make effort to bring the mind back to the object. And if your mind is too low, weak, losing its hold on its object, or falling into laxity, you should make an effort to awaken and cheer up. These are occasions when effort is required. Beginners must be very careful and vigilant every minute. Beginners need to be watchful all the time and immediately apply the antidotes when faults arise. Stability and confidence are cultivated through the correct application of the antidotes.

But if your concentration is not broken, there is no need to fix it. When the obstacles are nonexistent and your mind is on the object without laxity or excitement, you should drop your efforts to apply the antidotes. Simply remain with equanimity. This advice is for those with some experience in śamatha practice—practitioners who have periods of meditation when neither of the two obstacles arise. Such a practitioner can be confident that his or her mind is able to stay on a chosen object for a stretch of time. When you can successfully meditate without obstacles or disturbances for half an hour, or even a few minutes, and are confident that you are able to stay on the object clearly and evenly, you should just remain that way without disturbing your mind by mistakenly applying the antidotes. You should relax your effort. It is a fault to apply the antidotes when there is no laxity or excitement.

Relaxing your effort to apply the antidotes does not mean you release your hold on your object of meditation. Tsongkhapa is not saying that you should relax and let go too much. He says that you should continue to hold your object with tempered strength. If you lose that strength, subtle laxity can result. Because it is important not to sacrifice your tempered strength, you should not cultivate abiding in equanimity every time the obstacles are absent. In the beginning there may be periods that are free of obstacles when it is useful to maintain your introspection. But after you have some experience and have a special kind of confidence, you can relax a bit and abide in equanimity when the obstacles are not present.

Now the hypothetical student asks Tsongkhapa, "What does *equanimity* mean here?" There are three types of equanimity. The first is to be neutral or impartial with respect to feelings that are pleasant and unpleasant. The second is to have an equal attitude toward all sentient beings; this is one of the four immeasurables. This form of equanimity has both a subjective and objective aspect. The subjective side is for you to have an absolutely equal feeling toward all beings without any discrimination or bias; there is no sense of liking one person, wanting good things for that person, and disliking somebody else, wanting bad things to happen to him or her. The objective sense of immeasurable equanimity is meditating on how wonderful it would be if all sentient beings had happiness and freedom from misery; how wonderful it would be if all sentient beings were free from attachment and hatred; and how wonderful it would be if all sentient beings were loving and compassionate toward each other equally. The third sense of equanimity refers to the times in śamatha meditation when there is no need for some kind of special effort; the mind remains focused on its object effortlessly, naturally, spontaneously, and perfectly. This is equanimity with respect to application; you do not need to be concerned about, or apply, the antidotes to potential laxity or excitement. Asaṅga's *Śrāvaka Levels* defines the third type of equanimity in the following way:

> What is equanimity? As your mind attends to objects of meditation associated with śamatha and vipaśyanā, it is focusing with calm settling, spontaneous mental engagement, a sense of mental well-being, effortless mental functioning after becoming serviceable, and a mental balance free from the afflictions.

Equanimity, in this context, is a mind that is balanced in that it is free of both laxity and excitement. It is calm and able to peacefully remain on an object of either śamatha or vipaśyanā. It is like a steady candle flame: it requires effort to light a candle, but once lit does not require further effort. Similarly, once you have made the initial effort required for equanimity, your mind naturally and spontaneously abides that way. Another quality of equanimity is a peaceful sense of well-being. Because the mind has become supple and flexible, it has a degree of mental dexterity. This makes the mind serviceable. It is a useful tool, an instrument suitable to work on other types of meditation.

Asaṅga's *Śrāvaka Levels* also describes the signs of equanimity:

> What are the signs of equanimity? The object of meditation places your mind in equanimity; your mind is not overflowing with effortful perseverance with respect to the object of meditation.

What does equanimity look like? It is when the focus of your mind is settled and is neutral with regard to its effort. Your mind is neutral in the sense of not needing to make an effort to eliminate laxity or excitement.

Tsongkhapa also addresses the appropriate time for cultivating equanimity by again citing Asaṅga:

> When is the time for equanimity? In terms of śamatha and vipaśyanā, when your mind is free of laxity and excitement.

When you are meditating on an object of śamatha or vipaśyanā and your mind experiences no laxity and excitement at all, that is the time to utilize this equanimity.

Tsongkhapa says that his explanation of the method to develop and practice flawless śamatha accords with the teachings of Maitreya in *Separation of the Middle from the Extremes*. Here, Maitreya outlines the five faults that hinder the generation of śamatha and the eight antidotes to those faults:

> Staying with that perseverance,
> Your mind becomes serviceable, and you attain all goals.
> This comes from eliminating the five faults
> And relying on the eight antidotes.
> The five faults are laziness,
> Forgetting the instructions,
> Laxity and excitement,
> Non-application, and application.
> The eight antidotes are the basis [aspiration], that based on it
>   [perseverance],
> The cause [faith], the effect [mental pliancy],
> Not forgetting the object of meditation,
> Recognizing laxity and excitement,
> Application to eliminate them,
> And calmly stabilizing your mind when they have been quelled.

Maitreya's stanza is a quintessential condensation of the advice for developing śamatha. Knowledge of the five faults, the eight antidotes to those faults, and their application is at the core of successful śamatha practice. The first line, "Staying with that perseverance," refers to the special effort that is the primary cause of śamatha. The result of this perseverance is that your mind becomes supple. You achieve both a mental and a physical pliancy; neither the body nor the two extreme obstacles of laxity or excitement bother the mind. Free from those two obstacles, the mind is able to stay perfectly and spontaneously in whatever meditation you wish. Therefore the mind is described as "serviceable."

With the achievement of śamatha, you attain many mundane and supramundane abilities. The phrase "you attain all goals" indicates the attainment of a yogi's supranormal powers—such as walking on water, penetrating the ground without resistance, emanating physical forms, and so forth—upon the basis of śamatha. These miraculous physical feats are possible only for those who have the foundation of śamatha. They are not something you can buy; they are internal supranormal accomplishments that result from intensive practice.

There are six types of supranormal powers or knowledges. The first five are primarily the results of the achievement of śamatha. The sixth requires even higher additional realizations. The five common supranormal powers are:

1. The divine eye is the supranormal ability to see beyond the ordinary range of eyesight. Certain visual barriers no longer obstruct your vision.
2. The divine ear, clairaudience, is the supranormal ability to hear beyond the range of the ordinary hearing. Much like with the divine eye, certain ordinary auditory barriers no longer obstruct your ability to hear.
3. Recollection of former births and seeing future births is the supranormal ability to see past lives and the next rebirth.
4. Miraculous power is the supranormal ability to fly, walk on water, penetrate the ground, and so forth.
5. Knowing others' minds is the supranormal ability to read others' minds. This knowledge is limited to seeing only the minds of people who are of an equal or lesser level of spiritual development than you. Even with this power you cannot see into the minds of superior or higher beings.

These five are called the common supranormal knowledges. They are "common" in that any yogi—Buddhist or non-Buddhist, ārya or non-ārya—who practices the techniques and attains perfect mental stabilization achieves them. Even ordinary individuals, those who have yet to achieve arhatship or buddhahood, can achieve them. These five powers may be common, but they are extremely useful for bodhisattvas who want to attain the goal of perfect enlightenment in order to benefit other sentient beings. In order to attain buddhahood, bodhisattvas must accumulate an immense amount of merit through helping others. To be of maximum help to others, bodhisattvas can use the various types of supranormal knowledge to clearly see what teachings and engage in whatever actions will benefit others the most.

The sixth supranormal knowledge is uncommon. It is knowledge that all the defilements have been eliminated. It is the supranormal ability to see, through yogic perception, that all your defiled afflictions have been removed from the root. The "complete removal of all defiled afflictions from the root" is the attainment of arhatship. Ordinary people who have not had a direct realization of emptiness obviously cannot do this. It is an uncommon power because only beings like arhats and buddhas can do it. In fact, not even all arhats have this knowledge. All arhats know they have uprooted the afflictions but not all realize it directly.

In short, without the achievement of śamatha and the various forms of supranormal knowledge that derive from it, you are limited in your ability to attain your spiritual goals. This is why Maitreya and Tsongkhapa state that śamatha is the basis or foundation for the achievement of all spiritual goals. Just as you cannot walk without feet, you cannot achieve your spiritual goals without cultivating śamatha.

Maitreya goes on to explain that you use perseverance to rely on the eight antidotes in order to eliminate the five faults. This will eventually result in the attainment of śamatha and all the spiritual goals that rely on it. We have gone over these to some extent earlier,[14] but Tsongkhapa reiterates and elaborates on them here. The five faults are: (1) laziness, (2) forgetting the instructions (3) laxity and excitement, (4) non-application of the antidotes when obstacles occur, and (5) application of the antidotes even if no obstacles are present.

The first four of the eight antidotes—faith, aspiration, perseverance, and mental pliancy—counter the fault of laziness. Each of the other four faults has one corresponding antidote. The first of the four antidotes to laziness, faith, is a type of confidence built upon the foundation of knowing the benefits of śamatha, its nature, and how it is achieved. Having faith, or trust, in the value of śamatha becomes the cause of the second antidote: the aspiration to achieve it. This, in turn, is the basis of perseverance, the third antidote. The stronger your desire, the stronger your perseverance will be. When you have this persevering spirit, even if circumstances are difficult, you will yearn to practice. This combination of perseverance founded on aspiration is the real antidote to laziness. To summarize, perseverance comes from aspiration, aspiration comes from strong faith, faith comes from understanding, and understanding is a result of study.

The result of perseverance is mental and physical pliancy. After extensive training, you no longer experience uneasiness, hardship, or difficulty; your mind naturally remains where you focus for as long as you wish. Pliancy is the fourth antidote to laziness. In one sense, the first four antidotes are all aspects of perseverance. There are two aspects of perseverance relating to its cause, one from the point of view of its result, and perseverance itself.

You can understand these antidotes in another way, by looking at the types of laziness they counter. The first type of laziness is the laziness of attachment to other activities. Because you do not see the value of śamatha, instead of engaging in meditation practice, you allow your mind to go to other, seemingly more interesting, activities and objects of attention. The antidote to having no interest in meditation practice is the faith or conviction that comes from learning its value. The second type of laziness is procrastination. Even though you may see the purpose of meditation and want to do it, you put it off. You tell yourself, "I'll do it later; right now I'm tired." You postpone your practice for tomorrow, or next year, because for some reason it is difficult to do now. Perseverance grounded in strong aspiration is the antidote to this type of laziness. The third form of laziness is deprecating yourself. This is basically the laziness of low self-esteem. You understand the special qualities and value of śamatha, and you wish you could practice, but you lack the belief that you can actually do it. Exerting perseverance itself is the antidote to this self-denigration. From this great effort, the result will be mental pliancy.

After you overcome laziness and sit down to meditate, you may forget what you are supposed to do. Forgetting the instructions is obviously a big obstacle to accomplishing your goals. Simply put, the antidote to this is mindfulness. You need to recollect the instructions you have received. When you know what to do and actually try to meditate single-pointedly on an object, the third fault—the obstacles of laxity and excitement—must be dealt with. The antidote to these is introspection—the mental vigilance that identifies laxity and excitement.

The next two faults are non-application of antidotes when they are needed and the application of antidotes when they are not needed. The first is counteracted by a strong intention to be vigilant and to apply proper antidotes when obstacles arise. The latter is counteracted by the eighth antidote, equanimity—keeping the mind in a neutral state, not engaging in any effort to apply an antidote when there is no need for it. Accurate assessment of your mental state and acting appropriately—either applying the antidotes if necessary or remaining in equanimity—is the key to countering these last two faults.

Tsongkhapa singles out the proper application of these antidotes as the perfect method for achieving śamatha. Of course, all of the teachings about śamatha Tsongkhapa provides in the *Lamrim Chenmo* are important. The point here is that virtually all the great Indian masters who have written on the subject of śamatha stress the five faults that are obstacles to achieving it and the eight antidotes that serve as remedies to the faults. You will find this in Kamalaśīla's three *Stages of Meditation* and in Atiśa's autocommentary on *Lamp for the Path to Enlightenment*.

These instructions are not only for śamatha practice, they are also relevant and necessary for tantric practice. Although a practitioner should learn these things when beginning śamatha practice, tantric yogis are also taught them in the context of the highest among the four classes of tantra, the unsurpassable yoga tantras. Why? Because, as said above, all of the supranormal attainments have their foundation in the achievement of śamatha. It is śamatha that makes the mind serviceable. Therefore Tsongkhapa warns us not to consider this subject to be a merely scholastic area of study. The second chapter of the first section of the *Integration Tantra* (*Saṃpuṭa-tantra*) states:

> The concentration of yearning inspiration, the foundation of the supranormal abilities associated with remedial application, is based in solitude, it is based in freedom from attachment, and it is based in cessation. There is thorough transformation by means of correct elimination. With this yearning you meditate without being very slack or elated...

The Indian master Sthiramati presents the same ideas in his *Explanation of "Separation of the Middle from the Extremes."* In this commentary on Maitreya's text, he describes the four methods to establish this foundation for accomplishing spiritual goals, including the achievement of supranormal qualities. Tsongkhapa summarizes them as:

> (1) Achieving it through fierce yearning, (2) achieving it through prolonged perseverance, (3) achieving concentration by discriminating examination of the object of meditation... and (4) achieving one-pointedness of mind based on having in your mind seeds of earlier concentration.[15]

This is simply a condensation of the teachings above.

Even if you practice with great effort for a thousand years, you will not achieve śamatha if you do not utilize the proper method. Perfect mental stabilization is difficult to achieve and develops gradually. The mind that is in complete control of where it places its focus is critical to the achievement of further goals on the path.

· 5 ·

Attaining Śamatha

(2") The stages in which the mental states develop
    (a)) The actual stages in which the mental states develop
    (b)) The process of achieving them with the six forces
    (c)) How the four attentions are involved in this
(c') The measure of successful cultivation of śamatha
    (1') A presentation of the dividing line between accomplishing and
        not accomplishing śamatha
    (a") A presentation of the actual meaning
    (b") The marks associated with attention, and the elimination
        of qualms

(2") THE STAGES IN WHICH THE MENTAL STATES DEVELOP

THIS SECTION of the text deals with the more and more refined and capable mental states that develop through your practice to attain śamatha. Three topics are treated under this heading: the nine stages, the six forces, and the four ways of fixing your attention. In some texts this subject is discussed by way of just one or perhaps two of these topics. Tsongkhapa explains all three in his *Lamrim Chenmo*.

(a)) THE ACTUAL STAGES IN WHICH THE MENTAL STATES DEVELOP

First Tsongkhapa discusses the nine stages through which your mind progresses in dependence upon the correct methods. The stages occur in a specific order; śamatha occurs after the ninth. This particular presentation of the process of developing mental stabilization is derived from the Perfection of

Wisdom sutras, the teachings of yogis, and the treatises of great masters, like Kamalaśīla's three *Stages of Meditation*.

The teachings demarcate the stages to indicate the milestones along the path to śamatha. But without personal experience, it is difficult for much of this to make sense. Nevertheless, the teachings do describe certain signs when you reach certain levels: the strength and power of specific antidotes, whether an antidote is fully functioning, the degree to which an obstacle is eliminated, and so forth. You can gauge your progress if you keep these signs in mind as a sort of barometer for your experience. Keeping these things in mind when you practice allows you to make adjustments accordingly until your goals are realized.

The first stage is called *mental placement*. This is when your mind's attention is initially drawn to your internal meditation object. Your attention is pulled away from external objects and begins to internalize and focus on the object of meditation. No matter which of the many objects of meditation suitable for practicing śamatha you have chosen, this first stage involves placing your mind on that internal object of focus. For example, if you want to visualize a buddha image, first take a look at a statue or painting, examine it, then bring it into your mind and visualize it. Then look again. Go back and forth a few times. Eventually the image in your mind will become clearer. When visualizing internally you are not actually using your visual sense. Nonetheless, in your visualizations you must establish the color, shape, size, and so forth.

As discussed above, it is all right to be satisfied with an image that is a bit vague. In the beginning you may only be able to hold that rough image for a very short time, perhaps just a second, before you lose it. When you lose your focus on the object of meditation, do not follow your mind to another topic or visualization. Letting your mind chase after other objects can become a habit. Some people let this sort of thing go for hours and hours during which thousands of images come and go. In other contexts this may be fine, but if you are trying to achieve śamatha, this is an obstacle. You become accustomed to having streams of images go through your mind every time you sit down to meditate. Therefore, as soon as your mind shifts away from the image you want, stop and go back again. Do not remain on the changed image or merely observe whatever comes up.

In the beginning interruptions can be frequent. On the first stage of śamatha training, your mind is like a child that does not want to sit still in one place. As soon as you focus on your object, your mind begins to drift away. And when there are frequent interruptions, the object is not held clearly. At this stage, there is no continuity and almost no meditation. Your mind is quite easily distracted because it has been under the power of the senses your whole life. It can take months before significant progress occurs. You should not expect to achieve perfect śamatha in one week. However, once you overcome this initial difficult period, it becomes easier. A spontaneous ability to stay on the object and go deeper will manifest. But this comes later. On the first stage, your focus on the internal mental object may last for just a few seconds. However, you have recognized that distraction is the enemy.

The second stage is called *continuous placement*. It is given this name because now your mind remains on its object for a period of time. Previously, on the first stage, there was almost no continuity; as soon as your mind was placed on the object, it went away, and you had to bring it back. In contrast, *Ornament for the Mahayana Sutras* explains that on the stage of continuous placement, there is an undistracted continuity of the mind on the object. This may only be for a minute, perhaps even less at first. Even a minute can be a long time for a beginner. But when you are able to stay focused for some duration on the object of meditation, and it is exactly as you desired, that is continual placement. The difference between the first and second stages is the duration of your attention.

On the second stage you become very conscious of what your mind is doing. Usually people do not watch their minds. Here, you actually pay attention to your mind and its focus on the object. At first it may seem that your mind is more easily distracted in meditation than it is during your normal daily activities. When you sit down to meditate, it may seem like you get distracted almost immediately. Some people decide that they must stop meditating because it leads to much more distraction than usual. This is incorrect. Do not discourage yourself in this way. This kind of thinking is harmful to your practice and does not reflect the reality of the situation. The mind is always getting distracted; in just a few seconds you can get sidetracked without even noticing it. What is different at this stage is that with a little bit of training, you begin to recognize what your mind is doing.

During the first two stages the mind has very little actual stabilization. The two faults of excitement and laxity are prominent, and the object of meditation is often unclear. One indication that you have reached the second stage is that you are able to remain focused on your object for about a minute—about the time it takes to say one rosary of the mantra *Oṃ maṇi padme hūṃ*.

The third stage is called *patched placement*. Now you can quickly return your mind to the object of your śamatha meditation. There are still times when your mind becomes forgetful due to a lack of mindfulness and slips into laxity. At other times in your meditation practice, an external object may distract your attention. This stage is called *patched placement* because you can patch up those gaps in your focused practice.

What is the difference between the second and third stages? The primary difference is the length of time you remain distracted. On the first and second levels the length of time you are distracted is much longer. On the first two stages you develop the ability to have a continual placement of your mind on the object for perhaps a minute. On the third level, the duration of distraction becomes shorter. As soon as you become distracted you are able to bring your mind back. You can repeatedly fix your focus by reapplying the mind to the object again. The special antidotes at this stage are mindfulness and introspection.

The fourth stage is called *close placement*. Tsongkhapa draws on several Indian sources to explain this stage. Kamalaśīla's first *Stages of Meditation* says that on the stage of patched placement, you are aware that your mind has fallen under the power of distraction, and you abandon the distraction. On the stage of close placement, having stopped the distraction, you employ a strong effort to place your mind on the object. In other words, on the fourth stage, after refocusing on your object, you direct your energy to remaining on the object. At this stage, the ability of your mind to remain single-pointedly focused becomes stronger and stronger. The level of your mind's proficiency in focusing continues to increase. Ratnākaraśānti says in *Instructions for the Perfection of Wisdom* (*Prajñāpāramitā-upadeśa*) that although the untrained mind is naturally expansive, extends to different objects, and lacks a tendency to focus, on this stage of śamatha training, you repeatedly withdraw from that outward-looking state to one where your focus is single-pointed and directed inward. You draw your attention inward to a single object and exert an effort to remaining there. Applying strong effort to bring your attention to a more subtle and focused awareness helps to counteract the tendency of the mind to scatter again. There is still a degree of subtle distraction, but from this point on, it is not so extreme that your attention gets wholly separated from its object. There is no longer a need to "patch" your concentration, as on the third stage.

Similarly, *Ornament for the Mahayana Sutras* encourages us to exert greater energy and to deepen our degree of inward focus on our object of meditation on this stage. It is difficult to internalize on the early stages. Even when you can internalize, it is difficult to remain on the object. On the fourth level, when you bring your attention back to the internal object of meditation, you work on strengthening your ability to remain focused on your object. Asaṅga's *Śrāvaka Levels* discusses the role mindfulness plays here. When through introspection you become aware that your mind is distracted to external objects, mindfulness brings your mind back to your object. Once it is brought back to the object, and the strength of your mindfulness continues to build, there will be less of a tendency for your mind to stray externally and become distracted again.

Mindfulness is the primary antidote needed to complete both the third and fourth stages. The fourth stage is far superior to the first three stages of śamatha training because this is the first time mental wandering ceases. There may be some subtle excitement, but you never completely lose your object of meditation. Nonetheless, you still have to apply the appropriate antidotes when subtle faults arise. By the end of the fourth stage, mindfulness is fully developed. This does not mean that all its functions are accomplished; it means that the power of mindfulness has developed completely.

The fifth stage is called *taming*. What does it mean for the mind to be tamed? Tsongkhapa says that because you have reflected upon the good qualities, benefits, and value of śamatha, you take delight in meditative concentration. *Ornament for the Mahayana Sutras* makes the same point, "Then, when you see the advantages, your mind is tamed in concentration." From knowing the benefits of śamatha practice you feel happy and enthusiastic about your practice. You are less attracted to the distractions of the senses that caused trouble at earlier stages. In other words, this knowledge makes you gain energy to viligantly apply the antidote of introspection to combat the other primary fault, laxity. The gross level of laxity is tamed on this stage.

Mindfulness was the primary antidote on the third and fourth stages because distraction was still present. But from the fifth stage on, introspection is the primary antidote because it combats the overly internalized mind that tends to sink into laxity and sleepiness. When your mind can still be distracted externally, you put a great deal of effort into tying the mind to its object of meditation, but with so much energy drawing the mind inward, you risk going too far and falling into laxity. This can occur more often on the fourth stage. The primary difference between the fourth and the fifth stage is that the fifth includes a powerful introspection that controls the gross levels of both laxity and excitement to the extent that they actually cease. On the fourth level, some gross obstacles may remain, but they have definitely all been tamed by the fifth stage. This is another reason why the fifth stage is called *taming*.

Tsongkhapa also draws on the *Śrāvaka Levels* to explain this stage. According to that text, from the very beginning of the fifth stage, you regard the "ten signs" as problematic and disadvantageous. The ten signs are the five objects of the physical senses (sights, sounds, and so forth), the three poisons (desire, hatred, and ignorance), and the marks of male and female. All of these are objects to which you may have found yourself attracted in the past, and this attraction can lead to distraction. Now, as a result of having contemplated the disadvantages of being distracted by these ten signs, you no longer get excited by them. Your mind does not scatter when you perceive them.

The sixth stage in the ascent to śamatha is called *pacification*. This stage builds on the strength and orientation of the fifth stage. On the sixth stage, from seeing the disadvantages of a distracted mind, any reticence in your desire to practice to develop śamatha ceases. This is stated succinctly in *Ornament for the Mahayana Sutras*, "Because you see the faults of distraction, you quell dislike for the meditation." The *Śrāvaka Levels* explains that the mind is normally drawn to objects of desire; the mind proceeds from those objects to desirous thoughts and then to disturbing afflictions. From the very start of the stage of pacification, you clearly recognize all of this as problematic, and your mind does not get drawn to these objects and become disturbed. On this stage a special kind of powerful introspection cuts off such distractions, subduing them before they take hold. It is a very powerful vigilance that looks at what is coming, what is ready to come, and what is attempting to come. It can apply appropriate antidotes before they actually arise.

What is the difference between the fifth stage and the sixth stage? On the fifth stage, it was important to take delight in positive thinking about practice. But when you cheer up, the mind can get aroused, and this can lead to distraction. At this point any such distractions are of course subtle, for gross distraction has already been eliminated. But because they are so subtle, they are in some ways more insidious, because they can go unnoticed. Pabongka Rinpoche's *Liberation in the Palm of Your Hand* says there are greater dangers of subtle laxity arising in the fifth stage than in the sixth. He does not say that it never arises in the sixth stage but that there is less danger. It goes on to say that both the fifth and sixth stages are "established by the power of introspection." From the sixth stage onward, the development of introspection is complete and it is powerful.

The seventh stage is called *complete pacification*. "Complete" here refers to a mental state where uneasiness, attachment, melancholy, lethargy, and sleepiness, among other uncomfortable states of mind, are more fully subdued. Attachment and the distraction it causes, for example, are more finely pacified. Lethargy and sleepiness are also more fully subdued at this seventh stage. The lack of unpleasant mental feelings, uneasiness, agitation, a foggy mind, and so forth, are all signs that the seventh stage has been achieved. *Ornament for the Mahayana Sutras* says, "As soon as attachment, melancholy, and so forth arise, they are pacified." In other words, whenever these faults arise, the mind is immediately able to pacify them. According to the *Śrāvaka Levels*, at this point in your development, if secondary afflictions do arise, or are on the verge of arising as a result of forgetfulness, you will not give in to them; you will put them down before they flourish. When the temptations arise, they are recognized with introspection and abandoned.

What is the difference between the sixth and seventh stages? On the sixth stage practitioners are slightly worried about subtle forms of excitement and laxity arising. On the seventh stage suspicion and worry about the arising of subtle faults is not really present. Although the danger of their arising is not great, you still need to persevere and exert the appropriate effort to apply the antidotes if they are called for. Pabongka Rinpoche's *Liberation in the Palm of Your Hand* explains that while the fifth and sixth stages are established through the power of introspection, the seventh stage is signified by the complete ripening of both powerful antidotes: mindfulness and introspection. A special perseverance also distinguishes the seventh stage. It is through the power of this perseverance that even the subtle forms of the two faults are abandoned.

The eighth stage is called *one-pointed attention*. This refers to the ability to meditate single-pointedly on your chosen object. Of course, all of the stages involve one-pointed meditation, but this one is much more advanced. On the eighth stage some persevering effort is still needed to remain concentrated. As long as you exert effort, you are able to concentrate for as long as you wish without the obstacles of laxity and excitement. At this point your focused concentration is almost natural and spontaneous but not quite. The *Śrāvaka Levels* says, "By means of application you have no hindrance, and since you continuously establish a flow of concentration, you make a single channel." The "single channel" here indicates one-pointed attention.

The ninth stage is called *balanced placement*. This refers to an even, unruffled state of mind when it is placed on the object. Now there is equipoise. Kamalaśīla's *Stages of Meditation* refers to this quality as "equanimity." Equanimity means that your mind is no longer affected by excitement or laxity. Unlike on the eighth stage where some persevering effort was required to maintain your concentration, on the ninth stage no effort is needed. Your mind is naturally calm, focused, and completely without fear of the two major obstacles. Maintaining attention is not a struggle in any way at all. The *Śrāvaka Levels* says that your mind is effortlessly and spontaneously concentrated:

> As a consequence of dedication, familiarization, and frequent practice, you reach the path of both spontaneous and natural attention. With no application and with spontaneity, your mind enters into a flow of concentration that is without distraction. In this way it is concentrated.

Natural and spontaneous single-pointed attention comes as a result of regular practice in repeatedly focusing your mind on its object. Through continuous effort, concentration becomes natural, and effort is no longer needed. Your mind is able to continuously concentrate without any sort of distraction. The ninth stage is the direct, or immediate cause, of śamatha. After the ninth stage, actual śamatha is achieved. Actual śamatha is distinguished by a subtle bliss and physical and mental pliancy.

(b)) The process of achieving them with the six forces

The nine stages are achieved through six forces: the force of hearing, the force of reflection, the force of mindfulness, the force of introspection, the force of perseverance, and the force of acquaintance. Each force causes the accomplishment of certain positive qualities and the dissolution of certain negative qualities.

The first of the six forces, the *force of hearing* is the power behind the accomplishment of the first stage, mental placement. It is the starting point. Because you have studied the teachings on śamatha, you know the type of object to choose, the way to focus your attention on the object, and the other aspects of the practice. These things must be learned before they can be put into practice. Traditionally these teachings were passed on orally. There was not the wide availability of books as there is today; you learned from hearing the instructions given to you by your teacher. However, this force also refers to learning through reading and studying how to internalize your mind and focus on the desired object. At this point your familiarity with the meditation practice is dependent upon what you have learned, not your own experience.

The second force, the *force of reflection*, is the power behind the achievement of second stage, continuous placement. Now your mind can focus on the object with a bit of continuity. You accomplish this by reflection and mental control; this comes from within; it is not dependent on analysis of what you studied. The force of reflection is repeatedly placing your focus on the object. By doing this again and again, your mind becomes able to remain continuously, for at least some time, on its object.

The third force is the *force of mindfulness*. Both the third and fourth stages of śamatha are achieved through the power of mindfulness. On the third stage, patched placement, whenever your mind strays from its object, mindful recollection of your object pulls your mind back. This is the first function of mindfulness: drawing your attention back to the object when your mind has become distracted. This establishes a degree of bonding between your attention and your object of meditation. As your mindfulness becomes more developed, the duration of your mind's focus on its object increases, and you achieve the fourth stage, close placement. Now the second function of mindfulness is used: when mindfulness is strong, it prevents the mind from straying from the object.

The fourth force, *the force of introspection*, is behind the accomplishment of the fifth and sixth stages, taming and pacification. Introspection is the mental spy that maintains a watchful eye on the activities of the mind; it sees the faults of excitement and the signs of secondary afflictions. These signs include qualities like dullness, lethargy, vagueness of attention, over-internalizing, and so forth. When these occur, introspection sees them for what they are, and on this basis you apply the antidotes that keep them from developing further.

The fifth force, *the force of perseverance*, brings about the seventh and eighth stages, complete pacification and one-pointed attention. Through perseverance, or joyous effort, you are able to abandon even the most subtle thoughts and afflictions that obstruct achievement of these two stages. As previously mentioned, there is still a subtle degree of distraction and laxity at the seventh stage. The force of perseverance immediately applies the appropriate antidote when even mere indications of these subtle faults arise. Due to this perseverance these subtle faults do not arise, or if they do they are immediately removed.

The emphasis here is on the effort that is exerted to counteract the faults, no matter how small or subtle they may seem. This special attention and effort is required because at this level the mind is so internalized and focused on its object that you can easily confuse these obstacles as being part of meditative concentration or think that the subtle signs are not a big deal. In fact, it is easy for subtle laxity and subtle excitement to go almost unnoticed if some effort of perseverance is not applied. By applying this powerful force on the seventh stage, on the eighth stage no interruption at all occurs in your meditative concentration. The subtle obstacles cannot destroy your concentration when they are immediately addressed. Thus, at the eighth level, with some effort, you can remain continuously on the object.

The sixth force is *the force of acquaintance*. It brings about the ninth stage, balanced placement. This is the power of being well acquainted with all the above. Equipoise arises naturally from becoming so familiar with the teachings, practice, and the achievements of the earlier stages. You can concentrate for as long as you like on whatever you wish without any effort.

Tsongkhapa says that his explanation accords with the account of these subjects in Asaṅga's *Śrāvaka Levels*. He warns that some other explanations are not trustworthy. A good summary of the progression through the nine stages is found in Pabongka Rinpoche's *Liberation in the Palm of Your Hand*. He says that during the first two stages, your mind is largely under the power of distraction. Even if you are able to focus your mind on the object for a few continuous moments, your mind gets distracted again and again. From the third stage through the seventh stages, meditative stabilization increases. Nevertheless there still is some interruption by laxity and excitement. At the eighth stage there are no longer any interruptions, but you still need to exert some effort. Concentration does not come completely spontaneously, but with perseverance you can remain as long as you wish. When the ninth stage is achieved, concentration is effortless and natural. Pabongka Rinpoche likens the progression through the stages to fighting a battle. At first the enemy is very strong. As your success in battle increases, the power and strength of the enemy decreases. Eventually, as your confidence builds and the enemy becomes weaker and weaker, you only have to keep watch a little bit. You do not need to exert that much effort. This is the situation on the eighth stage when excitement and laxity are very weak. Introspection is no longer needed, though there may be some effort needed from time to time.

Tsongkhapa uses another analogy to explain going through the stages to the ninth stage. When you memorize a text for daily recitation, at first you have to read it repeatedly and put a lot of effort into trying to memorize it. As you become more accustomed to reciting the text, it requires less effort. Finally you become so completely familiar with the text that reciting it from memory is absolutely effortless. This is what the ninth stage of śamatha is like. Through the power of familiarity, remaining single-pointedly focused on the object of meditation becomes effortless.

Tsongkhapa now explains the nine stages of the development of śamatha in reverse order to show why each stage is necessarily preceded by its antecedent. The immediate cause of śamatha is the ninth stage, on which the mind is able to spontaneously concentrate on its object without any effort. In order for that kind of concentration to arise, you need to rely upon mindfulness and introspection. On the eighth stage your mind can remain on its object without interruption from laxity or excitement, but it still requires some perseverance to do this. The eighth and ninth stages are very similar in that meditative stabilization occurs without interruption on both of them. But the eighth level requires you to make some small effort in the application of mindfulness and introspection. The eighth stage has to arise before the ninth; it is the cause of the ninth stage. In order for the eighth stage to arise, you must have mastered the ability to immediately recognize subtle laxity and subtle excitement as soon as they occur and apply the appropriate antidote. This is what occurs on the seventh stage. So the seventh stage is a necessary cause of the eighth stage. Similarly, in order to be able to immediately stop any fault that is about to arise with powerful introspection on the seventh stage, earlier you must have clearly seen the faults of a distracted mind and the secondary afflictions and have intense introspection monitoring your attention so that the mind does not give in to them. In other words, the antidote of vigilant introspection is put to work on the fifth and sixth stages. On the fifth stage introspection becomes strong, and on the sixth stage it is fully developed. Before you can do that, you must have accomplished the third and fourth stages. On the third stage mindfulness swiftly recalls the object of meditation when you become distracted; and on the fourth stage, mindfulness prevents gross distraction from your object. Of course, in order to be able to harness the power of mindfulness, your mind must be able to fix upon the object of meditation, and you must have an undistracted continuity of concentration. These are the first and second stages; they must precede the third stage.

Tsongkhapa now summarizes how to progress through the stages. Understanding this will help you recognize the stages and know the most effective way to proceed. First you must understand and follow the instructions you have received regarding how to set your mind on the object. Repeatedly reflect on how to fix your attention, and then apply the methods to bring about some continuity of attention. Then, if your mindfulness declines and you become distracted, quickly recall your meditation object. Next, generate powerful mindfulness that prevents distraction before it occurs. After that, see the faults of laxity and excitement and develop intense introspection. Then, even if subtle faults arise you immediately recognize them and stop them. Upon eliminating the faults, use the power of perseverance to lengthen your meditation. After mastering the ability to meditate uninterrupted by the hindrances with perseverance, your concentration will become effortless.

Many people are confused and think they will have achieved śamatha when they are on the ninth stage. The ninth stage has so many of the qualities of śamatha that it is easy to mistake it for śamatha itself. It is a common misconception that the clear concentration without discursive thought that is achieved on the ninth stage is high special insight. But this is not the wisdom of an ārya directly realizing emptiness. According to the *Śrāvaka Levels*, some people think the ninth stage is the achievement of the completion stage of highest yoga tantra because on the ninth stage clarity and a lack of discursive thought is accompanied by bliss. Do not be confused in this way. The ninth stage is merely the last step on the way to achieving śamatha. In fact, not only is it not a tantric achievement, it is not even necessarily Buddhist. The practice and achievement of śamatha is not unique to Buddhism; many aspects of it are shared with other Indian religions. Although some of the details as they are explained here are uniquely Buddhist, like using an image of the Buddha as your object of meditation, śamatha practice in general predates Buddhism. The qualities of the experience that sometimes get confused with high tantric realizations are in fact qualities in common with non-Buddhist practices of śamatha. In summary, even if you have obtained the ninth stage, where your mind can spontaneously and effortlessly stay on its object, you still have not achieved the actual state of śamatha. Real śamatha is characterized by mental and physical pliancy. If you do not have this special pliancy, you have not yet attained śamatha, much less vipaśyanā.

The importance of this explanation is made clear in two concise stanzas from Tsongkhapa's *Condensed Points of the Stages of the Path*:

> Concentration is the king that reigns over the mind;
> When left, it is as unwavering as the king of mountains;
> When set forth, it engages with all objects of virtue;
> It induces the great bliss of a serviceable body and mind.
>
> Knowing this the great accomplished yogis
> Constantly apply meditations destroying the enemy of distraction.
> I, a yogi, have practiced in this manner;
> You, who aspire for liberation, should do likewise.[16]

Concentration gives you the power to control your mind. When you have achieved this meditative stabilization, you are able to firmly set your mind on your chosen object without any distraction or laxity. Your mind will be as stable as a mountain. Once you have achieved this, you will experience great physical and mental bliss as well as a special kind of mental and physical pliancy. Seeing the incredible benefit of cultivating śamatha, great yogis apply effort toward conquering the enemy of distraction.

(c)) How the four attentions are involved in this

The development of śamatha can also be explained by correlating the nine stages to what are called the four attentions. This presentation is found in Asaṅga's *Śrāvaka Levels*:

> With respect to these nine mental states, know that there are four types of attention: (1) tight focus, (2) intermittent focus, (3) uninterrupted focus, and (4) spontaneous focus. Now in the first two mental states of mental placement and correct mental placement [i.e., continuous placement], there is the attention of tight focus. In the next five mental states of withdrawn mental placement [i.e., patched placement], close placement, taming, pacification, and complete pacification, there is the attention of intermittent focus. In the eighth mental state of single channeling [i.e., one-pointed attention], there is the attention of uninterrupted focus. In the ninth state of concentrated awareness [i.e., balanced placement], there is the attention of effortless [i.e., spontaneous] focus.

The first attention is called *tight focus* and corresponds to the first two of the nine stages. It is a very tight, or tense, way of maintaining your attention on the object. It is similar to twisting several wires or threads together to increase their tensile strength. This requires a great deal of focused energy. Your mind is as sharply focused as it is when you are walking along a cliff edge. You cannot relax and let your attention lapse; you must be intensely aware.

The second of the four intentions, *intermittent focus*, is associated with the third through the seventh stages. Each of these stages has a degree of continuity of focus, but the focus is interrupted from time to time, thus breaking up extended meditation sessions.

The third attention is called *uninterrupted focus* and is associated with the eighth stage, one-pointed attention. The eighth stage is characterized by long periods of continuity; your meditative concentration is not broken at all by laxity or excitement. Nevertheless, it still requires some effort.

The fourth attention is called *spontaneous focus* and is associated with the ninth stage, balanced placement. The ninth stage is a fully concentrated mind with effortless stabilization of the mind on its object. Because there is no effort at all needed at this point, it is called spontaneous.

Tsongkhapa now has a hypothetical opponent ask why the first two attentions are not reversed in terms of the stages to which they relate. In other words, why are the first two mental states not correlated with intermittent attention, since that aptly describes their manner of attention to the object? And why aren't the next five mental states correlated with tight focus, since that seems like an apt description for them.

Tsongkhapa explains that the first two mental states are mostly characterized by distraction. There is actually very little concentration at these early two stages. It does not make much sense to speak of intermittent focus for the first two stages when the actual times of focused attention are extremely short and are separated by long periods of distraction. During the very brief periods when focus is present on the two initial stages, it is very tight. In contrast, the following five mental states have progressively longer durations of concentration. They all have a degree of continuation of focus, albeit with interruptions. Therefore describing their attention as intermittent is appropriate. These two groups of mental states—the first two stages and the next five stages—are similar in that they all have tight focus; they are dissimilar in that the latter group also has intermittent focus.

Tsongkhapa goes on to say that if you really want to accomplish śamatha, you should establish the necessary causes and conditions to bring it about. These necessities include the environmental conditions, internal physical and mental conditions, knowledge about obstacles and antidotes, and so forth. Then, if you continuously persevere in the practice, you will achieve śamatha. If you try to cut corners, only making a strong effort to practice now and then, and sometimes dropping your practice, you will not achieve it. Āryaśūra's *Compendium of the Perfections* illuminates the importance of perseverance:

> With constant yoga
> Strive to accomplish meditative stabilization.
> Fire does not arise from friction
> If you repeatedly slack off.
> Likewise, do not stop striving at the method of yoga
> Until you reach a special state.

If you are serious about cultivating śamatha, frequent or long breaks between your meditation sessions are detrimental. You harm the strength of your practice if you do a little meditation but spend much more of your time thinking about or doing things like relaxing, walking, running, shopping, and so forth. Āryaśūra likens this to trying to start a fire by rubbing two sticks. You need continuous friction to produce heat and finally start a fire; if you only intermittently rub the sticks together, you will not cause a flame. Similarly, the cultivation of śamatha takes consistent determined effort. This is not meant to suggest that if you cannot completely dedicate yourself to this practice, then you should not do it at all. Most practitioners do not do intense śamatha practice in the beginning. You may plant the seed for future serious practice by doing a little every day in the morning or evening. This will make meditation a habit.

When you do dedicate yourself with the intention of actually achieving śamatha, you should properly prepare yourself both physically and mentally. You should be single-minded about this. You will need a quiet place with all the necessary external conditions. You should also prepare the internal conditions. Not just any type of meditation practice will result in śamatha. Achieving śamatha involves the application of specific antidotes to specific types of faults and obstacles. You will need dedicated effort to achieve your goal; you should expect that it could take several months or even years. Eventually you will be able to achieve śamatha.

(c') The measure of successful cultivation of śamatha

How do you know when you have achieved śamatha? What signs indicate such an achievement? The way to measure successful cultivation of śamatha is divided into three subtopics:

(1') A presentation of the dividing line between accomplishing and not accomplishing śamatha

(2') A general presentation of the way to proceed along the path on the basis of śamatha (chapter 6)

(3') A specific presentation of the way to proceed along the mundane path (chapter 6)

(1') A PRESENTATION OF THE DIVIDING LINE BETWEEN ACCOMPLISHING AND NOT ACCOMPLISHING ŚAMATHA

Tsongkhapa explains the qualities of śamatha and the signs that you have achieved it because many practitioners, some who are nowhere near the actual achievement of śamatha, think they have accomplished the goal. There are two subtopics: (a") a presentation of the actual meaning, and (b") the marks associated with attention, and the elimination of qualms.

(a") A PRESENTATION OF THE ACTUAL MEANING

First Tsongkhapa presents what actually constitutes śamatha. Then he addresses other definitions of śamatha and explains whether they are correct or incorrect. He begins with a hypothetical opponent asking about the difference between the ninth stage of the preparatory practice and the actual state of śamatha. The questioner says, "Haven't you achieved śamatha when you can effortlessly meditate with a stabilized mind for as long as you like without any laxity or excitement? What else do you need?"

Tsongkhapa replies that at the ninth stage the mind is able to focus on its chosen object for as long as it wants without any excitement or laxity. There is no lack of strength, clarity, or energy in such a mind. What distinguishes this state from śamatha is mental and physical pliancy. Before achieving pliancy the mind may be content, but the body is not, or vice versa. When śamatha has been achieved, it is not like that; the mind and body act cooperatively spontaneously. The body does not interrupt the mind, and the mind does not interrupt the body. The body has a kind of light feeling. It is only after the ninth stage that this special dexterity of body and mind arises. Therefore, because there is no pliancy on the ninth stage, it is only an approximation of śamatha. This is clearly stated in the *Sutra Unraveling the Intended Meaning*:

> Bhagavan, when bodhisattvas direct their attention inward and focus it upon their minds, what is this attention called for as long as physical pliancy and mental pliancy are not achieved? Maitreya, this is not

śamatha. You should say that it is associated with an aspiration that approximates śamatha.

In a similar vein, Kamalaśīla wrote in the second *Stages of Meditation* that pliancy is an integral part of śamatha:

> For you who have cultivated śamatha in this way, when your body and mind become pliant and you have mastery over your mind in directing it as you wish, at that time you know that you have accomplished śamatha.

Kamalaśīla describes śamatha in the first *Stages of Meditation* as attention that remains focused on its object for as long as you wish without any need to rely on the antidotes. The second *Stages of Meditation* makes it clear that this definition also implies the presence of pliancy in śamatha. Maitreya's *Ornament for the Mahayana Sutras* and *Separation of the Middle from the Extremes* as well as Ratnākaraśānti's *Instructions for the Perfection of Wisdom* among others make this same point: one of key qualities that distinguishes śamatha from the mental state of the ninth stage is this special pliancy.

So what is this special pliancy? It is not mere suppleness or flexibility. This special pliancy is a kind of wind-energy, *prāṇa* in Sanskrit. It is a vehicle for the mind and instills a harmonious mental and physical disposition. This wind-energy goes through the body clearing away all physical dysfunction, hardships, difficulties, and hindrances. When the wind has eliminated these hindrances, the body becomes light, flexible, and supple. The body becomes tamed and is much closer to the mental nature. It produces a pleasant feeling in the body. The body becomes harmonious with the mind, and both have complete dexterity.

Even as a result of ordinary athletic training, there are instances when the body can do almost unbelievable things. Great athletes like Olympic gymnasts or high-wire walkers are good examples of the mind commanding the body to do incredible things. The body learns to cooperate with the mind. Take the example of the high-wire walker. In the beginning of training for this kind of activity, the athlete focuses intensely on how he or she is walking. If his mind goes somewhere else, he may fall down. Eventually with enough training the mind and body work together, and he is able to walk the entire length of the wire without falling. The yogic practice of śamatha uses internal energy—a kind of subtle wind—that corrects physical hindrances. The result is pliancy. With pliancy, if you want to sit in one position, concentrating and meditating even for many weeks or months, your body will easily comply with that wish and not be a hindrance.

As this energy-wind goes throughout the body, the brain experiences a feeling of slight weight that is not unpleasant. It is difficult to give an analogy for this sensation because nothing is quite like it. Barely touching your shaved scalp is probably the closest I can get to describing it. When you shave your head—which you may never do if you are not a monk or nun—there is no hair left, just your bare scalp. When your hand softly and lightly brushes against your scalp, you will feel a mild sensation. The wind coursing through the body is a subtle tangible feeling like that. It produces a subtle sensation of being touched. It is like a pleasant internal touch.

Between the two types of pliancy—mental and physical—mental pliancy arises first. Mental pliancy is the antidote to certain mental hindrances and difficulties that obstruct perfect meditation. After you remove the afflictions that keep you from taking joy in your practice, your mind will be serviceable for any type of meditation. Mental serviceability is almost synonymous with mental pliancy. It then causes an energy to surge through your body. This is the cause for physical pliancy. The physical pliancy of śamatha is a subtle feeling pervading your body. As it touches the entirety of the inside of your body, you feel a subtle sensation of physical bliss. That bliss is then produced in the mind. Thus, between the two blissful states—mental and physical—physical bliss occurs first. It then serves as a cause for a special mental bliss to arise.

When bliss first occurs, you are still on the ninth stage. The ninth stage is spontaneous meditation that creates a gross pliancy and then gross bliss. Until it becomes subtle pliancy, it is not śamatha. Further, because this gross bliss is on the ninth stage, it is associated with the desire realm. Why? Because the achievement of śamatha marks achievement of the preparatory stage of the first meditative absorption of the form realm.

Tsongkhapa then has his imaginary questioner ask, "If pliancy is what comes first and distinguishes śamatha from the previous states, how is pliancy achieved and how does it lead to śamatha?" Asaṅga's *Compendium of Knowledge* defines pliancy and addresses these questions:

> What is pliancy? It is a serviceability of the body and mind due to the cessation of the continuum of physical and mental dysfunctions, and it has the function of dispelling all obstructions.

The "dysfunctions" are obstacles that make your body and mind unfit for cultivating virtue. They are the afflictions that keep you from taking joy in the removal of disturbing mental, emotional, and physical states. When these obstacles are eliminated, your body and mind become serviceable. The previous heavy sluggishness of your body is replaced with a feeling of lightness and buoyancy, and your mind has no resistance to focusing on virtue.

What are the signs indicating perfect pliancy is about to occur? The first indicator, the slight feeling of being touched throughout the interior of your body, arises from the gross wind element going through your body like a cleaner of obstructions. This is an early sign that pliancy will occur. Physical hindrances are eliminated after that; all your aches and discomfort are gone. Your mind and body no longer pull in separate directions. Eventually you do not feel like your body is separate from your mind; it is almost as if your body has absorbed your meditation object. At the point of that feeling of mental and physical unity, physical pliancy arises. Tsongkhapa cites Asaṅga's *Śrāvaka Levels* on this point:

> The portent of the proximate occurrence of obvious, easily discernible one-pointedness of mind and mental and physical pliancy is a sensation of the brain becoming heavy; but this is not a harmful characteristic. As soon as this happens, you eliminate the mental dysfunction belonging to the category of affliction that obstructs your delight in eliminating affliction, and the mental serviceability and mental pliancy that are the remedy for this dysfunction arise.

As noted, serviceability is nearly the same as pliancy, or suppleness. In some texts, a yogi's suppleness is compared to carding wool. To card wool, you take rough clumps of wool and comb them into strands. Eventually it becomes very soft and smooth, and the thin threads are very workable—they have a soft suppleness and flexibility. The same text also says:

> Due to [pliancy's] occurrence, an energy-wind—included among the great elements—that is conducive to the arising of physical pliancy courses through the body. When it flows, you are freed of the physical dysfunction that belongs to the category of afflictions and that obstructs your delight in eliminating afflictions; and physical pliancy, the remedy for this affliction, saturates the entire body, so that it seems as if you are filled with this energy.

Tsongkhapa says that physical pliancy and the delightful sensations that accompany it are definitely of the body. Some other scholars have said that this is a mental experience. He cites the master Sthiramati's *Explanation of the "Thirty Stanzas"* (*Triṃśikā-bhāṣya*) on this point:

If a distinctive physical sensation is qualified by delight, recognize this to be physical pliancy. If your mind is delighted, your body becomes pliant.

Sthiramati's comments are actually a citation from a sutra. What does it mean? The first time that mental bliss arises, it is a little bit rough and intense. It is a wonderful feeling but is not real peace. It almost seems that you will lose your concentration, but you do not. It is similar to how you feel when you receive some wonderful news. For a few moments you feel as if you cannot stand it. The initial bliss eventually settles into a neutral feeling that is suitable for perfect concentration. Sometimes that neutral feeling is called *subtle bliss*. But it is not actually a joyful feeling; it began with a type of bliss but has become neutral. You have not yet obtained special pliancy, or the bliss of pliancy, until it cools down. This does not mean that pliancy is exhausted or disappears. It means that when the bliss and pliancy have settled down, they become very subtle, like a shadow. When that feeling of excited joy has dissipated, your mind is able to firmly remain on its object without any internal or external disturbances. Your mind becomes unshakeable and is suitable for perfect concentration. This marks the attainment of śamatha, and concomitantly, reaching the preparatory stage of the first stabilization or meditative absorption in the form realm. Asaṅga summarizes this quite succinctly in his *Śrāvaka Levels* when he writes:

> When this first arises, you experience delight, a great sense of bliss, attention to unsurpassed delight, and manifest delight. Following this, the force of pliancy that first arose slowly becomes very refined, and your body becomes endowed with shadow-like pliancy. You eliminate delight, your mind becomes stabilized with meditative serenity, and you focus on the object of meditation with exceptional śamatha.

Tsongkhapa follows Asaṅga in describing those who achieve this state of śamatha as having "attention." This is a way of saying that those who achieve śamatha are those who are on the level of the first meditative equipoise of the upper realms—specifically, the preparatory stage of the first stabilization of the form realm. *Śrāvaka Levels* says:

> Thereafter, the novice yogi is endowed with attention and is included in the ranks of those who are called "attentive." Why? Because this person has achieved the small type of attention on the level of meditative equipoise that first experiences the form realm. Therefore this person is called "attentive."

(b") THE MARKS ASSOCIATED WITH ATTENTION, AND THE
ELIMINATION OF QUALMS

There are five particular marks that indicate achievement of śamatha. You will recognize these signs in yourself. Others may be able to see certain aspects of them as well.

The first sign or mark of achieving śamatha is the accomplishment of some degree of the following: a mind belonging to the form realm, physical pliancy, mental pliancy, and a single-pointedness of mind.

Tsongkhapa says the second mark is "the ability to purify afflictions either by means of the path bearing the aspects of calmness and coarseness, or the path bearing the aspects of the truths." The two means of purifying the afflictions referred to here are the mundane and supramundane paths. The mundane path, here referred to as "bearing the aspects of calmness and coarseness," subdues the afflictions of the lower realms by comparing the gross suffering of each level of existence with the relatively superior experience of the next higher one. This will loosen attachment to one level of existence at a time. The supramundane path, "the path bearing the aspects of the truths," does not involve a comparative meditation. It entails meditating on the suffering of the whole of samsara, on the truth of cessation, on the ultimate truth of emptiness, and so forth, to permanently eliminate all the afflictions from the root.

Once you have achieved śamatha, you are on the preparatory stage of the first level of the form realm. There, it is possible to apply either of these two approaches, or paths, to purifying the afflictions. Before achieving śamatha, no matter what meditation you do, you will not actually purify the afflictions; at best, you will temporarily subdue them. Even after achieving śamatha, if you pursue the mundane path, then you will only subdue the afflictions temporarily because removing afflictions from the root requires a direct realization of emptiness. But the short-term suppression on the mundane path is far more effective than the temporary suppression of afflictions without śamatha. On the mundane path, you will be able to subdue those afflictions for the rest of that particular life. At death those afflictions will still be subdued, and you will have a high rebirth in the next life as a result. Therefore, if you have actually subdued the afflictions belonging to the desire realm and take rebirth in a higher realm as a result of meditation on the mundane path, this is a sign of the achievement of śamatha. And when you are able purify the afflictions from the root, it is also a sign of having achieved śamatha.

The third mark of achieving śamatha is that as soon as you start to focus on your object of meditation, meditative equipoise that is completely free of the obstacles along with mental and physical pliancy naturally come quite quickly.

If they do not come quickly, you have not really achieved what you think you have. The quick onset of meditative equipoise and mental and physical pliancy is a sign of actually achieving śamatha.

The fourth mark is the nonoccurrence of the five obstacles that are primarily associated with the desire realm. In other words, you have almost no attraction to and attachment for the objects of your five physical senses because you have achieved the superior mental state of the first meditative equipoise of the form realm. Attachment to sensory objects and pleasure is a quality of the desire realm. This attachment, along with the afflictions of anger, hatred, stinginess, envy, and so forth, which are typical with a desire realm mentality, almost never occur after achieving śamatha.

The fifth mark is that when you arise from meditation, there is still some physical and mental pliancy present. Even during nonmeditative periods your mind is more stable and calm, and your body will spontaneously and naturally follow. Every ordinary daily activity you undertake will be much easier. This happens because of your mental and physical pliancy during meditation.

These signs of the achievement of śamatha were also taught by Asaṅga in *Śrāvaka Levels.*

> These are the marks of a novice who is endowed with attention: You achieve the small degree of a mind that experiences the form realm, physical pliancy, mental pliancy, and one-pointedness of mind. You have the opportunity and ability to practice with objects of meditation that purify afflictions. Your mindstream becomes smooth, and you are enveloped by śamatha.

"Enveloped by śamatha" means that your mind is more attentive in every situation, not just during the meditation session. The same text also says:

> When your mind is perfectly drawn inward, settled and focused, mental and physical pliancy occur ever so swiftly; you are not afflicted by physical dysfunction, and for the most part the obstructions do not operate.

Prior to attaining śamatha, when you focus on an object of meditation, mental pliancy does not arise quickly. After śamatha is achieved, as soon as you focus your mind on an object, mental pliancy comes. In addition, you are not bothered by physical hindrances. Once śamatha is achieved, no achy feelings or physical pain will occur. And mental obstacles, like attachment to the pleasing objects of the desire realm, anger, stinginess, and so forth, will also not arise for the most part. The following quote, also from Asaṅga's text, reinforces this point:

> Even when you rise from meditation and move about, you still have a certain degree of physical and mental pliancy. Recognize such experiences to be purified characteristics and signs of possessing attention.

After achieving śamatha some physical and mental pliancy carries over into the postmeditation period. You are naturally more mindful no matter what you are doing—walking, shopping, working, and so forth.

As soon as you have achieved single-pointed concentration, you naturally have mental and physical pliancy in your practice. One of the special qualities of śamatha meditation is that every time you engage in single-pointed concentration, pliancy is increased. As pliancy increases, the stabilization of your single-pointed concentration becomes stronger and firmer. Each nurtures and relies on the other: pliancy helps strengthen single-pointed concentration, and single-pointed concentration helps strengthen pliancy. *Śrāvaka Levels* says:

> Just as your physical and mental pliancy increase, so does your mental one-pointedness upon the object of meditation increase; and just as your mental one-pointedness increases, so does your physical and mental pliancy increase. These two phenomena—mental one-pointedness and pliancy—are based upon each other and are reinforced by each other.

In summary, when your mind is serviceable, the mind and its vehicle—a subtle wind-energy—perform the same function harmoniously. They go together like electricity flows through a wire. At that time, physical pliancy arises. There are no hindrances. This mental and physical pliancy assist your concentration. Your concentration brings forth additional serviceable energy.

Now Tsongkhapa responds to questions raised by hypothetical opponents. The first questioner asks, "In the framework of the five Buddhist paths, where does the mental state of meditative equipoise and its accompanying subtle mental and physical bliss occur?" In other words, do you achieve śamatha before the first of the five paths? Or is it on the path of accumulation, or the path of preparation, or the path of seeing, or the path of meditation, or the path of no further training? Many people assume these qualities arise somewhere high on the Mahayana path. Remember, some people think that these states of mind—bliss due to the physical and mental pliancy accompanying a mind in equipoise with perfect clarity—are beyond the five paths of the sutra vehicle and indicate the achievement of the highest level of tantric attainment.

Tsongkhapa's answer is not what such people hope. Following the texts of authoritative teachers like Asaṅga and Kamalaśīla, as well as Buddhist scriptural teachings like those in Maitreya's corpus, he tells us that the attainment of śamatha is not even uniquely a Buddhist achievement. Even non-Buddhists can attain śamatha, and by following the mundane path they can temporarily subdue all their afflictions up through and including the third level of the formless realm. This is not a minor accomplishment. In order to be born in the first meditative absorption of the form realm, you must have achieved śamatha and temporarily gotten rid of afflictions belonging to desire realm. Nevertheless, it is not something unique to Buddhism.

Śamatha is part of the Buddhist path to liberation only when it is imbued with renunciation—the wish to be utterly free of samsara and all its entanglements. In other words, your primary motivation for practice is to achieve total emancipation from samsara because you realize the faults of being born anywhere from the hells up to the peak of worldly existence. So when Buddhists refer to the five paths, they are referring to striving for an accomplishment that is higher than that reached on the mundane path. The supramundane path requires a correct understanding of selflessness in order to abandon the egotistic view controlled by ignorance that is the ground of samsara. Achievement of śamatha is necessary for a direct realization of selflessness, or emptiness, without error. And if your renunciation of samsara and desire for liberation is for yourself alone, then your śamatha is part of the Hinayana path. It is only when it is additionally imbued with the altruistic wish to achieve buddhahood in order to benefit others that it becomes a part of the Mahayana path.

There are different systems of thought when it comes to vipaśyanā. The different philosophical schools' explanations about emptiness, the object of insight, and other related topics are not similar. However, there is no disagreement in their explanations of the nature of śamatha, how to achieve it, the way it arises in your mental continuum, its measures and boundaries, and how it differs from vipaśyanā.

The five books of Maitreya and Asaṅga's works commenting upon them (*Bodhisattva Levels, Compendium of Determinations, Compendium of Knowledge,* and *Śrāvaka Levels*) always separately explain the nature of śamatha and vipaśyanā and the way to train in them. They teach how śamatha is achieved through the nine levels of concentration and teach a different method to develop vipaśyanā. For the former, you block any kind of analytical thought that arises while working on any of these nine stages; when training in vipaśyanā, analysis is instrumental and essential. The Madhyamaka *Stages of Meditation* texts (those by Kamalaśīla, Jñānakīrti, and so forth) and Ratnākaraśānti's *Instructions for the Perfection of Wisdom* also explain that training in vipaśyanā is an entirely separate enterprise from the training in the nine stages of śamatha.

Tsongkhapa next addresses a hypothetical opponent who asks, "Isn't any meditation in which your mind is focused, not thinking about anything, and not analyzing anything, a concentration on emptiness?"

When some scholars assert that vipaśyanā is emptiness yoga, by "emptiness" they mean a mind of no thinking, no analytical reasoning, no discursive thought, and the like. They conflate the statement from the *Śrāvaka Levels* that explains śamatha as being single-pointed nondiscursive awareness with the profound nondiscursive awareness of meditation realizing emptiness directly. In other words, they think that because śamatha is a type of nondiscursive awareness combined with bliss and clarity, it must be a meditation on emptiness—it must be vipaśyanā. If, as they seem to think, any single-pointed awareness is a direct realization of emptiness, then there would be no need for analysis at all in the process of coming to realize emptiness.

There are various uses of the term *nondiscursive*. The ordinary sense of nondiscursive, as when used to describe śamatha, only means that it is a mind that is not actively analyzing its object. There is no examination "This is this; that is that" and so on. In the sense that there is no analytic investigation of the characteristics of the object, it is single-pointed awareness. But even śamatha has a slight degree of discursiveness from the point of view that the object of meditation is a universal, a generic image. A *universal* is by definition a concept, and concepts are a type of thought. Thus all śamatha meditation, except for the direct realization of emptiness beginning on the path of seeing, is conceptual or discursive in the sense of relying on a universal. *Śrāvaka Levels* says:

> At that time, this [concentration] attends to an image without discursive thought, and it exclusively focuses mindfulness one-pointedly upon the object. It does not examine it, nor classify it, nor investigate it, nor ponder it, nor analyze it.

In the same vein, Kamalaśīla says in the first *Stages of Meditation*:

> The nature of śamatha is nothing more than a one-pointed mind. This is the general characteristic of all meditative śamatha.

Thus when śamatha is spoken of as nondiscursive, it means that it is a meditation that is focused without analytical activity.

There is quite a different sense of the term *nondiscursive* when it is used to describe an ārya's profound nondiscursive realization of emptiness. Tsongkhapa explains the meaning of nondiscursive in this context by giving a brief explanation of vipaśyanā. Vipaśyanā, or insight, is an analytical wisdom that knows how the self and phenomenal things—subjects and objects—appear to the mind, how they actually exist, whether they exist as they appear, whether they are empty of inherently existing as they appear, and so forth. To gain this understanding, you have to investigate and analyze the reality of the self and phenomenal things. This is vipaśyanā practice. The mind analyzes and searches for an ultimate nature in things. This analysis goes more and more deeply until there are no further depths to penetrate. It is like going down a long, deep tunnel. When you finally reach the end, you realize there is no ultimate nature or inherent existence in anything. Everything, the self and all phenomena, is empty of any type of inherent existence. So it is analysis that leads you to understand emptiness—the lack of an inherent nature in things. You then make that understanding of emptiness the object of your śamatha meditation. In other words, you focus your mind on that understanding of emptiness and abide on that realization without analysis. At this point, when the mind is focusing on emptiness in equipoise without analysis, it is completely free of discursive thought.

Thus the profound nondiscursive wisdom that realizes emptiness requires analysis first. The single-pointed awareness of śamatha does not engage in any such analysis and is not dependent on such analysis. There are nondiscursive awarenesses that lack the slightest cognition of emptiness, and there is nondiscursive awareness that meditates on emptiness. Single-pointed focus on an object of meditation is not the same as vipaśyanā; simply concentrating without thinking or analysis does not mean that you are engaging in the profound nondiscursive awareness of an ārya in equipoise. Śamatha meditation is only profound nondiscursive awareness when its object is emptiness. This is realized directly by an ārya on the path of seeing or above.

Those who mistakenly understand nondiscursive awareness, believing that because śamatha is single-pointed nondiscursive awareness it is meditation on emptiness, misconstrue the three terms used in canonical sources for the ultimate nature of reality: signless, objectless, and empty. They incorrectly think that the realization of these is simply an empty blank mind. They do not see that real understanding and direct realization of the ultimate requires learning and analysis. Realization of emptiness, objectlessness, or signlessness is not simply a blank stare into space. Wisdom does not come from just blocking out all thought. The ordinary mind incorrectly perceives phenomena; to correct this ingrained misperception, a practitioner must investigate the true nature of reality. After the depths of reality are penetrated by analytic wisdom, you combine śamatha with analytic wisdom to see more deeply. The single-pointed awareness of śamatha is the powerful tool that will bring this insight into direct perception. You must stabilize your mind, in other words develop śamatha, so that you have this powerful mental instrument. With śamatha, when you set your mind on the empty nature of all phenomena—the conclusion of your analysis—you are engaged in profound nondiscursive awareness.

This can actually occur on the paths of accumulation or preparation. You don't necessarily have a direct realization of emptiness the very first time you apply śamatha to your analytical meditation on emptiness. To rephrase, when analytic insight has reached an understanding of emptiness and that analytic conclusion is the object of single-pointed awareness, that too is profound nondiscursive awareness, even though it precedes the direct realization of an ārya. Of course, the direct realization of emptiness by an ārya is also profound nondiscursive awareness.

Tsongkhapa strongly rejects any other interpretation; he says that to view it otherwise is a misreading of both sutra and tantra sources. He singles out the Chinese master Hvashang, who lost the great debate at Samye to Kamalaśīla, as a proponent of such an erroneous view. According to Hvashang, a realization of emptiness is equated to emptying the mind of all thought. In his view, all thoughts, whether virtuous or nonvirtuous, obscure reality. According to Hvashang, there is no object of meditation in meditation on emptiness. Therefore any meditation without analytic or discursive thinking is a meditation on emptiness. To him, being free means that the mind is blank and clear.

According to Tsongkhapa, it is important that you do not confuse the bliss, clarity, and nondiscursive awareness of śamatha that focuses on an object like the breath with the profound nondiscursive yogic insight of a direct realization of emptiness. Misunderstanding this critical point will be harmful to your practice because you will not bother to study. Without study you will not even achieve śamatha, much less insight. If you just want to relax, a blank mind is fine. But if you want to achieve liberation from samsara, then you must engage in analytic meditation. The afflictions that keep you bound in samsara are only removed by wisdom realizing emptiness. A blank mind will not take you to the goal of liberation. The real counter-force to ignorance is wisdom penetrating the depths of reality. Do not literally read terms like *objectless* or *signless* and take them to mean that profound meditation is merely a blank mind without an object. In this context these terms mean that there is no inherently or truly existent object or characteristic. When the *Heart Sutra* (*Prajñāpāramitā-hṛdaya*) says, "There is no eye, no ear, no nose," it means that there is no inherently existing eye, no inherently existing nose, and so forth. It does not mean they do not exist at all. Ignorance cannot be alleviated by a blank mind that does not realize anything. Single-pointed focus on an object of meditation is not the same as vipaśyanā.

In summary, simply focusing on an object of meditation without analytical examination does not make it a meditation realizing emptiness. It does not make the meditation a profound nondiscursive awareness. Insight, or vipaśyanā, begins with analysis. Śamatha is an instrument to support vipaśyanā. Before a direct realization of emptiness, you must achieve śamatha. A profound nondiscursive insight occurs after the instrument of śamatha is utilized to focus on emptiness as its object. In the "Insight" chapter of the *Lamrim Chenmo*, Tsongkhapa explains vipaśyanā in great detail and describes the union of the śamatha and vipaśyanā.

✢ 6 ✢

Śamatha as Part of the Path

(2') A general presentation of the way to proceed along the path on the basis
of śamatha

(3') A specific presentation of the way to proceed along the mundane path

  (a") The need to achieve śamatha before proceeding on the path bearing
  the aspects of calmness and coarseness

  (b") On the basis of śamatha, the way to freedom from the attachment
  of the desire realm

———◆———

NOW THAT WE have established the dividing line between accomplishing
and not accomplishing śamatha, we can discuss the way to proceed along
the path on the basis of having achieved śamatha. In this chapter, Tsongkhapa
discusses śamatha in the course of the mundane path. The discussion of śamatha
on the supramundane path, where śamatha in conjoined with vipaśyanā, is
treated in volume 5 of this series.

(2') A GENERAL PRESENTATION OF THE WAY TO PROCEED
ALONG THE PATH ON THE BASIS OF ŚAMATHA

How should you practice the path after having achieved śamatha? What do
you do next? Is it enough that your mind can stay spontaneously and comfortably on its object with vivid clarity and without distraction? Or is there
something you must do with this skill?

Śamatha, on its own, does not remove the afflictions like greed, hatred, jealousy, and the like. Merely remaining single-pointedly focused on an object will
not, by itself, result in liberation from samsara. But while śamatha alone will
not solve your problems, when it is used as an instrument with other things, it
is a highly effective tool.

For a Buddhist, the main purpose of achieving śamatha is to develop vipaśyanā, the wisdom that overcomes the afflictions. Śamatha is the foundation that supports the achievement of that goal. As we have discussed, there are two ways to go about removing the afflictions: temporarily or permanently. Temporary removal means to subdue the afflictions. To remove them permanently means to completely uproot them so they will never arise again. Temporary removal of the afflictions is effected on the mundane path; it is called "mundane" because it does not lead to complete liberation. Permanent removal of the afflictions depends on vipaśyanā; this is done on the supramundane path. It is called "supramundane" because it leads to liberation from samsara. These are the only two options; there is nothing higher. Asaṅga's *Śrāvaka Levels* makes this point:

> Thus the yogi who has achieved attention and has entered the small delight of elimination of the afflictions has two ways to progress and no others. What are these two? They are the mundane and supramundane.

When you have attained śamatha, you can choose to cultivate the insight of the mundane path or the insight of the supramundane path. Whichever you choose, continued practice of śamatha is important. You must practice again and again so that it becomes stronger and firmer. Building the strength of pliancy and the stability of your concentration will be helpful in combating the afflictions. This is true whether it is combined with the wisdom of either the mundane or supramundane paths. As you continue to practice and your stable attention and pliancy grow, you grow more skillful at recognizing the increasingly evident signs of śamatha and insight. Regarding this, Asaṅga says that the beginner who has just achieved śamatha must decide whether to pursue the mundane or supramundane path:

> In regard to this, the novice yogis who are endowed with attention reflect, "I shall proceed by either the mundane or the supramundane path," and they frequently apply themselves to this attention. Commensurate with how much they pass the days and nights in frequent practice, their pliancy and mental one-pointedness increase, expand, and are broadened. When their attention becomes firm, stable, and solid, when it engages pure objects at will, and when it is imbued with the signs associated with śamatha and vipaśyanā, at that time they strive at their practice along the mundane path or the supramundane path, whichever they wish to follow.

When striving to develop śamatha, your primary effort is nonanalytical concentration to acquire a stabilized and focused mind. After you achieve śamatha, you resume analytical meditation. And because your mental stabilization is strong, your analysis becomes better; you do not lose focus on the object of your examination. Earlier I used an analogy of a little fish in a large bowl of water. The fish is like vipaśyanā and the bowl of water is the foundation of śamatha. The fish can swim all around, examining the nature of things, without disturbing the stability of the water at all. Once you have śamatha, analytical meditation does not disturb your mental stabilization. That is a sign that you are ready to begin vipaśyanā meditation practice.

If you choose to engage in mundane vipaśyanā meditation at this point, your primary focus is on comparing your current state with the next higher level in terms of its relative calmness and coarseness. This temporarily subdues the afflictions associated with the lower level. For example, you compare the relative peace and ease of the first level of the form realm to the suffering and impurities of the desire realm. Through this kind of comparison, you subdue the desire-realm afflictions. Then you compare the coarseness of the first level of the form realm to the superior qualities of the second level of the form realm. This process continues up to the peak of cyclic existence, the highest meditative attainment of the formless realm. This is a part of vipaśyanā practice. After doing it for some time, like with the achievement of śamatha, a special physical and mental pliancy is achieved.

Or, once you achieve śamatha, you may choose to immediately proceed to the supramundane path. In this case, according to *Śrāvaka Levels*, you engage in vipaśyanā practice focusing on the sixteen aspects of the four noble truths. Each of the four truths has four attributes that you investigate individually with analytic meditation. The sixteen aspects of the four noble truths are explained from the perspective of the Vaibaṣīka school in texts like Vasubandhu's *Treasury of Knowledge*.

Sometimes people get confused about the mundane and supramundane paths. Part of the problem is the usage of the terms. Sometimes mundane and supramundane are used to distinguish the activities of āryas from non-āryas; sometimes they are used to distinguish the ultimate goals of the specific practices. In the first sense, any practice done by a non-ārya—someone who has not yet had a direct realization of emptiness and thus not yet attained the path of seeing—is mundane by definition. And any practice done after achieving the path of seeing through a direct realization of emptiness is an ārya-level path and hence is supramundane. In the sense being discussed here, however, the difference is the goal of liberation from samsara as opposed to the goal of a higher state within samsara. Here, even if you are not yet an ārya and are still on the path of accumulation or preparation, if you are meditating on the sixteen aspects of the four noble truths, or selflessness, emptiness, or any of these kinds of meditations on the actual path to liberation, it is called a supramundane path.

Tsongkhapa goes on to have a hypothetical questioner ask, "What type of person chooses the mundane path upon achievement of śamatha?" Tsongkhapa first addresses this with a quote from Asaṅga's *Śrāvaka Levels*:

> What persons proceed in this life solely by the mundane path and not by the supramundane path? There are the following four types of persons: (1) all those who are not Buddhists; (2) those who adhere to this [Buddhist] teaching but, while they have practiced śamatha well, are of dull faculties; (3) similarly, those who are of sharp faculties but whose roots of virtue have not matured; and (4) bodhisattvas who wish to achieve enlightenment in the future but not in this life.

As Asaṅga says here, there are non-Buddhist yogis who achieve śamatha and proceed along the mundane path. Because they have a strong belief in the self, they do not have any enthusiasm for the meditation on selflessness found on the supramundane path. As long as they hold to the idea of a permanent self, they do not practice vipaśyanā meditation that entails the wisdom realizing emptiness. Though they may make their way through the four levels of the form realm and up to the peak of cyclic existence in the formless realm, they will not remove the afflictions from the root. Their mundane path will only temporarily subdue the afflictions; they will not achieve liberation from samsara. Some non-Buddhists simply remain in nonanalytical śamatha meditation and enjoy that.

Second, there are Buddhist practitioners who have a very strong familiarization with śamatha meditation and enjoy it very much but their intellectual abilities are not very sharp. They haven't done much study or analytical meditation about the nature of reality in the past, and they therefore have difficulty understanding the profound and subtle meaning of selflessness and emptiness. As a result, they do not enjoy analytical meditation so much. When texts refer to people with dull faculties, they specifically mean that the person has not yet cultivated the capacity to understand the profound teachings. For such people the comparison meditations of the mundane path are easier.

A third type of person who may choose the mundane path is someone who is quite sharp mentally and may even have an intellectual understanding of selflessness and emptiness, but who does not have enough virtue or merit for a true, direct realization of emptiness. Such people are not able to rise to the supramundane path of an ārya in this lifetime. Even though they are able to cultivate an understanding of emptiness, they remain on the mundane path.

Finally, there are some bodhisattvas who want to obtain enlightenment but not in this lifetime. Since a bodhisattva has to accumulate a vast store of merit over a long time, he or she may choose to focus on accumulating merit in this life and proceed to the supramundane path leading directly to enlightenment in the next life. This is how Hinayana texts, such Vasubandhu's *Treasury of Knowledge*, describe the bodhisattva path. For example, according to the Vaibhāṣikas, Buddha Śakyamuni received teachings in Tuṣita heaven in his previous life. In his final samsaric rebirth he accomplished the final four paths, from the path of preparation up to enlightenment. Vasubandhu says in his *Treasury of Knowledge*:

> For our Teacher and the rhinoceros-like pratyekabuddhas,
> All paths from preparation to enlightenment
> Are on the last meditative stabilization.
> Prior to that are the aids to liberation [the path of accumulation].

According to the Sautrāntika, the other Hinayana school, the supramundane path is followed only in the last life of a bodhisattva destined for buddhahood. Buddha Śākyamuni engaged in three countless eons of accumulation of merit. After that he needed one more life to attain enlightenment. It was because of this long period during which he accumulated merit that he was able to traverse the four remaining paths and achieve enlightenment in one meditative session in his last life. It would have been premature for him to enter the supramundane path in one of those previous lifetimes. This is why a bodhisattva would choose to engage in the mundane path. Obviously, this Hinayana explanation of the bodhisattva path differs from Mahayana explanations found in treatises of masters like Asaṅga.

In short, śamatha is necessary as a basis for subduing the afflictions temporarily on the mundane path for Buddhist and non-Buddhist yogis as well as on the supramundane path for Buddhists. It is the foundation for both and a very important fundamental practice for all types of practitioners. Śamatha must be achieved before successfully proceeding in either of the two ways. This is a point of agreement for all Buddhists, both Hinayana and Mahayana. When it is said that Mahayana practitioners must achieve śamatha, this includes both those practicing the sutra vehicle and those practicing the tantric vehicle. The teachings on śamatha in tantric scriptures are, for the most part, similar to those of the sutra system. The main elements of training in mental stabilization are present: the five obstacles and eight antidotes, the way of relying on the antidotes, the nine stages, pliancy and its subtle bliss, and so forth. The primary difference is the object of meditation used by tantric yogis. For example, on the tantric path, the object may be the divine body of the meditational deity visualized in front of you, or you may visualize yourself as the deity. Other potential objects might be a letter, a mantra, or an implement held by the deity.

With this in mind, the *Sutra Unraveling the Intended Meaning* says that all Hinayana and Mahayana meditations are subsumed within the two categories of śamatha and vipaśyanā. Thus cultivating expertise in both is very important. You achieve śamatha first because that is the foundation for the direct realizations of vipaśyanā.

One finds many reasons to develop śamatha. For example, it makes attainment of the supranormal powers possible and enables you to take rebirth in the upper realms. Both Buddhist and non-Buddhist yogis seek such goals. But according to Tsongkhapa, the most important purpose of śamatha is its critical role in the generation of vipaśyanā. There are two types of vipaśyanā: common and uncommon. Common vipaśyanā is insight that is common to everybody—non-Buddhists and all Buddhists. This is the vipaśyanā that is developed through the analytical comparison-type meditations that result in the temporary subduing of the afflictions. Uncommon vipaśyanā is the wisdom that is able to remove the afflictions from the root; it is the way to achieve liberation from samsara. It is the direct realization of selflessness or emptiness. It is uncommon in that it is the unique teaching of the Buddha.

Although common vipaśyanā has many excellent qualities and can fulfill many goals, it isn't absolutely essential. You may gain supranormal powers and a feeling of peace. But even if you progress through the form and formless realms, no matter how long you practice with common vipaśyanā, it will not result in emancipation or the removal of afflictions. If you are looking for liberation from samsara, either for yourself or for all sentient beings, cultivating uncommon insight should be your primary concern. Uncommon vipaśyanā—a direct realization of emptiness—is necessary for achieving the goal of liberation. Therefore Mātṛceṭa's poem titled "Praise That Falls Short" from the first chapter of his *Praise in Honor of One Worthy of Honor* (*Varṇāha-varṇe-bhagavato-buddhasya-stotre-śakya-stava*) says:

> Those opposed to your teaching
> Are blinded by delusion.
> Even after venturing to the peak of cyclic existence,
> Suffering occurs again, and cyclic existence is maintained.
>
> Those who follow your teaching—
> Even if they do not achieve actual meditative absorption—

Turn away from cyclic existence,
While under the steady gaze of the eyes of Māra.

The one worthy of honor is, of course, the Buddha. "Those opposed to your teaching are blinded by delusion" refers to people who remain under the sway of ignorance because they do not cultivate uncommon vipaśyanā and thus are unable to remove the afflictions that are the root of suffering. They are "blinded" because they do not see with the wisdom understanding the ultimate truth; they do not realize selflessness or emptiness. Though they may follow the common path to the peak of cyclic existence, they remain in samsara. As long as there is ignorance, the afflictions will reemerge, and these practitioners will fall to a lower rebirth after death. It does not matter how much they have practiced śamatha, they will have to experience the misery of lower realms again.

The next four lines praise the teachings of the Buddha. "Those who follow your teachings" refers to practitioners who meditate on the four noble truths and so forth and eventually obtain the highest realization—the truth of emptiness. When the poem says, "even if they do not achieve actual meditative absorption," it is referring to those who are on the preparatory stage of the first meditative absorption of the form realm. At that point they choose to follow the supramundane path rather than doing the mundane comparison meditations that would result in achieving the actual first absorption of the form realm. Following the supramundane path does not necessitate this step. The practitioners referred to here begin the supramundane path on the preparatory stage of the first level of the form realm and bypass achievement of the actual first meditative absorption. Liberation from samsara does not require achievement of the actual first meditative absorption of the form realm.

When the poem says that such people "turn away from cyclic existence," it means that they achieve liberation. When they engage in supramundane vipaśyanā meditation, even if the "steady gaze of the eyes of Māra"—in other words, the afflictions—are trying to interrupt their practice, they will be unharmed because the power of this liberating insight removes the afflictions from the root. This is illustrated by the life story of the Buddha. At the cusp of his enlightenment under the bodhi tree, Māra tried many evil tricks to interrupt Śākyamuni Buddha's meditation. According to the story, every attempt he made to distract the Buddha failed. For example, Māra hurled weapons, but they turned into flowers before reaching Śākyamuni. Because the Buddha had developed perfect love and perfect wisdom, nothing could affect him. In the same way, once you have a realization of emptiness, you will not be harmed by Māra and will achieve freedom from samsara.

Tsongkhapa says that all of the accomplishments along the path to liberation depend up the achievement of śamatha. His contemporaries knew what he meant, but modern readers need a bit more explanation. When the Buddha taught the śrāvakas, he said that on the path to arhatship, there are four fruits, or results, achieved along the way. Each of the fruits corresponds to a specific degree of removal of afflictions from the root. The four fruits are: stream winner, once-returner, nonreturner, and the actual fruit of arhatship. These fit into the context of the five paths according to the śrāvakas. The first two paths, the path of accumulation and the path of preparation, are preparatory in that they do not include a direct realization of selflessness. The last three—the paths of seeing, meditation, and no more learning—are called *ārya* paths because they entail a direct realization of selflessness. All four of the fruits are ārya paths. The stream-winner fruit is achieved at the end of the path of seeing. Stream winners have removed the grossest, or biggest, afflictions of the desire realm and the upper realms. These gross-level afflictions are referred to as "the afflictions abandoned on the path of seeing."

In addition to categorizing the afflictions as big, medium, and small, they can be described as either constructed or innate. The grossest, biggest afflictions are constructed because they are grounded in erroneous philosophical or religious views. For example, a religious system might propound that there is a permanent soul; this tenet influences the followers of that religion to strongly grasp that view. Such an afflicted view is constructed through a religious or philosophical system of reasoning. It is not innate and is therefore grosser.

Innate afflictions are a bit different. Unlike the constructed afflictions that arise from holding erroneous philosophical views, innate afflictions are subtler. Everybody—even animals, insects, and children—has these innate afflictions without being aware of them. You do not need a dogmatic philosophical or religious view to have desire, hatred, an egotistic view of self, and so forth. Even after you achieve a direct realization of emptiness and so are on the path of seeing, the innate afflictions are not removed immediately. Long periods of meditation on emptiness combined with other methods are required. According to texts like Vasubandhu's *Treasury of Knowledge* as well as Mahayana path-system scriptures like Maitreya's *Ornament for Clear Knowledge*, the innate afflictions are divided into nine levels. We have already discussed how this works. To recap, the first three are the most rough; these are categorized as big-big, big-intermediate, and big-small. The same type of threefold division is applied to the intermediate and small levels of innate afflictions: intermediate-big, intermediate-intermediate, intermediate-small, and so forth. So there are nine levels of afflictions associated with the desire realm, nine with each of the four levels of the form realm, and nine with each of the four levels of the formless realm. All told there are eighty-one innate afflictions in the threefold world system.

After an ārya has a direct realization of ultimate truth, he or she works to remove the innate afflictions. The gradual path removes them one by one through eighty-one steps. First you remove the innate afflictions of the nine levels of the desire realm, then each of the nine of the first level of the form realm, and so forth on up through the peak of cyclic existence, the highest level of the formless realm. After all eighty-one innate afflictions are removed, you achieve arhatship. Those who have removed the three grossest and three intermediate desire-realm afflictions attain the fruit of once-returners. They will achieve arhatship with one more rebirth at most. It is possible that they will not need to return at all, but at most once-returners will have one more samsaric rebirth in the desire realm. Of course, if such a yogi is a bodhisattva, he or she can willingly take rebirth in the desire realm in order to be of benefit to sentient beings. But they will no longer be compelled to take rebirth due to the power of karma and afflictions. If a once-returner dies before achieving arhatship, he or she may be born in the upper realms until finishing that achievement. When all nine afflictions of the desire realm are removed, the yogi is described as a nonreturner. The Buddha did not distinguish any other fruit between that point and the removal of the remaining seventy-two upper-realm afflictions that results in arhatship. After the achievement of nonreturner status, the next fruit is that of arhatship.

There is another way to eliminate the afflictions that is faster, but it requires more skill. This approach removes the afflictions simultaneously. "Simultaneous" does not mean that the eighty-one innate afflictions are removed all at once. It means that they are removed in groups of nine at a time. First the biggest innate afflictions from all nine levels are removed together. In other words, the biggest of the gross-level afflictions of the desire realm, four form-realm levels, and four formless-realm levels are removed at once. Then the big-intermediate ones are all removed at once, and so forth. So a practitioner who utilizes this method progresses through nine steps, removing nine afflictions at a time, culminating in arhatship. Yogis who take this simultaneous approach will go directly from the preparatory stage of the first meditative absorption directly to arhatship, because they remove the last and subtlest of the innate afflictions of all nine levels simultaneously. Because the smallest of the small desire-realm afflictions is removed at the same time as all the small-small afflictions of all the form- and formless-realm levels, the practitioner skips the absorptions of the upper realms. This yogi will not achieve the fruits of once-returner and nonreturner because he or she goes directly from stream winner to arhat.

Even those practicing highest yoga tantra cannot achieve their goal if they have not developed śamatha. There are two stages of highest yoga tantra: the generation stage and the completion stage. Śamatha is achieved during the generation stage. Deep single-pointed concentration is required for a clear and vivid meditation of all the minute details of the mandala, deities, and so forth.

In summary, all of the fruits of the path depend upon the cultivation of śamatha. Both the gradual and simultaneous systems for removing the afflictions are only possible on the foundation of the stable mind of śamatha. If you have not achieved śamatha, you will not be able to cultivate vipaśyanā. Without that, neither of the two approaches to arhatship is possible, because afflictions are only removed from the root on the basis of a direct realization of emptiness.

(3') A SPECIFIC PRESENTATION OF THE WAY TO PROCEED ALONG THE MUNDANE PATH

This section explains the way to practice the mundane path. There are two topics here:

- (a") The need to achieve śamatha before proceeding on the path bearing the aspects of calmness and coarseness
- (b") On the basis of śamatha, the way to freedom from the attachment of the desire realm

(a") THE NEED TO ACHIEVE ŚAMATHA BEFORE PROCEEDING ON THE PATH BEARING THE ASPECTS OF CALMNESS AND COARSENESS

To proceed on the mundane path successfully, you must first attain śamatha. Once śamatha is achieved, you decide whether to proceed along the mundane path or supramundane path. If you choose the mundane path, vipaśyanā meditation does not analyze the truth of emptiness as it would on the supramundane path. Here, on the mundane path, your analysis is the means to subdue attachment. It involves an analysis and comparison of the characteristics and qualities of the desire realm as well as those of the four levels of each of the form and formless realms.

When you have accomplished the ninth stage in the development of śamatha, and are on the preparatory stage of the first level of the form realm, you are called a "beginner at attention." At that point you have not yet begun to do the comparison meditation of the desire realm and first level of the form realm. To make this comparison, you need to study what the desire realm is and what its qualities are. You also analyze the characteristics of the first stage of the form realm. For example, what is wrong with the desire realm? What mental and physical conditions characterize a desire-realm rebirth? What is its general nature? Compared to the misery, ugliness, shortness of life, and so forth of the desire realm, the first level of the form realm is quite subtle, calm, and peaceful. When you turn your attention to discerning these characteristics, you are called a "beginner at purifying afflictions."

The point Tsongkhapa emphasizes here is that you must develop and increase your stabilization beyond the ninth stage and attain actual śamatha in order to progress along the mundane path. Six progressive levels of attention will be required to subdue the mental afflictions of the desire realm and attain actual śamatha and the first meditative absorption of the form realm. (These attentions will be discussed in detail in the next section.) Here, the point is that only when this process of six levels of attention is complete and all nine desire-realm afflictions are subdued do you achieve the actual first part of the meditative absorption of the form realm. Until then you are just on the preparatory stage of the first meditative absorption. Since you can only achieve the actual first meditative absorption from the basis of the preparatory first meditative absorption, and that requires the achievement of the ninth stage of the development of śamatha, even progress on the mundane path requires śamatha.

(b") On the basis of śamatha, the way to freedom from the attachment of the desire realm

Since śamatha is the foundation upon which vipaśyanā can be cultivated, and vipaśyanā is the antidote to the afflictions, once you have achieved śamatha, you should cultivate one of the two types of vipaśyanā: mundane or supramundane. Obviously, if vipaśyanā is needed merely to remove the afflictions of the desire realm temporarily, it goes without saying that it is necessary for removing from the root the afflictions that keep you bound in samsara as well as the knowledge obstacles that prevent you from attaining buddhahood.

Sometimes people say that insight, or vipaśyanā, removes afflictions from the root while śamatha suppresses them temporarily. Tsongkhapa makes it clear that this is not entirely correct. Śamatha alone does not fully suppress the afflictions, even temporarily, without being combined with mundane insight. Explications in which śamatha is said to suppress the afflictions include the insight of the mundane path in the explanation of śamatha. In the present context, Tsongkhapa stresses the necessity of śamatha for any type of vipaśyanā. To illustrate, Tsongkhapa explains the vipaśyanā of the mundane path—specifically, how to gain freedom from the attachment of the desire realm. This method involves six types of attention as an antidote to the attachment of the desire realm. The *Śrāvaka Levels* says:

> For the sake of freedom from the desire realm, diligent yogis use the seven types of attention and subsequently achieve their freedom. The seven types of attention are: the attention of the (1) discernment of characteristics, (2) arisal from belief, (3) isolation, (4) delight or withdrawal, (5) analysis, (6) final application, and (7) the result of final application.

Although the *Śrāvaka Levels* suggests that there are seven attentions, not six, Tsongkhapa explains that the text is saying that the first six are causal and result in the seventh, which is the actual first meditative absorption of the form realm. These six types of attention are all analytical meditative states. It is important to note that no matter how definite your discernment of the faults of the desire realm and of the good qualities of the first level of the form realm, until you focus upon that analytical knowledge with śamatha, you will not be able to suppress the afflictions. And no matter how much you cultivate śamatha, if you do not analyze with discernment, you will not be able to eliminate the afflictions. You need both śamatha and vipaśyanā to be able to subdue the afflictions of the desire realm. The six attentions are antidotes to the three levels of desire-realm afflictions—big, intermediate, and small—but none can be applied without first having achieved śamatha.

The first attention, *discernment of characteristics*, is knowing the qualities and characteristics of the desire realm and the first level of the form realm. This requires study and research, because this knowledge does not come about naturally. This is still a preparatory level, and the afflictions are not yet subdued. It is not a direct antidote. It is not yet actual insight. First, you look at the qualities and characteristics individually, and then you summarize the general coarseness of the desire realm in contrast to the general calm peacefulness of the first level of the form realm.

The second attention is called *arisal of belief*. While the first attention is primarily study and examination of the specific characteristics of the desire realm and first level of the form realm, the second attention accustoms you to these qualities through meditation. The first attention includes some meditation, but the second attention is primarily meditation. As your familiarity deepens through meditation, recognition of the faults of the desire realm and good qualities of the first meditative absorption of the form realm become integrated into your core beliefs. Although this meditation is not focusing on selflessness, the *Śrāvaka Levels* makes it clear that this type of analytical meditation is a type of vipaśyanā.

The first two attentions are said to correspond to the first two of the five paths in that the first attention is similar to the path of accumulation and the second attention is similar to the path of preparation. In the context of these first two types of attention you cultivate śamatha and vipaśyanā sequentially. First you repeatedly analyze the qualities of the desire realm and the first level of the form realm. Then you make the conclusion of that analysis the object of your śamatha meditation. Nevertheless, these two are still not antidotes to the afflictions belonging to the desire realm. Both are of the preparatory level.

On the basis of your familiarity with the alternating meditations on the second attention, the third attention, called *isolation*, arises. This is the direct antidote to the gross level of afflictions in the desire realm. In other words, you become isolated, or free, from the gross mental afflictions of the desire realm.

The fourth attention is called *delight*, or *withdrawal*. This is the antidote to the intermediate level of desire-realm afflictions. Achieving freedom from the gross and intermediate levels of affliction produces delight or joy. Thus, this is called the attention of delight. However, getting too overjoyed may bring about the danger of distraction. Therefore a bit of withdrawal from the extreme delight is also a characteristic of this attention.

The fifth attention is called *analysis*. Since the gross and intermediate afflictions of the desire realm were subdued with the fourth attention, all that remains are the subtle ones. In postmeditation sessions, because none of the gross or even intermediate-level afflictions are present, your situation seems really good. The subtle afflictions are not noticeable, so you may be tempted to think that all the afflictions have been removed. Therefore this is a time that requires analysis of whether you have truly achieved the actual first meditative absorption. This analysis can involve examining objects, situations, and places where your attachment was previously very powerful. It is like testing yourself; you check to see whether some attachment still exists. This analysis will help you to rid yourself of the arrogance that mistakenly assumes that you are completely free of desire-realm afflictions. This prepares you to go on and deal with the subtlest afflictions.

The sixth attention is called *final application*. It also utilizes an alternation of śamatha and mundane vipaśyanā. This attention removes the smallest, most subtle afflictions of the desire realm. Because it is the direct antidote to the last of the desire-realm afflictions, it is the immediate cause of freedom from the desire realm and achieving the actual first meditative absorption of the form realm.

The seventh, *the result of final application*, is the state of the actual first meditative absorption. It refers to the achievement of the goal, whereas the first six are the method. Among the six causal attentions, three of them are direct antidotes to the afflictions: the third, fourth, and sixth. The other attentions are preparatory to those.

Becoming thoroughly familiar with the faults of the desire realm and good qualities of the first level of the form realm is a very powerful antidote to counteract and keep down the afflictions. When the desire-realm afflictions are removed in this way, it is like the afflictions are in a deep sleep. They are not functioning or manifest on the surface, but they remain latent. Even though the afflictions are not destroyed and you have not become free of samsara, this method protects you from the afflictions during this lifetime. Very occasionally circumstances may allow the afflictions to arise, but generally they will not. Even though the afflictions are not completely destroyed from the root, at the time of death you may achieve rebirth in an upper realm.

This method of the six attentions is used in a similar step-by-step process to successively remove the afflictions of each of the upper realms. When you have achieved the actual first meditative absorption of the form realm, you use the same techniques to compare the faults of that level with the more pleasant situation of the second meditative absorption. This is done to successively subdue the afflictions all the way up through the third formless realm, called *nothingness*. The faults of the third level of the formless realm can be compared to the more subtle and pleasant qualities of the fourth formless realm, called the *peak of cyclic existence*. But as there is nothing higher or better in samsara than the peak of cyclic existence, there is nothing better to compare it to, and so this comparative method cannot eliminate your attachment to that state.

In summary, the mundane path cannot completely free you from samsara. The mundane path can suppress seventy-two of the eighty-one afflictions of samsara—that is, those of the desire realm, the four levels of the form realm, and the first three levels of the formless realm. It cannot free you from the last nine afflictions of the peak of cyclic existence. The mundane path enables you to achieve the levels of the form and formless realms and obtain the five types of supranormal knowledge. But it is not a cause for liberation.

Because the mundane path is common to both Buddhists and non-Buddhists, you do not need to receive instructions that are exclusively or uniquely Buddhist. Nevertheless, if you gain a thorough understanding of what is entailed on this path, it can help you to eliminate incorrect ways of doing other Buddhist practices.

Not only will the mundane path not liberate you from samsara, it actually binds you to samsara. Although the comparative meditations lessen your attachment to lower realms, they maintain and increase your attachment to upper realms, which are also part of samsara. In other words, the mundane path causes you to create the karma for rebirth in upper samsaric realms. Therefore you will not achieve true satisfaction through śamatha practice alone nor through its union with mundane vipaśyanā. For ultimate release from the suffering of samsara, you must strive for the supramundane vipaśyanā that knows emptiness directly.

Tsongkhapa relied upon many sources for his explanation of śamatha. He compiled the essence of these important teachings in this chapter of the *Lamrim Chenmo* so that we would have reliable instructions to help us achieve it. He urges us to learn from the following authoritative texts directly: The Perfection of Wisdom sutras teach the profound meaning of emptiness and also explain how to achieve śamatha by way of the nine stages. The great Madhyamaka exegete Kamalaśīla explains śamatha in accordance with those sutras in his three *Stages of Meditation*. The intended meaning of the Perfection of Wisdom sutras is expanded by Maitreya in his *Ornament for the Mahayana Sutras*. Asaṅga summarizes and expands upon Maitreya's teachings and the sutras in many works, such as *Bodhisattva Levels, Compendium of Knowledge*, and *Compendium of Determinations*. And in *Śrāvaka Levels* Asaṅga goes into extensive detail on the way to develop śamatha and vipaśyanā as indicated in his *Compendium of Bases* (*Vastu-saṃgrahaṇī*). Ratnākaraśānti's *Instructions for the Perfection of Wisdom* is also a principal source for these teachings. And the teachings on the five faults or obstacles to achieving śamatha and the eight antidotes that address them are taught principally in Maitreya's *Separation of the Middle from the Extremes*.

Some practitioners of śamatha are not familiar with the attentions and meditations that are discussed here. Some may have briefly skimmed some famous texts and studied a little, so they have heard the terms, but they do not thoroughly understand them. Without a proper understanding of these subjects, you will fail to see their purpose. When you do practice, you will have many misconceptions about the practice and the realizations you may achieve. Only when you study the various authoritative sources and teachings will you know how to proceed most effectively and avoid mistakes on the path that cultivates śamatha. From understanding these teachings, you will not fall into the trap of thinking the ninth stage is not a desire-realm mind. You will not confuse the spontaneity and concentration of the ninth stage to be anything other than what it is. You certainly will not believe you have achieved the completion stage of highest yoga tantra. You will not mistake a mundane single-pointed nonanalytical concentration for a profound nondiscursive wisdom realizing emptiness directly. Nor will you be confused about terms like objectless, signless, and empty.

Tsongkhapa concludes his discussion of śamatha with advice in the form of a poem:

> Profound are the descriptions of the stages for achieving
>   concentration
> Well taught in the sutras and the great commentaries.
> Those of little intelligence do not precisely comprehend them,
> Projecting the faults of their own minds upon others.
>
> Thinking, "There are no instructions there for sustaining
>   nondiscursive awareness,"
> They do not look for them in texts that have them,
> And they think they have found them
> After diligently seeking them where they do not exist.
>
> Such people fail to distinguish between
> Even the concentrations of Buddhists and non-Buddhists.
> What need, then, is there to mention
> Their precisely distinguishing the differences
> Between concentrations of the Mahayana and Hinayana
> And of the Vajrayāna and Pāramitāyāna!
> Seeing this situation, I have explained in simple words
> The way to sustain concentration as taught in the classics.
>
> O friends who have trained for many years in the classics,
> Do not discard your precious gem
> In favor of others' costume jewelry,
> But recognize you have something of great value!
>
> There is nothing apart from the meaning of the instructions
> In the treatises you have studied. Knowing this,
> The Master of Sages said, "There is bliss in the forest
> For those of great learning." Analyze these words.

May even those meditators who place their hopes in sheer
    determination,
Though they have not first acquired a proper discernment
Of how to practice and the measure of success
For the path of a fully nondiscursive, focused serenity,
Come to know precisely the way to sustain
Meditation in reliance on the learned.
Otherwise, there is less harm if they take for a while
A refreshing break from the teachings of the Conqueror.

This explanation of the way to achieve serenity
Using the treatises of Maitreya and Asaṅga
Is for the sake of preserving for a long time
The teachings of the Conqueror.

The first stanza states that instructions on the practice of śamatha were well taught by the Buddha and thoroughly explained in the great commentaries. However, some people think that there are no authoritative teachings on how to practice śamatha in these scriptures and commentaries. They believe that there are special instructions, a few singular words of advice, which will be all they need. If they get these special instructions—these few secret words with dynamic power—they think they will not need to put any effort into learning the great texts. They ignore the authoritative sources, look elsewhere for instructions, and are misled. You should not think that way. The teachings in the great scriptures are the special instructions. When those of little intelligence ignore those instructions, do not understand them, and do not attain the results that they desire, it is certainly not the fault of the deep and profound scriptures and commentaries. It is the fault of these mistaken practitioners' own minds.

Many of those who do not study these excellent teachings do not distinguish between the way Buddhists and non-Buddhists present the path to śamatha. They think it does not matter whether they are following a Buddhist or non-Buddhist path and get quite confused. If they do not understand the common distinctions between Buddhists and non-Buddhists, how will they distinguish between the Mahayana and Hinayana, or between the Vajrayāna and Pāramitāyāna? Each of these approaches has distinct techniques and viewpoints that are important and should not be mixed up. Without proper study, it is impossible to properly understand these things. Then confusion will be brought into your practice. Upon seeing all this confusion, Tsongkhapa drew forth the essence of the instructions of authoritative Indian masters and presented them in straightforward language so that they could be easily understood.

Now that you have found a reliable source of instruction on śamatha, you should study it well. After you have studied you must use these teachings. When you are practicing, refer to them. These teachings are not for scholastic edification; they are to be used in practice. Therefore, Tsongkhapa urges those who have studied the great Indian treatises and scriptures for many years not to abandon them when they begin meditation practice. Some people think that they must jettison everything they studied if they want to achieve realizations. That is incorrect. Tsongkhapa says that would be like trading a real jewel—the excellent teachings in the classic texts—for costume jewelry—a misunderstanding of the path. He urges those who have studied to value the great jewel of their learning by integrating what they have learned into their practice.

Tsongkhapa quotes from the *Individual Liberation Sutra* (*Prātimokṣa-sūtra*). There the Buddha says, "There is a bliss in the forest for those of great learning." This means that when people who have studied for a long time go to a solitary place to meditate, they will find great peace and bliss. This is because they have everything they need. They know and understand the teachings. Therefore they can engage in fruitful practice immediately; they have no hesitation, doubt, or other difficulties. In contrast, when someone who has not studied and does not understand the teachings goes into retreat, they will not have a pleasant or productive experience. When they get to their hermitage, they will not know what to do. They will have no confidence. They will be hesitant, and everything they do will be uncomfortable.

As I've discussed, there are people who have heard that śamatha is non-discursive, so they try to stop every kind of mental activity whatsoever. They regard all thought as the enemy and try to abolish it when it arises. Believing this is the correct method is the result of not properly understanding the practice or the measurement of real śamatha. Although there may be some special instances where cessation of thought is useful, ignorantly doing it for a long time is a great obstacle to attaining positive results.

Tsongkhapa prays that those who have sincere determination but fall into such misconceptions come to rely on learned and skillful teachers. Then they can learn the nature of the practice, the goals, obstacles, antidotes, and so forth. If this does not happen, Tsongkhapa says it is better to take a break from practice than to reinforce bad habits with repetition. Instead of being helpful, incorrect practice can be harmful.

The Buddha taught people how to achieve spiritual goals according to their predispositions and mental capacities. Accordingly, if you want to exert great effort toward a spiritual goal, you should take the Buddha's advice. Exert effort to learn those instructions and apply them. You will not achieve your goal even if you spend your entire life working hard in a misdirected way.

Tsongkhapa based his explanation of śamatha and the way to achieve it on the teachings of the Buddha and the way the Buddha's teachings were explained by Maitreya and Asaṅga, among others. He summarized those teachings in the *Lamrim Chenmo* so that they could benefit as many people as possible and endure for a long time. His motivation was to provide reliable teachings that will help people actually achieve śamatha. Please work hard to study these teachings, and then put your understanding into practice.

This concludes the section on śamatha in the *Lamrim Chenmo*. The vipaśyanā section that follows is extremely difficult. It requires its own volume.

Appendix: Outline of the Text

THE OUTLINE USED in this commentary was created by Tsongkhapa to organize his massive text. We have used the same outline so that readers of this commentary can refer to the relevant sections of the original Tibetan and the English translation of the *Lamrim Chenmo*. To make it as easy as possible for readers to use this commentary along with the English translation of the *Lamrim Chenmo*, the Lamrim Chenmo Translation Committee and Snow Lion Publications graciously gave us permission to use their format of the outline headings. We also follow their practice of including the outline for each chapter's content at the beginning of the chapter. While our translation of some terms differs from the English translation of the *Lamrim Chenmo*, these differences are minimal and should not cause any confusion.

In this appendix, two sets of numbers follow each outline topic. The first number refers the reader to the page on which this topic is discussed in this book. The second number refers the reader to the page in the edition of the Tibetan text published in Xining by the mTsho sngon People's Press (1985) and reprinted in Dharamsala by Ganden Bar Nying (1991). To find the page number in the English translation of the *Lamrim Chenmo*, *The Great Treatise on the Stages of the Path to Enlightenment*, the reader should refer to appendix 1 of that work.

CHAPTER 1
ŚAMATHA AND VIPAŚYANĀ

2" In particular, how to train in the last two perfections [9, 468]
    (a) The benefits of cultivating śamatha and vipaśyanā [10, 468]
    (b) How śamatha and vipaśyanā include all states of meditative concentration [16, 470]
    (c) The nature of śamatha and vipaśyanā [17, 471]
    (d) Why it is necessary to cultivate both [19, 475]
    (e) How to be certain about their order [30, 480]

CHAPTER 2
PREPARING FOR ŚAMATHA MEDITATION

CHAPTER 3
FOCUSING YOUR MIND

CHAPTER 4
DEALING WITH LAXITY AND EXCITEMENT

CHAPTER 5
ATTAINING ŚAMATHA

CHAPTER 6
ŚAMATHA AS PART OF THE PATH

Glossary

Abhidharma (*chos mngon pa*). One of three major sections of the Buddhist canon, containing texts that systemize and classify the essence of the Buddha's teachings found in the sutras. This body of commentarial texts is encyclopedic in that it deals with Buddhist ontology, psychology, cosmology, the operation of karma and affliction, the path to liberation, and the nature of its stages and attainments.

afflictions (*nyon mongs*; Skt: *kleśa*). *See* mental afflictions.

arhat (*dgra bcom pa*). A person who has attained nirvana, the final goal of the Hinayana path.

ārya (*'phags pa*). A person who has achieved a direct realization of emptiness, thus technically designating them as "superior" (*ārya*) in the spiritual sense. One who has attained the path of seeing.

attentions. *See* seven attentions of the mundane path of insight; four attentions.

balanced placement (*mnyam par 'jog pa*). Equipoise. The ninth stage of development of śamatha. It does not require effort to remain focused on the object of meditation. *See also* nine stages of śamatha.

bliss of śamatha (*gzhi gnas kyi bde ba*). The bliss experienced when actual śamatha is achieved. There is no discomfort because the body is in complete harmony with the mind.

bodhicitta (*byang chub kyi sems*). The altruistic mind of enlightenment. The desire to become a buddha in order to benefit other sentient beings caught in the misery of samsara.

calm abiding. *See* śamatha.

close placement (*nye bar 'jog pa*). The fourth stage in the development of śamatha. After attention is replaced on the object meditation, particular effort is made to remain there. *See also* nine stages of śamatha.

complete pacification (*rnam par zhi bar byed pa*). The seventh stage in the development of śamatha. The mind can immediately pacify whatever faults arise through completely developed mindfulness and introspection. *See also* nine stages of śamatha.

concentration. *See* meditative stabilization; samādhi.

continuous placement (*rgyun du 'jog pa*). The second stage in the development of śamatha. There are short periods of continued abiding on the object. *See also* nine stages of śamatha.

desire realm (*'dod khams*; Skt: *kāmadhātu*). All beings in the samsaric world live in one of three realms: the desire, form, or formless realms. Particular types of afflictions dominate each realm; the predominant affliction in the desire realm is desire or attachment—in particular the craving for the sensual pleasures.

eight antidotes. These eight are used to counteract the five faults in the practice of śamatha. (1) Faith, (2) aspiration, (3) perseverance, and (4) mental pliancy combat the first of the five faults. (5) Mindfulness combats the second, (6) introspection combats the third, (7) applying the antidotes combats the fourth, and (8) not applying the antidotes counteracts the fifth.

emptiness (*stong pa nyid*; Skt: *śūnyatā*). Emptiness or suchness is the ultimate nature of all phenomena: the absence of inherent existence.

equanimity (*btang snyoms*; Skt. *upekṣā*). There are three different uses of the term equanimity. The first (*tshor ba btang snyoms*) is being neutral or impartial with regards to feelings such as pleasant or unpleasant. The second, as one of the four immeasurables (*tshad med btang snyoms*), is an equal feeling for all beings without discrimination or bias. The third is in the context of śamatha meditation (*'du byed btang snyoms*) and refers to the times when there is no need to apply antidotes to laxity or distraction because the mind is engaging its object effortlessly and naturally.

excitement (*rgod pa*; Skt: *auddhatya*). The distracted, desirous state that disturbs one's meditative stability. According to Asaṅga's *Compendium of Knowledge*, "It is an unquiet state of mind, considered a derivative of attachment, which pursues pleasant objects and acts as an impediment to śamatha."

faith (*dad pa*; Skt: *śraddhā*). A special kind of trust and conviction that is built upon knowledge.

final application (*sbyor ba mthar thug pa*). The sixth of the seven attentions of the mundane path of insight. This attention uses an alternation of śamatha and mundane vipaśyanā to remove the smallest, most subtle afflictions of the desire realm. Because it is the direct antidote to the last of the desire-realm afflictions, it is the immediate cause of freedom from the desire realm and achieving the actual first meditative absorption of the form realm. *See also* seven attentions of the mundane path of insight.

five aggregates (*phung po lnga*; Skt: *pañcaskandha*). Form, feeling, discrimination, compositional factors, and consciousness. Ignorance causes us to grasp at these impermanent collections as a unitary, inherently existent self. This self-grasping is a fundamental cause of our perpetual suffering in cyclic existence.

five faults in the practice of śamatha. The five faults are laziness (*le lo*), forgetting the instructions (*gdams ngag brjed pa*), laxity and excitement (*bying rgod*), non-application of the antidotes when obstacles occur (*'du mi byed pa*), and mistaken application of antidotes although no obstacles are present (*'du byed pa*). They are combatted by the eight antidotes.

five paths (*lam lnga*). The five consecutive paths culminating in nirvana or enlightenment. These consist of: (1) the path of accumulation (*tshogs lam*), on which one begins to amass the accumulation of merit and wisdom; (2) the path of preparation (*sbyor lam*), on which one prepares for a direct realization of emptiness; (3) the path of seeing (*mthong lam*), on which one sees emptiness directly and nonconceptually for the first time; (4) the path of meditation (*sgom lam*), on which one continuously familiarizes oneself with the emptiness that was initially directly cognized on the path of seeing; (5) the path of no further training (*mi slob lam*), in which there is no longer any need to abandon further obstacles or develop new realizations. At this point the final fruit of one's spiritual journey is achieved: those who followed the Mahayana path attain complete buddhahood, while those who followed the Hinayana path attain arhatship.

five omnipresent secondary consciousnesses. *See* secondary consciousnesses.

force of… *See* six forces.

form realm (*gzugs khams*; Skt: *rūpadhātu*). Along with the desire realm and the formless realm, this is one of the three realms of samsaric existence. Its basic divisions are the four concentrations or meditative absorptions (*bsam gtan*; Skt: *dhyāna*). Each absorption has a preparatory stage. The actual absorption is attained after sustained practice on its associated preparatory stage.

formless realm (*gzugs med khams*; Skt: *arūpadhātu*). Along with the desire realm and the form realm, this is one of the three realms of samsaric existence. It has four levels called the *four formless absorptions* (*gzugs med snyoms 'jug*; Skt: *samāpatti*). Because the beings in this realm do not possess obstructive form, the formless realm is without a physical dimension.

four attentions (*yid la byed pa bzhi*). The types of mental engagement used on the nine stages of the development of śamatha: (1) tight focus (*bsgrims te 'jug pa*) corresponds to the first two of the nine stages and refers to a very tight way of maintaining focus on the object of meditation; (2) intermittent focus (*bar du 'chad cing 'jug pa*) corresponds to the third through seventh stages and is marked by an increasing degree of continuity of focus; (3) uninterrupted focus (*skabs su 'chad pa med par 'jug pa*) corresponds to the eighth stage and is characterized by long periods of meditative concentration unbroken by laxity or excitement; (4) spontaneous focus (*lhun gyis grub par 'jug pa*) is an effortless uninterrupted focus of the mind on its object corresponding to the ninth stage, balanced placement.

four meditative absorptions. *See* form realm; meditative absorption.

four fruits (*'bras bu bzhi*): stream winner (*rgyun du zhugs pa*), once-returner (*lan cig phyir 'ong ba*), nonreturner (*phyir mi 'ong ba*), and arhat (*dgra bcom pa*). These are levels of spiritual attainment. *See individual entries.*

four formless absorptions. *See* formless realm.

four immeasurables (*tshad med bzhi*; Skt: *apramāṇa*). Also known as the *four limitless thoughts*: (1) compassion—thinking how wonderful it would be if all sentient beings were free from all forms of misery; (2) love—thinking how wonderful it would be if they all possessed the highest happiness; (3) equanimity—thinking how wonderful it would be if all sentient beings felt equanimity toward each other, without hatred or attachment; and (4) joy—thinking how wonderful it is that some beings have already obtained the highest happiness, some have intermediate happiness, and some at least have some small pleasure and rejoicing in their happiness and good fortune. The virtue of this way of thinking is measureless, or limitless.

generic image. A concept. *See* universal.

insight (*lhag mthong*; Skt: *vipaśyanā*). Wisdom that knows reality. It is cultivated through discerning analysis and then stabilized within meditation. There are two types of insight: mundane and supramundane.

intermittent focus. *See* four attentions.

introspection (*shes bzhin*; Skt: *samprajñāna*). A mental factor that, like a spy, constantly observes what is happening within one's mind-body continuum. It is the tool that observes the way the mind is holding its meditational object and determines whether it is abiding on the object properly or not. Sometimes translated as "vigilance."

knowledge obstacles (*shes sgrib*; Skt: *jñeyāvaraṇa*). Subtle propensities for self-grasping that remain after the removal of the mental afflictions. These obscurations block attainment of omniscience.

lamrim (*lam rim*). Literally, "stages of the path." The lamrim method is a progressive system of teachings and meditations organized to lead the practitioner from the very beginning of the spiritual path all the way to buddhahood.

laxity (*bying ba*; Skt: *laya*). "Mental sinking." A weakening of the mind's apprehension of its object. A lack of clarity of the focal object and a sinking of the mind in an excessively internal focus. It has both gross and subtle forms. *Subtle laxity* is a slight loosening of the mind's hold and a vagueness as the mind sinks into itself. Since it never loses the object, it can be confused for deep meditation and thereby become a major obstacle to śamatha. *Gross laxity*, on the other hand, is a coarser dullness or darkness that may even lead to falling asleep. Laxity can be either virtuous or neutral but never nonvirtuous.

lethargy (*rmugs pa*; Skt. *styāna*). A heaviness of body and mind that renders them unserviceable for śamatha practice; a lassitude due not to physical exhaustion but to a foggy boredom and mental darkness. It can be a cause for laxity but should not be confused with laxity. Lethargy of the body is when it accompanies one of the five sense consciousnesses, where it assists all the primary and secondary mental afflictions. With subtle and coarse forms, it can be either neutral or nonvirtuous.

Madhyamaka (*dbu ma*). A Mahayana school of philosophy based on the writings of Nāgārjuna. It is called the "Middle Way" school because it teaches the doctrine of emptiness (*śūnyatā*) as a middle position between the extremes of nihilism and inherent existence. *See also* Prāsaṅgika Madhyamaka.

major and minor marks. *See* thirty-two major and eighty minor marks of a buddha.

meditative absorption (*bsam gtan*; Skt: *dhyāna*). There are four meditative absorptions of the form realm. The actual first meditative absorption is marked by the achievement of the single-pointed focus and pliancy of śamatha. *See also* form realm.

meditative stabilization. A general term for the cultivation of meditative focus. Also, the name used for the fifth of the six perfections. *See also* meditative absorption; perfections; samādhi; śamatha.

meditational deity (*yi dam*). A tantric form of a buddha that a practitioner worships as well as strives to become. The deity guides the practitioner along the path to enlightenment; the practitioner's subsequent enlightenment will be experienced in the form and nature of that yidam.

mental afflictions (*nyon mongs*; Skt: *kleśa*). There are two types of afflictions: innate (*lhan skyes kyi nyon mongs pa*) and intellectually acquired (*kun btags pa'i nyon mongs pa*). Innate mental afflictions are obscuring mental states, such as desire, hostility, and ignorance, that are the obstacles to emancipation. These nonvirtuous mental states obscure the mind from seeing reality in its true nature and motivate actions (*karma*) that cause one to continue to be born in cyclic existence. Intellectually acquired mental afflictions are learned wrong views based on philosophical tenets. Secondary afflictions (*nye nyon*) are subtle mental factors that accompany the egotistic view but may be ethically neutral. In the practice of śamatha, these include such mental factors as distraction, forgetfulness, dullness, lethargy, vagueness of attention, and overinternalizing.

mental placement (*sems 'jog pa*). First of the nine stages in the development of śamatha. Here, the mind's attention is pulled away from external objects and begins to internalize on the object of meditation, however the mind is easily distracted. *See also* nine stages of śamatha.

mental pliancy (*sems shin tu sbyangs pa*). After you remove the afflictions that keep you from experiencing a special joy in your practice, the mind is serviceable for any type of meditation. Mental serviceability is almost synonymous with mental pliancy. Mental pliancy is the antidote to certain mental hindrances and difficulties that obstruct perfect meditation. It causes an energy to surge through your body; this energy is the cause for physical pliancy. *See also* eight antidotes.

mindfulness (*dran pa*; Skt: *smṛti*). Recollection. It is the active way the mind holds its object. It is a mental factor that functions to hold the mind to its object, not letting the mind forget about or move away from its object. It also refers to the quality of mind that does not forget which objects are suitable to engage in and which should be avoided. It is the function of the mind that is continuously present on the object.

mundane path (*'jig rten pa'i lam*). A method of temporarily subduing the afflictions by utilizing the single-pointed, concentrated mind of śamatha to compare the faults of the level of existence you are trying to transcend with the relative subtlety of the next higher state. This method, common to both Buddhists and non-Buddhists, can lead to the highest levels of formless meditative absorption and rebirth in form or formless realms. However, because it does not eliminate the mental afflictions from the root, it does not result in complete freedom from samsara. *See also* supramundane path.

nine stages of śamatha. (1) Mental placement (*sems 'jog pa*), the mind's attention is pulled away from outer objects and begins to internalize on the object of meditation, however the mind is easily distracted; (2) Continuous placement (*rgyun du 'jog pa*), there are short periods of continued abiding on the object; (3) Patched placement (*blan du 'jog pa*), longer periods of concentration on the object because the mind is quickly and repeatedly brought back to its object of meditation once it has been distracted or slipped into laxity; (4) Close placement (*nye bar 'jog pa*), after attention is replaced on the object meditation, particular effort is made to remain there; (5) Taming (*dul bar byed pa*), the process of controlling or subduing the mind by reflecting on the advantages of śamatha and taking delight in it; (6) Pacification (*zhi bar byed pa*), the elimination of any reticence for meditation practice or dislike for concentration; (7) Complete pacification (*rnam par zhi bar byed pa*), the mind can immediately pacify whatever faults arise through completely developed mindfulness and introspection; (8) One-pointed attention (*rtse gcig tu byed pa*), with effort, an ability to meditate single-pointedly on the object of meditation for as long as you wish; (9) Balanced placement (*mnyam par 'jog pa*), no effort is required to remain focused on the object of meditation.

nonreturner (*phyir mi 'ong ba*; Skt: *anāgāmin*). Third of the four fruits: stream winner, once-returner, nonreturner, and arhat. When an ārya has removed all nine desire-realm afflictions on the supramundane path, that yogi becomes a nonreturner. Such a being is no longer compelled by karma and the afflictions to be reborn in the desire realm.

object (*yul*). Something that is known by consciousness.

object of meditation (*dmigs pa*). Something that is observed by consciousness in meditation.

one-pointed attention (*rtse gcig tu byed pa*). The eighth stage in the development of śamatha. With effort, an ability to meditate single-pointedly on the object of meditation for as long as you wish. *See also* nine stages of śamatha.

once-returner (*lan cig phyir 'ong ba*; *sakṛdāgāmi*). Second of the four fruits: stream winner, once-returner, nonreturner, and arhat. When a person has removed six of the nine desire-realm afflictions, he or she is called a once-returner because such a being will remove the final three afflictions after only one more rebirth.

pacification (*zhi bar byed pa*). The sixth stage in the development of śamatha. Based on the strength of the fifth stage, the elimination of any reticence for meditation practice or dislike for concentration. *See also* nine stages of śamatha.

patched placement (*blan du 'jog pa*). The third stage in the development of śamatha. Longer periods of concentration on the object are possible because the mind is quickly and repeatedly brought back to its object of meditation once it has been distracted or slipped into laxity. *See also* nine stages of śamatha.

path of... *See* five paths.

perfections (*phar phyin*; Skt: *pāramitā*). The activities of practitioners on the Mahayana path after they have developed bodhicitta. The six perfections are generosity, ethical discipline, patience, perseverance, meditative stability, and wisdom.

perseverance (*brtson 'grus*; Skt: *vīrya*). A genuine enthusiasm for and concerted effort in practicing the path and cultivating virtue, central to keeping the mind on the object of meditation in śamatha. It has been commonly translated as "joyous perseverance," "diligence," "effort," "enthusiasm," and "vigor." *See also* eight antidotes; five faults in the practice of śamatha; perfections; six forces.

physical pliancy (*lus shin tu sbyangs pa*). The body ceases to inhibit the mind's ability to remain single-pointedly focused on its object. Pain or discomfort no longer distract the mind. *See also* pliancy.

pliancy (*shin tu sbyangs pa*). Dexterity. A serviceability of the body and mind. *See also* physical pliancy and mental pliancy.

Prāsaṅgika Madhyamaka (*dbu ma thal 'gyur pa*). A branch of the Mahayana school of philosophy based on the writings of Nāgārjuna. The Prāsaṅgika is distinguished from the other Madhyamaka school, the Svātantrika Madhyamaka, on issues such as which scriptures are definitive, how to posit conventionalities, and how to prove the ultimate. *See also* Madhyamaka.

pratyekabuddha (*rang sangs rgyas*). "Solitary realizers," so called because in their last lifetime prior to attaining liberation they stay alone—they do not interact with a teacher. Prior study and practice over many lives enable them to be silent and solitary during their last lifetime, in which they attain the state of a Hinayana arhat.

primary consciousness (*gtso sems*). The five sense consciousnesses and mental consciousness. These function with accompanying consciousnesses. *See also* secondary consciousnesses.

samādhi (*ting nge 'dzin*). In general, a virtuous undistracted mind. A meditative stabilization or concentration on a particular object. A correct fixation: a mental factor that holds the mind single-pointedly and continuously on an examined functional thing or mental object.

śamatha (*zhi gnas*). Serenity, or "calm abiding," accompanied by physical and mental pliancy and their concurrent forms of bliss. The ability of the mind to abide, or remain, focused on an object of observation with complete freedom from distraction and from mental laxity for as long as desired. The term *śamatha* refers both to the practice for developing this capacity and to the attainment itself.

Sautrāntika (*mdo sde pa*). One of the four schools of Buddhist tenets, a non-Mahayana school, whose name means follower of the sutras.

secondary afflictions. *See* mental afflictions.

secondary consciousnesses (*sems 'byung*). According to the upper schools, any primary consciousness must have at least five omnipresent accompanying secondary consciousnesses: feeling, discrimination, intention, contact, and attention. The Vaibhāṣika and the lower Abhidharma accept that there are ten omnipresent mental factors. There are many more secondary consciousnesses that are not omnipresent. *See also* primary consciousness.

serenity. *See* śamatha.

seven attentions of the mundane path of insight (*yid la byed pa rnam pa bdun*). After completing the nine stages in the development of śamatha, six progressive levels of attention are required to subdue the mental afflictions of the desire realm. The seventh attention is the result, i.e., attainment of the actual first form-realm meditative absorption. The first six attentions are analytical meditative states on the preparatory level of the first form-realm meditative absorption. The attentions are: (1) discernment of characteristics (*mtshan nyid so sor rig pa*), (2) arisal from belief (*mos pa las byung ba*), (3) isolated attention (*rab tu dben pa*), (4) delight or withdrawal (*dga ba sdud pa*), (5) analysis (*dpyod pa'i yid la byed pa*), (6) final application (*sbyor ba mthar thug pa*), and (7) the result of final application (*sbyor ba mthar thug pa'i 'bras bu*)—this last is the actual state of śamatha that is free from attachment to the desire realm. *See also* final application; mundane path.

siddhi (*grub pa*). Spiritual attainments or supernormal powers or knowledge.

sinking. *See* laxity.

six attentions. *See* seven attentions of the mundane path of insight.

six forces (*stobs drug*). (1) The force of hearing (*thos pa'i stobs*) is the power of hearing and studying the teachings on śamatha. This is the cause of achieving the first stage, mental placement. (2) The force of reflection (*bsam pa'i stobs*) is the cause of the second stage of śamatha, continuous placement, where the mind can be tied to its object for some duration. The power comes from inside the mind rather than from listening to instructions. (3) The force of mindfulness (*dran pa'i stobs*), bringing the mind back to its object when it has gone astray, causes the third and fourth stages of śamatha. (4) The force of introspection (*shes bzhin gyi stobs*) is the force behind the fifth and sixth stages of śamatha. The introspective mental spy keeps a watchful eye on the activities of mind, watching for the faults and signs of laxity and excitement as well as other afflictions. (5) The force of perseverance (*brtson 'grus kyi stobs*) brings about the seventh and eighth stages of śamatha. It is enthusiastic, diligent effort that does not hesitate at all to apply antidotes even when the first signs of subtle faults arise. (6) The force of acquaintance (*yongs su 'dris pa'i stobs*) brings about the ninth stage of śamatha, balanced placement. This is the power derived from familiarity and experience with all the teachings and explanations regarding śamatha practice.

six perfections. *See* perfections.

spontaneous focus. *See* four attentions.

śrāvakas (*nyan thos*). Literally "hearers," such practitioners strive for their own liberation from samsara. They receive this name because—unlike pratyekabuddhas—they rely on listening to their teachers' instructions through the course of their spiritual practice.

stream winner (*rgyun du zhugs pa*; Skt: *śrotāpanna*). First of the four fruits. It is attained when one enters the supramundane path by attaining a direct realization of emptiness.

supramundane path (*'jig rten las 'das pa'i lam*). The method of practice, unique to Buddhism, leading to the direct realization of emptiness, which destroys karmic seeds from the root. *See also* mundane path.

supranormal knowledge or power (*mngon par shes pa*). The six supranormal powers are: miraculous powers, the divine eye, clairaudience, the knowledge of others' thoughts, recollection of past lives and knowledge of the next birth, and knowledge that the mental afflictions have been terminated. The first five are mundane supranormal powers, and the sixth is supramundane.

taming (*dul bar byed pa*). The fifth stage in the development of śamatha. The process of controlling or subduing the mind by reflecting on the advantages of śamatha and taking delight in it. *See also* nine stages of śamatha.

thirty-two major and eighty minor marks of a buddha (*mtshan dang dpe byad bzang po*). These are distinctive features of the form body of a buddha indicative of his supreme attainment, like elongated earlobes and an uṣṇīṣa protruding from the crown of his head. One common source of this list is Maitreya's *Ornament for Clear Knowledge*.

tight focus. *See* four attentions.

two accumulations (*tshogs gnyis*). The accumulations of merit and wisdom are the causes to attain enlightenment. The accumulation of merit comes from the practice of bodhicitta and the first five perfections. The accumulation of wisdom is the practice of the sixth perfection, culminating in direct realization of the ultimate nature of reality.

uninterrupted focus. *See* four attentions.

universal (*don phyi*). A generality, sometimes referred to as a "generic image," is a technical term utilized in epistemology and logic to refer to conceptual constructs, such as the idea of a tree in one's mind in contrast with a "particular" instance of an actual, unique tree in the world.

Vaibhāṣika (*bye brag smra ba*). The first of the four schools of Indian Buddhist tenets.

vigilance. *See* introspection.

Vikramaśīla. One of several great Buddhist universities of classical northern India.

vipaśyanā (*lhag mthong*). *See* insight.

wisdom (*shes rab*; Skt: *prajñā*). Wisdom in its perfected form is realization of the final nature of all phenomena; it is direct comprehension of emptiness, the lack of inherent existence of self and phenomena.

yogi (*rnal 'byor pa*). An assiduous Dharma practitioner. Because they put the various teachings into strict daily practice, yogis and yoginis (the feminine form of the word) often adopt an ascetic lifestyle.

Notes

1. *King of Samādhi Sutra* 4.24.

2. We have chosen to translate the term *rigs* as "essence" rather than "lineage" here, in contrast to page 20 of the *Lamrim Chenmo* translation. See the explanation in the text following the quotation.

3. *Engaging in the Bodhisattva Deeds* 9.40.

4. More extensive discussions of Hva Shang Mahayana's ideas are found in volumes 1, 3, and 5 of this series.

5. See section (c) above.

6. *Treasury of Knowledge* 6.8.

7. The ten nonvirtues are divided into three categories: nonvirtues of body, speech, and mind. The three nonvirtues of body are killing, stealing, and sexual misconduct. The four nonvirtues of speech are lying, divisive speech/slander, harsh speech, and idle gossip. The three nonvirtues of mind are greed, ill will, and wrong views.

8. *Treasury of Knowledge* 6.5.

9. See volumes 1 and 2 of this series for detailed explanations of these meditations and practices.

10. A detailed explanation of how to meditate on love and bodhicitta, based on the extensive teachings found in Indian canonical texts, is found in volume 3 of this series, pp. 61–106.

11. *Engaging in the Bodhisattva Deeds* 9:1.

12. *Engaging in the Bodhisattva Deeds* 7:69.

13. *Engaging in the Bodhisattva Deeds* 5:28.

14. In chapter 2, see (1") How to develop flawless concentration, particularly the first subtopic: (a)) What to do prior to focusing the attention on an object of meditation.

15. Tsong kha pa, *Great Treatise*, vol. 3: 70.

16. *Lam rim nyams mgur*. A translation by Thupten Jinpa of this brief text can be found at http://www.tibetanclassics.org/Jinpa_Translation.html.

Bibliography

CLASSICAL WORKS CITED

Bodhisattva Levels
    Bodhisattva-bhūmi
    Byang chub sems dpa'i sa
    author: Asaṅga
    P5537, vol. 110

Commentary on the "Compendium of Valid Cognition"
    Pramāṇa-vārttika
    Tshad ma rnam 'grel
    author: Dharmakīrti
    P5709, vol. 130

Commentary on the Difficult Points of the "Lamp for the Path to Enlightenment"
    Bodhi-mārga-pradīpa-pañjikā
    Byang chub lam gyi sgron ma'i dka' 'grel
    author: Atiśa
    P5344, vol. 103

Commentary on the "Ornament for the Mahayana Sutras"
    Sūtra-alaṃkāra-bhāṣya
    mDo sde'i rgyan gyi bshad pa
    author: Vasubandhu
    P5527, vol. 108

Compendium of Bases
    Vastu-saṃgrahaṇī
    Sa las gzhi bsdu ba
    author: Asaṅga
    P5540, vol. 111

Compendium of Determinations
    Yoga-caryā-bhūmi-viniścaya-saṃgrahaṇī
    rNal 'byor spyod pa'i sa rnam par gtan la dbab pa bsdu ba
    author: Asaṅga
    P5539, vol. 110

Compendium of Knowledge
Abhidharma-samuccaya
Chos mngon pa kun las btus pa
author: Asaṅga
P5550, vol. 112

Compendium of Teachings Sutra
Dharma-saṃgīti-sūtra
Chos yang dag par sdud pa'i mdo
P904, vol. 36

Compendium of the Perfections
Pāramitā-samāsa
Pha rol tu phyin pa bsdus pa
author: Āryaśūra
P5340, vol. 103

Compendium of Trainings
Śikṣā-samuccaya
bSlab pa kun las btus pa
author: Śāntideva
P5336, vol. 102

Engaging in the Bodhisattva Deeds
Bodhisattva-caryāvatāra
Byang chub sems dpa'i spyod la 'jug pa
author: Śāntideva
P5272, vol. 99

Explanation of "Separation of the Middle from the Extremes"
Madhyānta-vibhāga-ṭīkā
dBus dang mtha' rnam par 'byed pa'i 'grel bshad
author: Sthiramati
P5534, vol. 109

Explanation of the "Thirty Stanzas"
Triṃśikā-bhāṣya
gSum cu pa'i bshad pa
author: Sthiramati
P5565, vol. 113

Fundamental Verses of the Middle Way
Mūlamadhyamaka-kārikā
dBu ma rtsa ba'i tshig le'ur byas pa
author: Nāgārjuna
P5224, vol. 95

Great Final Nirvāṇa Sutra
Mahāparinirvāṇa-sūtra

Yongs su mya ngan las 'das pa chen po'i mdo
P789, vol. 31

Heart of the Middle Way
Madhyamaka-hṛdaya
dBu ma'i snying po
author: Bhāvaviveka
P5255, vol. 96

Heart Sutra
Prajñāpāramitā-hṛdaya
Shes rab kyi pha rol tu phyin pa'i snying po
P160, vol. 6

Individual Liberation Sutra
Prātimokṣa-sūtra
So sor thar pa'i mdo
P1031, vol. 42

Instructions for the Perfection of Wisdom
Prajñāpāramitopadeśa
Shes rab kyi pha rol tu phyin pa'i man ngag
author: Ratnākarśānti
P5579, vol. 114

Integration Tantra
Saṃpuṭa-tantra
Yang dag par sbyor ba'i rgyud
P26, vol. 2

King of Samādhi Sutra
Samādhi-rāja-sūtra
Ting nge 'dzin gyi rgyal po'i mdo
P795, vol. 31

Lamp for the Path to Enlightenment
Bodhi-patha-pradīpa
Byang chub lam gyi sgron ma
author: Atiśa
P5343, vol. 103

Levels of Yogic Deeds
Yoga-caryā-bhūmi
rNal 'byor spyod pa'i sa
author: Asaṅga
P5536, vol. 110

Moon Lamp Sutra
Candra-pradīpa-sūtra
Alternate name for the *King of Samādhi Sutra*

Ornament for Clear Knowledge
Abhisamaya-alaṃkāra
Mngon par rtogs pa'i rgyan
author: Maitreya
P5184, vol. 88

Ornament for the Mahayana Sutras
Mahāyāna-sūtra-alaṃkāra
Theg pa chen po'i mdo sde'i rgyan
author: Maitreya
P5521, vol. 108

Pile of Precious Things Collection
A collection of four dozen sutras in the Tibetan canon
Ratna-kūṭa-grantha
dKon brtsegs mdzod
P760, vols. 22–24

Praise in Honor of One Worthy of Honor
Varṇārha-varṇe-bhagavato-buddhasya-stotre-śakya-stava
Sangs rgyas bcom ldan 'das la bstod pa bsngags par 'os pa bsngags pa las
bstod par mi nus par bstod pa
author: Mātṛceṭa
P2029, vol. 46

Praise of Confession
Deśanā-stava
bShags pa'i bstod pa
author: Candragomin
P2048, vol. 46

Scriptural Collection of Bodhisattvas
Bodhisattva-piṭaka
Byang chub sems dpa'i sde snod
P760, vol. 23, chap. 12

Separation of the Middle from the Extremes
Madhyānta-vibhāga
dBus dang mtha' rnam par 'byed pa
author: Maitreya
P5522, vol. 108

Śrāvaka Levels
Śrāvaka-bhūmi
rNal 'byor spyod pa
author: Asaṅga
P5537, vol. 110

Stages of Meditation
Bhāvanā-krama
sGom pa'i rim pa
author: Kamalaśīla
P5310–5312, vol. 102

Sutra of Cultivating Faith in the Mahayana
Mahāyāna-prasāda-prabhāvanā-sūtra
Theg pa chen po la dad pa rab tu sgom pa'i mdo
P812, vol. 32

Sutra on the Samādhi That Perceives the Buddha of the Present Face to Face
Pratyutpanna-buddha-saṃmukhāvasthita-samādhi-sūtra
Da ltar gyi sangs rgyas mngon sum du bzhugs pa'i ting nge 'dzin gyi mdo
P801, vol. 32

Sutra Unraveling the Intended Meaning
Saṃdhi-nirmocana-sūtra
dGongs pa nges par 'grol pa'i mdo
P774, vol. 29

Treasury of Knowledge
Abhidharma-kośa
Chos mngon pa'i mdzod
author: Vasubandhu
P5590, vol. 115

"Treasury of Knowledge" Autocommentary
Abhidharma-kośa-bhāṣya
Chos mngon pa'i mdzod kyi bshad pa
author: Vasubandhu
P5591, vol. 115

OTHER WORKS CITED

Pabongka Rinpoche. *Liberation in the Palm of Your Hand* (*Rnam grol lag bcangs*). Compiled by Trijang Rinpoche. Translated by Michael Richards. Boston: Wisdom Publications, 1991.

Śāntideva. *A Guide to the Bodhisattva's Way of Life*. Translated by Vesna A. Wallace and B. Alan Wallace. Ithaca: Snow Lion Publications, 1997.

Tsong kha pa. *Condensed Points of the Stages of the Path* (*Lam rim nyams mgur*). In *Chos spyod* (*Dharma Practices*), 64–74. Sarnath, India: Central Institute of Higher Tibetan Studies, 1987.

———. *Foundations of All Good Qualities* (*Yon tan gzhir gyur ma* in *Byang chub lam gyi rim pa'i brgyud pa rnams la gsol ba 'debs pa'i rim pa "Lam mchog sgo 'byed" shes bya ba*). P6003, vol. 153.

———. *Great Treatise on the Stages of the Path to Enlightenment: Lam Rim Chen Mo.* Translated by the Lamrim Chenmo Translation Committee. Vol. 1: 2000, vol. 2: 2004, vol. 3: 2002. Ithaca, NY: Snow Lion Publications. Tibetan text: *sKye bu gsum gyi rnyams su blang ba'i rim pa thams cad tshang bar ston pa'i byang chub lam gyi rim pa.* Xining: mTsho sngon People's Press, 1985. Reprinted in Dharamsala: Ganden Bar Nying, 1991. P6001.

———. *Medium Stages of the Path. Byang chub lam gyi rim pa'i nyams len gyi rnam gshag mdor bsdus te brjed byang du byas pa.* P6061, vol. 153.

Vasubandhu (sLob dpon dByig gnyen). *Chos mngon pa mdzod kyi bshad pa.* Dharamsala: Council of Cultural & Religious Affairs of His Holiness the Dalai Lama, 1969.

———. *Chos mngon pa'i mdzod kyi tsig le'ur byas pa.* 3rd ed. Sarnath: Sarnath Legs bshad gter mdzod par khang, 1978.

———. *Abhidharmakośa and Bhāṣya of Ācārya Vasubandhu with Sphuṭārthā Commentary of Ācārya Yaśomitra.* 2nd ed. Edited by Swāmi Dwārikādās Śastri. Varanasi: Bauddha Bharati, 1981.

Index

Also Available from Wisdom Publications
by Geshe Lhundub Sopa

STEPS ON THE PATH TO ENLIGHTENMENT
A Commentary on Tsongkhapa's Lamrim Chenmo

Vol. 1: The Foundation Practices
Geshe Lhundub Sopa with David Patt and Beth Newman
Foreword by His Holiness the Dalai Lama

"An indispensable companion to Tsongkhapa's elegant and elaborate *Great Exposition on the Stages of the Path.*"—*Buddhadharma*

Vol. 2: Karma
Geshe Lhundub Sopa with David Patt
Foreword by His Holiness the Dalai Lama

"Those of us fortunate to have studied directly with Geshe Sopa well know what an inexhaustible fount of Buddhist learning and wisdom he is. With the publication of volume 2 of his comprehensive commentary on Tsongkhapa's classic *Lamrim Chenmo*, a much wider audience will further benefit from these unending riches."—William S. Waldron, Middlebury College

Vol. 3: The Way of the Bodhisattva
Geshe Lhundub Sopa with Beth Newman
Foreword by His Holiness the Dalai Lama

"From my first encounter with Professor Geshe Lhundub Sopa in 1962, I have been impressed with his kindness, patience, and thorough-going scholarship, qualities so strong that they obviously are based on profound realization. His compassionate forbearance shines throughout the heartfelt, practical explanations in these books."—Jeffrey Hopkins

LIKE A WAKING DREAM
The Autobiography of Geshe Lhundub Sopa
Geshe Lhundub Sopa with Paul Donnelly
Foreword by His Holiness the Dalai Lama

"Geshe Sopa is one of the greatest living Buddhist masters of his generation. This marvelous life story, rich in detail and told in his own words, will captivate the hearts and minds of anyone who reads it."—José Ignacio Cabezón, UC Santa Barbara

THE CRYSTAL MIRROR OF PHILOSOPHICAL SYSTEMS
A Tibetan Study of Asian Religious Thought
Thuken Losang Chökyi Nyima
Translated by Geshe Lhundub Sopa
Edited by Roger Jackson

"An impressive translation of a fascinating and vitally important book. Its broad scope and keen observation makes it an invaluable resource." —Guy Newland, Central Michigan University, author of *Introduction to Emptiness*

PEACOCK IN THE POISON GROVE
Two Buddhist Texts on Training the Mind
Geshe Lhundub Sopa with Leonard Zwilling and Michael J. Sweet

"It belongs on the shelf—and a readily accessible one at that!—of every scholar and every practitioner of Tibetan Buddhism."—Roger Jackson, Carleton College

About Wisdom Publications

Wisdom Publications is the leading publisher of classic and contemporary Buddhist books and practical works on mindfulness. To learn more about us or to explore our other books, please visit our website at wisdompubs.org or contact us as the address below.

Wisdom Publications
199 Elm Street
Somerville, MA 02144 USA

We are a 501(c)(3) organization, and donations in support of our mission are tax deductible.

Wisdom Publications is affiliated with the Foundation for the Preservation of the Mahayana Tradition (FPMT).